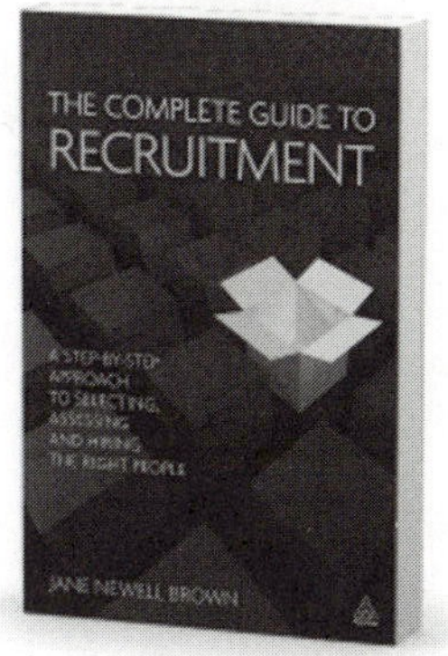

The Complete Guide to Recruitment

The Complete Guide to Recruitment

A step-by-step approach to selecting, assessing and hiring the right people

Jane Newell Brown

LONDON PHILADELPHIA NEW DELHI

Publisher's note

Every possible effort has been made to ensure that the information contained in this book is accurate at the time of going to press, and the publishers and author cannot accept responsibility for any errors or omissions, however caused. No responsibility for loss or damage occasioned to any person acting, or refraining from action, as a result of the material in this publication can be accepted by the editor, the publisher or the author.

First published in Great Britain and the United States in 2011 by Kogan Page Limited

120 Pentonville Road
London N1 9JN
United Kingdom
www.koganpage.com

1518 Walnut Street, Suite 1100
Philadelphia PA 19102
USA

4737/23 Ansari Road
Daryaganj
New Delhi 110002
India

ISBN 978 0 7494 5974 1
E-ISBN 978 0 7494 5975 8

British Library Cataloguing-in-Publication Data

A CIP record for this book is available from the British Library.

Library of Congress Cataloging-in-Publication Data

Brown, Jane Newell.
The complete guide to recruitment : a step-by-step approach to selecting, assessing and hiring the right people / Jane Newell Brown. – 1st ed.
p. cm.
ISBN 978-0-7494-5974-1 – ISBN 978-0-7494-5975-8 1. Employees–Recruiting. 2. Employee selection. I. Title.
HF5549.5.R44B6976 2011
658.3'11–dc22
2011000994

Typeset by Saxon Graphics Ltd, Derby
Printed and bound in India by Replika Press Pvt Ltd

CONTENTS

List of Figures viii
List of Tables ix
Acknowledgements x

Introduction 1

PART ONE The recruitment environment 3

01 Joined-up recruitment 5

Placing recruitment at the heart of a business 5
The employment cycle explained 7
Assessment 7
Engagement 8
Retention 9

02 The costs of poor recruitment 13

The recruiting life cycle of an organization 17

03 Engagement and retention 21

Engagement 21
Retention 34
Key retention drivers 41

04 Creating a great place to work 50

Vision and purpose 50
Leadership 51
Strategy 52
Communication 52
Career development 52
Learning opportunities 53
Community 53
Culture 54
People strategy 55

PART TWO Making great recruitment happen 57

05 Elements for successful recruitment 59

Elements for success 60
Element checklist 60

06 Developing a successful recruitment and talent strategy 71

Talent and recruitment strategy development 73
Strategic labour choices 87
Factors in choosing your recruitment strategy 102
Delivering your strategy into the business 107

07 A recruiting process fit for purpose 108

Business plan 111
What not to do 111
Objectives of any recruitment process 111
The overall process 112
A simple recruitment process in detail 115
Decide upon your attraction and assessment strategy 125
Choosing and engaging with an agency supplier – a 10-step approach 126
Recruiting for the role in-house – a five-step approach 128
Creating a shortlist 130

08 Attraction 134

How to develop a great recruitment brand 134
Indirect candidate attraction methods 139
Direct candidate attraction methods 146
Advertising 148
Attracting apprentices and graduates for schemes 158
Using recruitment agencies 161

09 **Assessment** 165

Legislative framework 169
Developing your assessment process 170
Determining who to hire and what to assess 171
What 'good' looks like 172
How to get started 172
Setting the assessment criteria 181
Different assessment methods 181
Presenting your business 200
Interviews 201

10 **On-boarding** 213

Completing the recruitment process 213
On-boarding from Day One and beyond 228
Transitioning into your team 232
'Joined-up' recruitment 239

Index 241

LIST OF FIGURES

FIGURE 1.1 The employment cycle 6
FIGURE 3.1 The joining life cycle 22
FIGURE 3.2 The employment life cycle 22
FIGURE 3.3 Application acknowledgement: informal 29
FIGURE 3.4 Application acknowledgement: formal 30
FIGURE 3.5 Key drivers for retention 36
FIGURE 3.6 Exit interview 38
FIGURE 4.1 Maslow's hierarchy of needs 54
FIGURE 5.1 The balancing act 68
FIGURE 6.1 SWOT analysis 74
FIGURE 6.2 Gap analysis: labour turnover rate 83
FIGURE 7.1 The recruitment process relationship 109
FIGURE 7.2 The recruitment cycle 110
FIGURE 7.3 A simple recruitment process 113
FIGURE 7.4 Example advertisement 130
FIGURE 8.1 Letter to identified talent 156
FIGURE 9.1 Assessment process 182
FIGURE 9.2 Invitation to assessment 196
FIGURE 9.3 Sample junior assessment centre format 198
FIGURE 9.4 Sample senior assessment centre format 199
FIGURE 9.5 STAR interviewing 209
FIGURE 10.1 A rejection letter template for a close-to-hire candidate 215
FIGURE 10.2 A rejection letter template post interview 216
FIGURE 10.3 A rejection letter post CV/application form 217
FIGURE 10.4 A poor example of a rejection letter 218
FIGURE 10.5 The magic circle 221
FIGURE 10.6 Informal offer letter 224

LIST OF TABLES

TABLE 1.1 Recruitment 'at the heart' 10
TABLE 2.1 Estimated cost of replacing staff 15
TABLE 2.2 Average loss per year against labour turnover 15
TABLE 3.1 CIPD Resourcing and Talent Planning Survey 2010 36
TABLE 3.2 Leaver's metrics 39
TABLE 3.3 Recruitment checklist 42
TABLE 3.4 On-boarding checklist 43
TABLE 3.5 Career development checklist 44
TABLE 3.6 Pay and benefits checklist 46
TABLE 3.7 Manager's/leader's checklist 47
TABLE 3.8 Commitment to people 48
TABLE 5.1 The elements of successful recruitment 60
TABLE 6.1 PESTLEC analysis 76
TABLE 6.2 Recruitment metrics 78
TABLE 6.3 Strategic labour choices 88
TABLE 6.4 Evaluating strategic choices for your business – blank template 99
TABLE 6.5 Evaluating strategic choices for your business – completed example 100
TABLE 7.1 Hiring requisition form 118
TABLE 7.2 Job description 119
TABLE 7.3 Person specification 120
TABLE 7.4 Combined job and person specification 121
TABLE 8.1 Candidate attraction methods 138
TABLE 8.2 AIDA advertisement build 151
TABLE 9.1 Assessment processes 167
TABLE 9.2 Role specification and competences 175
TABLE 9.3 Example of competence definition 177
TABLE 9.4 Job skills and competency matrix 178
TABLE 9.5 Choosing an assessment structure 183
TABLE 9.6 Telephone assessment form 189
TABLE 9.7 Question types 204
TABLE 9.8 Interview evaluation form 210
TABLE 10.1 An on-boarding template 234
TABLE 10.2 On-boarding meeting format: post month-one meeting 238

ACKNOWLEDGEMENTS

My thanks go to all who have contributed to this book and given of their valuable time.

Specifically I'd like to thank Andrew and Ed, whose forbearance at weekends has enabled 'the writing of books' to take place at all. You are a true example of a perfect family.

I'd also like to thank my lovely clients, without whom I would not have developed the knowledge base or experience in all areas of my practice. You need to remain nameless for confidentiality but I value both the professional and personal relationships that have developed from working together and hope for many more years of the same.

Thanks of course to Kogan Page for their continued faith in me.

Last, but by no means least my thanks to all the individual case study contributors, and organizations, who both demonstrate my view that richness of knowledge comes from learning from many others and show what a wide, diverse and challenging arena the business of recruitment is. They are:

Alex Snelling, Ann Swain, Amanda Marques, Brian Wilkinson, Carol Hammond, Claire Howe, Donna Miller, Elizabeth Frankland, Emma Kellaher, Gerry Wyatt, Graham Palfery-Smith, Hala Collins, Jack Grattan, Joe Perez, Salma Shah, Spencer King, Stephen Gilbert, Malcolm Menard, Maria Traynor, Mark Williams, Patrick Merlevede, Penny Davis, Richard Phelps, Roger Philby, Shirley Pruden, Spencer King, Stephen Gilbert, Sue Evans, Tara Ricks, Tracey Richardson

Aberdeen Group, Apsco, SHL, Dimensions International, Enterprise Rent-A-Car, graduate-jobs.com, Indigo Accountancy, Major Players, People Answers, PPS Works Ltd. Randstad, SHL

INTRODUCTION

This book takes you step by step through the entire recruitment process. It will show you exactly what to do for best results and how to do it, sharing tricks of the recruitment trade that you can adopt as well as suggesting when and how you might use external recruiters to best effect for your organization. It is ideal for students of recruitment or human resources but its core readership will be those for whom recruitment is not their first area of expertise but who still need to deliver 'right first time' efficient recruitment into their organizations, thereby contributing to their bottom line and future growth potential. They may be line managers, human resources practitioners, owner managers, internal recruiters – indeed, anyone wishing to improve their capability to recruit well and thus develop their business towards future success.

This book does not consider recruitment in isolation, however. While it does provide a highly practical approach with easy-to-copy tools and techniques for each stage of the recruitment process, it also considers a more 'joined-up' approach to be effective. So it looks at four interdependent elements of people in organizations: recruitment and then, alongside that, assessment, engagement and retention. I argue that without paying attention to all of these elements, an organization is missing the opportunity of being the best recruiter it can be. The book does not set out to be an expert in either of the other pre- and post-recruitment areas (engagement and retention) as there are many good texts on these topics already, but intends to provide a context within which great recruitment should sit and to consider how the issues interrelate with one another.

The book comprises two parts. Part One takes a look at the context within which recruitment operates and offers some thinking as to what needs to be in place for good recruitment to happen. I see recruitment as more than a process and a series of activities. For me it is more of a mindset and although an efficient process will play a big part in success, if we remove passion we lose the capacity to connect with people and thereby build a great organization.

Part One also considers 'what it takes' to be a successful recruitment organization. It considers the critical success factors to engage the whole business in the importance of good recruitment. It considers where the four elements outlined earlier relate to and join up with each other and what that means for those responsible for recruitment. It looks at each of the elements, detailing what each means, exploring in more detail engagement and retention and how they can contribute towards broader recruitment success. The costs of poor recruitment and choosing the wrong people can be vast – both the overt costs such as wasted advertising and also the hidden costs such as morale – and it considers how these might compute and therefore what the opportunity to recruit well can represent to the business both in terms of competitive advantage and also the opportunity to reduce costs. The final chapter in this section looks at what constitutes a great place to work. This provides in effect a checklist of areas of the business that need to be focused on to create a great place to work. While we recognize that the recruiter or hiring manager will not have influence over all, or sometimes even many, of these, it is useful to understand the environment within which great recruitment needs to sit to be successful. I take the view that recruitment can only be as good as the organization's capacity to retain and gain maximum potential from the people it hires. Evidence suggests that being a great place to work contributes strongly to return on people investment.

With the environment set up for success, Part Two of the book details each stage of the process towards successful hiring with a wide range of useful tools and techniques to support the internal and external process. The first chapter sets out all of the elements for successful recruitment. It provides a checklist for each of the elements so you can look at your own business and decide how it is faring and consider improvements in your process or strategy.

The following five chapters then tackle many of these elements in much more detail, with tips and techniques for success. They start with recruitment strategy and how to develop one that works for your business, goes on to look at the recruitment process, a key element and often one where success is prohibited rather than encouraged, considers how to attract your talent depending upon your particular circumstances and then how to assess it. It finishes with a chapter on bringing people over the threshold into your business and how to help them contribute quickly, to the benefit of both. How well the people within your business do starts with the recruitment process. If this is working well, then the business has a much greater chance of overall success.

The book is packed with case studies from successful people and organizations, as well as stories of my own, explaining what works well and providing inspiration to develop clever and forward-thinking recruitment techniques.

Above all, I hope this book makes us all think about looking at recruitment in a different way.

PART ONE
The recruitment environment

'Joined-up' recruitment

01

This chapter is the start of the first section. This section discusses all of the elements that need to be there for great recruitment to take place. It starts with exploring how recruitment relates to other aspects of an organization, goes on to look at the costs of recruiting badly and then gives pointers on retention and engagement to ensure that all your hard recruitment work doesn't just fly right out of the door.

Recruitment is often seen in organizations as a 'stand-alone' activity, handled either by a line manager, HR partners or an internal recruitment team. This means that the opportunity to grow and develop a business through the use of recruitment can often be missed. A 'joined-up' approach to recruitment, encompassing the retention, assessment and engagement of an organization's people as well as one that places recruitment at the heart of a business, will offer significantly increased returns on investment. And in fact, paying significant attention to assessment, retention and engagement will actually reduce the amount of time you need to spend on recruitment.

In this chapter the core activities to create a successful joined-up recruitment environment are explored so you can see how to make recruitment work successfully for your business.

Placing recruitment at the heart of a business

The need for recruitment is driven by the success or failure of other parts of the organization. If your business is highly successful and needs to grow, recruitment will be a prime driver of growth; the capacity to get the right skills in the right place at the right time at the right salaries will determine the capacity to keep up with, or drive, the growth curve. If your business hires the wrong people, loses more people than it hires and is unable to get them to deliver what's needed, then high volumes of recruitment can be a symptom of a wider problem. Either way, recruitment needs to be both a strong influencer in the business and to have regular board attention. The best recruitment, whether delivered by a busy line manager, a business owner or a recruitment specialist, has influence and is far-sighted. The ability to see how the skills of someone recently sourced or interviewed can impact the business positively is an essential skill for any business.

If your business is lucky enough to have a great specialist recruitment team, they can only be as successful as the rest of the business. They can hire great people but if these people are not on-boarded and inducted well, engaged with, developed and retained, then the investment in the great recruitment team will have been a waste of resources. If you have an HR team, you are dependent upon this team being able to hold in mind all aspects of the people process yet focus on each to create the greatest chance of success. If you don't have an HR or recruitment team, then you'll need to find a way of creating investment in your people from recruitment through to retention for yourself. But this is not a dark art. Often this means simply paying really good attention to all of the aspects mentioned above and joining them up so they become part of the whole rather than stand-alone elements. Practising joined-up recruitment means taking an interdependent approach as shown in Figure 1.1.

As you can see in Figure 1.1, good recruitment is dependent upon good assessment. Choosing the right people is likely to lead to strong engagement, in turn leading to retention, following back through to recruitment. It is a challenging balancing act to create focus on each area and yet to hold the whole in mind at all times.

For greatest ownership and success, the people responsible for recruitment need to be equally involved in the other areas. Recruitment consultants, whether internal or external, are judged upon whether they provide great people who stay with the business. In reality they rarely have any control

FIGURE 1.1 The employment cycle

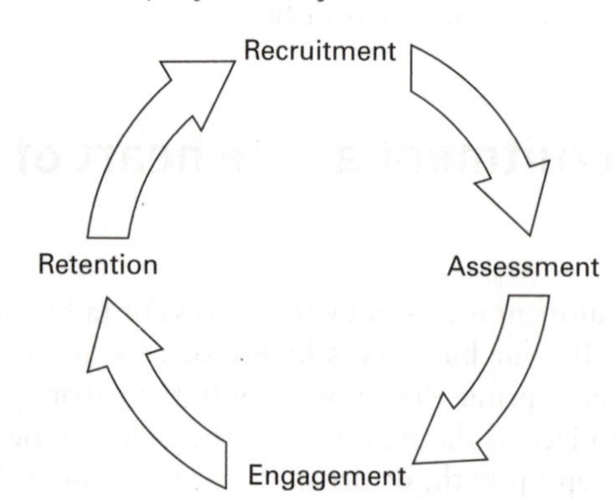

over this. Their main focus is getting people hired rather than focusing on making good hiring decisions. Holding recruiters more to account for the quality of their hires can be a good way of changing their focus from getting people into jobs towards a more holistic approach of making the whole employment cycle work better.

The employment cycle explained

Recruitment itself starts when a need for a task or series of tasks is recognized. Whether this is after someone leaving an existing job or identifying a new position, it will include one or both of the following activities:

- conducting a work analysis and defining the tasks to be done;
- determining the best way to get the tasks done.

Once it is identified that a job needs doing, the following activities need to happen:

- agreeing a budget and getting it signed off;
- drawing up a role and person specification along with salary and benefits;
- designing and implementing an internal and external attraction strategy;
- managing and running the assessment process;
- deciding which candidate(s) to offer;
- managing and running the offer process;
- managing and running the on-boarding process.

Assessment

Assessment can shift the chances of appointing someone who will perform in the role from a 30 per cent chance to a 60 per cent chance. Your assessment process will have a major impact on costs and team effectiveness; it must be valid, not open to discrimination claims and designed to assess the competences and behaviours needed in the role.

The candidate experience is also a crucial part of the assessment process. If they have a bad experience, they are likely to tell their friends, so there are two sides to assessment: the overall need to assess the candidate's capability to do the job and their experience of you as an employer and what that can do for your brand.

In designing your assessment process, you will consider what it takes to be successful in the role you want to hire and then identify how to assess that.

You will design a process either by yourself or with expert help, which will include one or more of the following assessment types:

- CV/application forms;
- psychometric/aptitude testing;
- verbal and numerical reasoning tests;
- business simulations/assessment centres;
- interviews.

Finally, you will need to choose your candidate and appoint them. Appointing may sound like a simple part of the recruitment process but in a candidate-short market (where applicants are in demand elsewhere) it can be a crucial part of the overall strategy.

Engagement

Although the phrase 'employee engagement' has a wider context, I am using it here in recruitment terms. So engagement means ensuring that you are able to hire the candidates you want to, they are sufficiently engaged with the process and your business, they accept your offers and that they join feeling really excited about the opportunity. Engagement is the capacity of the business to demonstrate that the organization can meet their objectives, whether these be as simple as providing for their family or furthering their knowledge in astrophysics.

To do this, it's important to understand the needs, drivers and motivations of your candidates. Turning your unsuccessful candidates down is as much part of the engagement process as offering them a role. Equally important are:

- negotiating the offer;
- writing the offer letter;
- designing the contract of employment;
- on-boarding;
- induction.

The engagement process starts at the very beginning of the recruitment process. It is a strong part of attraction and needs to build through the process at every point. It's often helpful to consider it in terms of consumer marketing and our engagement with the brands we associate with ourselves. The brand needs to make us feel comfortable and at home. We need to feel that we 'fit' the brand and it 'fits' us. So the initial attraction needs to be in place and then the story needs to build at every step, from the careers page of the website to the people answering the phone or sitting in reception when the candidate arrives for interview. Consider how your business or organization presents itself to prospective candidates, how it builds their brand experience and what you can do to improve it.

Having engaged and appointed your candidate, you'll need to ensure you get the best from them, and them from you, for the ultimate successful relationship. You'll need to retain them.

Retention

The capacity to retain and develop your talent lies at the heart of any people strategy. Retaining your people is supported by succession planning, well-being, career development, and engagement in its wider sense. It has a wide range of benefits. Some key things to think about are:

- setting labour turnover or attrition rate key performance indicators (KPIs) to focus the business;
- what the optimum levels of new people coming into the business are;
- how to be an employer of choice in your sector and beyond;
- how to be a 'great place to work';
- relationship building for long-term hiring;
- recruitment pipeline development and talent strategy, both internally and externally;
- internal career management;
- performance management and people development.

Once you have organized your business around the employment cycle, you'll then need to ensure you are geared up internally to make sure you can implement this well.

Insufficient attention is paid to recruitment as a professional discipline and as a crucial part of the people strategy. Research from the Great Place to Work Institute in the USA, which conducts an annual survey of organizations, tracked the financial performance of 'great place to work' companies against the stock market from 1998 and found they outperformed it by 15 per cent. To create a great place to work, you need staff you want to keep. You need make it easy for them to join and even easier for them to stay. This means putting recruitment at the heart of your organization.

Organizations that put recruitment 'at the heart' do all of the things in Table 1.1.

TABLE 1.1 Recruitment 'at the heart'

Recruitment 'at the heart' of an organization means:
Taking a 'top-down' approach; commitment from the board
Developing your employer brand
Developing your recruitment strategy
According status and value to the people in charge of your recruitment
Treating your external suppliers as partners

I'll look at these factors in a little more detail now.

Take a 'top-down' approach

The recruitment strategy is discussed and decided at the top of the business. It doesn't matter whether you are a start-up business with three founders or a multimillion-dollar business with hundreds of thousands of employees. Hiring the best people in a cost-effective and value-based way will add multiple zeros to your bottom line. If the board or the top team does not underpin and demonstrably support recruitment, the rest of the business will not take it seriously either. At this level the strategy and the performance measure of success should be set and monitored.

Develop your employer brand

Consider how you are perceived as an employer:

- Do you enter for and win awards?
- If you draw your labour force from the local market, how you are perceived locally? Do you have a local presence?
- Do you have an employer 'brand' or personality? What do you stand for? How do you differentiate yourself?
- What values does your business hold?
- How do you determine your reward strategy?
- Why would someone want to work for you?

Employment should be a mutually beneficial relationship. Both parties need to consider what value they can gain from the relationship; as in all good relationships if you consider first how you can look after your partner, it will increase the chances of success.

If you pay the same attention to marketing your business to your people as you do to marketing it to your customers, you will be working just as hard on your employer brand as you are on your customer brand.

Develop your recruitment strategy

Decide how recruitment can meet your business needs. Align your recruitment process with your strategic goals. If you do not have a current recruitment strategy, start by finding out what you currently do. Spend time with your hiring managers and observe and analyse the process from start to finish. Is it fit for purpose?

Recruitment should be as planned a process and as integral a part of the organization's planning cycle as managing the production line or delivering client work. Often it's much more ad hoc and panic driven.

Accord status and value to people in charge of your recruitment

Recruitment is often left to the line manager with no support, a junior staff member or an HR manager who would rather be doing something else. The most forward-thinking human resources directors or managing directors realize that it's easily the way in which they can add most value to the business in a clearly measurable way. Recruitment should be aligned to the other areas of the employment cycle and its success or failure measured.

If you have a specialist team, make it count. Position the team as an advice centre for all aspects of recruitment, internal and external. Have the team go out into the business and work face to face with the line managers. Help line managers use best practice to assess and recruit the best people; teach them how to develop a risk-reduced assessment process that is fit for purpose; take candidate attraction and any recruitment agency management away from them so they can focus on their core responsibilities.

If you don't have a specialist team, use the resources in the second half of this book to ensure you are using best-practice methods to reduce cost and increase success rates. Let your managers know that recruitment and assessment are one of the most important things they do.

Treat your external suppliers as partners

The time and effort you put into your suppliers will determine the level of value you receive from them. Think about how you like to work with your own customers or clients. If you have no information from them about what they want from you, what they are interested in buying, what they value you for and what is important about your product of service, how can you hope to meet their needs? Yet external recruiting suppliers are often expected to deliver excellence with little or no deep understanding of their client's business. Treat your suppliers as valued customers and you will reap the rewards of the time spent with them.

Before exploring in more detail how to do all of these important things, the next chapter looks at the overt and hidden costs involved in getting recruitment wrong. If you need convincing to focus on recruitment to help save money and maximize return from your people investment, the next chapter will go some way to help.

The costs of poor recruitment

02

Most organizations perceive recruitment as 'high cost'. Few see it as a good investment in the way that many see learning and development, research and development or business process re-engineering. It is easy to spend significant money on recruitment with little return, as recruiting poorly will both provide a low return and lead to increased costs. The challenge is to make the money spent worthwhile and to make sure it works. The risk–reward balance will be increased by harnessing each of the four areas of recruitment and talent management discussed in the previous chapter: recruitment, assessment, engagement and retention.

Recruitment in isolation will regularly mean the wrong choice is made and the candidate leaves before much contribution is made, or has to be asked to leave as they are not right for the job. Although there is sadly no such thing as perfect prediction of someone's capacity to perform well in a job, the odds can be increased significantly by employing best practice. Here I explore the consequences of not employing that best practice by taking a chance in recruitment. Few organizations would 'take a flyer' on a leadership trainer for the top team, give a new organizational structure 'a go', buy a company or launch a new product without exploring the likely feasibility and chance of success very closely. Yet time and again organizations treat recruitment very differently from other investments. The cost of failure mounts up.

Recruitment costs are made up of both overt and hidden costs:

- Overt costs, costs that have to be paid for, include: advertising to attract candidates, recruitment agency fees, dedicated in-house recruitment teams, training courses, employer branding costs, website design, liaison with universities, headhunting fees.

- Hidden costs, costs that drain the business but may not have an actual invoice attached, include: lack of knowledge transfer, on-the-job training, brain drain, management time, team spirit and morale, HR and payroll time.

All contribute to the financial drain on resources any organization will experience when someone leaves. Sometimes, of course, an employee leaving can have a positive impact on the resources of the business. A new employee may be more effective than one who has left. However, if we assume that the performance management systems within the business – the ways in which people's ability to do their job is measured and managed – are working, it is fair to assume that people leaving cost the business money.

There are various schools of thought on the quantifiable cost of people leaving. Research by the Chartered Institute of Personnel and Development (CIPD) shows that the average cost of replacing an employee is about £6,000. For many roles this wouldn't even cover the recruitment fees. Other models refer to costs of half of a year's annual salary; and recent research from PricewaterhouseCoopers (PwC) suggests the costs are even higher.

CASE STUDY

PwC's research reveals that the cost of replacing a competent member of staff equates to approximately a year of that person's salary, reflecting all costs associated with lost skills and productivity, cost of replacement and training of new recruits. Richard Phelps, human resource services partner at PwC, comments: 'Companies often vastly underestimate the financial benefits of retaining existing employees. With many businesses eager to maintain or grow staff levels as the economy starts to recover, it is crucial they consider the full costs of losing staff through resignation.'

PwC argues that these costs extend far beyond any employment agency fees and 'golden hello' incentives sometimes given to recruits from rival firms. The research factors in time spent interviewing candidates, particularly if a number of senior people are involved, reference checking and administration, the induction process and loss of competence before the new joiner is fully up to speed, revenue/productivity loss and customer disruption at the point the person leaves; not to mention the higher salaries often attached to new hires.

Consider too the likely loss of engagement and performance while someone looks for a new job and works their notice. As soon as someone hands in their notice the business begins to incur overt cost, but when the employee mentally disengages from their role, hidden costs are incurred and impact is felt. A disengaged employee may spread their feelings around the business, sometimes disengaging others. Less effort may be made within their role and there will certainly be time spent focusing on new opportunities, time attending interviews and mentally 'leaving' – so even before someone resigns, the business will have incurred hidden costs of recruitment.

Other hidden costs are time, such as the cost of the line or HR manager to replace the person. The smaller the business or the higher the value of the business proposition, the more impact one particular person leaving can have. Overt costs then will be the costs of advertising, recruitment agency fees, assessment processes if outsourced or if testing is involved, and the costs of induction courses and training within the business once the new person has joined.

Table 2.1 shows the potential impact on the business of losing a particular key role in the business.

Table 2.2 shows the potential costs to the bottom line of a particular level of staff turnover and the significant difference that a reduction in attrition (or, indeed, an increase in retention) can make on an organization. This money could then be reinvested in further retention through learning and development or improved recruitment processes to continue the retention spiral upwards.

TABLE 2.1 Estimated cost of replacing staff

Role	Cost of replacement
Chief executive	£75,000
Senior manager	£50,000
Line manager	£28,000
PA	£13,000
Skilled worker	£17,000
Worker	£10,000

TABLE 2.2 Average loss per year against labour turnover

SME with 150 people	
Average salary of £29,000	
20% labour turnover of 150 people	15% labour turnover of 150 people
150 × 20% × 2 (£29,000) = £435,000	150 × 15% × 2 (£29,000) = £326,250
Saving to bottom line	£108,750

Organizations in high-growth markets often use their line managers to spend a high proportion of their time recruiting. If the growth needs supporting by new people, in new roles coming into the business, then while this is a cost, it is unavoidable, and often the opportunity cost of not hiring people and therefore not being able to deliver to customers will be much greater than the costs associated with growing an organization quickly. Google in the UK reports its managers spending 30 per cent of their time hiring. Often recruitment costs can be one of the most obvious costs to a high-growth business. Any organization on a fast-growth trajectory will need to factor this into its business planning, especially if it is in a skill-short market.

CASE STUDY

For high-growth companies, recruitment costs can spiral out of control in a fast-growth market, says Shirley Pruden of DSC. 'Getting people on board suddenly becomes more important than cost, more important than quality and certainly more important than strategy or process. Managers need to deal with a wide range of suppliers, recruitment isn't planned, often the HR service is under-resourced or underdeveloped as the organizations we work with (typically tech or new markets) tend to be new and growing really quickly, certainly compared with the national average growth rate. So it is important that the business leaders are clear about their objectives and priorities and then we design the strategy around that. If they need to be first to market with a product, paying higher salaries to acquire the top talent, then acquiring that talent through a range of high-value suppliers may be the best option under some circumstances. Equally, line managers all "doing their own thing", recruiting from their personal contacts with a wide range of suppliers, can mean that economy of scale is not realized and the opportunity to gain value for the business is lost. We balance those needs but above all we provide fast-to-market solutions for companies who need that to maintain competitive edge.'

Recruiting costs will present different challenges throughout the life cycle of an organization. Typically organizations move through a range of recruiting solutions as they grow and develop. Your organization is likely to fit into one of the categories below. You may find it helpful to see if the analysis offers any help with challenges you are facing.

The recruiting life cycle of an organization

Phase one: start up

As businesses start up, they often resource new people through existing contacts, often both raising money and hiring through friends and family. The advantage of this is that they are mainly hiring 'known quantities' and people they can trust, with no external costs of hiring. The disadvantage, of course, is that often the entrepreneurs are not used to recruiting and may not seek the right evidence that the people can perform the role. There can often then be a mismatch between skills and delivery. Further, there may be some kind of existing relationship between the entrepreneur and the person they have hired, which may make working together difficult. This may not even show up in the early heady days of starting a business together but may come to light later as cracks emerge in philosophy or communication skills. Many small businesses fail because of the lack of ability of the founders or senior team to see eye to eye.

The costs of recruitment in this phase are mainly hidden and often do not show up until later in the cycle.

Key danger areas are: hiring friends of friends; not exploring enough of what happens if things go wrong; ignoring skills and capabilities; and allowing costs to determine skill levels, often at too low a level.

Advice here is to find someone who understands recruitment and design some good interviewing practices. Widen the net to look for good candidates and manage risk by avoiding compromise on skill level. Consider taking someone on a pro-rata basis or freelance at least initially to increase your buying power and skill level.

Phase two: from start-up to 20 to 50 people

Somewhere at this point the business runs out of contacts and starts recruiting outside its network. As it is unlikely to have a full-time HR manager, this may take one of two routes: placing advertising or using a recruitment agency. At this point in an organization's growth, recruitment costs can often be contained but the expertise to recruit well can be missing. It may be that no one in the organization is an experienced recruiter and in this situation hires are often made on the basis of 'chemistry' rather than match of skills and competences for the role. Most often the business at this point will still be housed in one large space, so the capacity of new people to fit in is perceived to be crucial. There is also still a hangover from the networking recruitment days of phase one, so the business is more likely to recruit friends than competences.

The costs of recruitment in this phase are likely to focus on making the wrong choices through lack of assessment. This may not show up for a while as people will be chosen for fit and may well then get on well with everyone. It may take some time for the lack of competence to show up and by then this person will be friends with everyone else and it will be difficult to challenge their performance, particularly as managers may also be unskilled at this. There can also be lack of knowledge on how to make a recruitment agency or advertising work for you, leading to overspending on the actual recruitment fees as well.

Key danger areas are: hiring for personality fit and not skills; using a recruitment agency without knowing how to build that relationship and achieve the best value for money; placing advertising without understanding the likely results and thus potentially wasting valuable advertising spend; and not centralizing or coordinating recruitment, so that everyone does their own thing – potentially costing even more money.

Advice here is to place all of the recruitment under one person's remit (can be an existing manager or director) so at least it can be coordinated centrally. Make this one person responsible for all of the attraction, eg finding candidates and coordinating the use of agencies and advertising, so that at least the process is streamlined. Continue to build good interviewing and recruiting practices and consider the issue of on-boarding to make the most of your investment in your new hire.

Phase three: medium-sized business of 50 to 350 (or even up to 1,000) people

From 50 people onwards there is likely to be some kind of recruitment or HR resource within the business, in which the focus on recruitment can be located. It will then be up to the particular make-up and needs of the business how this can best be organized. Typically here the business may be operating from a range of locations or may still be in one larger office; but after 50 people, individuals will be spread out in a building and not all together, so communication becomes more important and more challenging. No longer can best practice, new ways of working – or even gossip – spread of their own accord through the business, and attention needs to be paid to ensure everyone knows what is happening and how things should be done.

Organizations in high growth will need some kind of dedicated resource in recruiting as this is likely to be a large part of their spend. Typically this becomes clear when the finance director notices that a massive spend is going out on a range of recruitment agencies and that the business is dealing with a wide range of them at full fees. The finance director may also notice that the business is paying fees for people that others in the business know and could have put forward for nothing. Equally it may be that the HR team has become too busy with new people to focus on recruitment and line managers are struggling to meet their hiring quota. This in turn is leading to the company being unable to fulfil its customer orders – and finally the board decides something needs to be done.

The costs of recruitment here will be lack of leveraging purchasing power across the business with both recruitment agencies and advertising spend. Lack of coordinated effort and systems makes the process time-consuming and labour intensive. Lack of recruiting expertise, especially in new managers who may be being hired one day and then responsible for hiring the next. In very fast-growth companies, people will be hired with little regard to capability, as being up to headcount is most important. This phase heralds great opportunity for any recruitment agency to make high fees – after all, it is not their responsibility to choose the right people but simply to supply a qualified choice. This is probably the main danger point in terms of wasting real money through recruitment.

Key danger areas are: a scattergun approach; not maximizing the use of resources; not on-boarding new starters well as there is so much to be done; skipping detailed assessment; and making the wrong hiring choices.

Advice here is to professionalize recruitment. Place recruitment with an experienced recruiter rather than HR, either internally or externally. Build strong and good relationships with your recruitment agencies, negotiate a good deal on fees but not so much that they prefer to work for your competition and see you as a hunting ground. Make it easy for suppliers to work with you; give good briefings; take the trouble to 'sell' them the business so they do the same with your potential candidates; give fast feedback on CVs and candidates. Agree a modus operandi, and treat it as a partnership. Introduce an applicant tracking system and rationalize advertising spend, checking what works and what doesn't. Introduce a 'friends' finder scheme internally to encourage new people joining to put their network forward as candidates. Reward this in some way to reduce agency fees. Maximize internal recruitment and promotions both to reduce cost and create a strong developmental environment for your people, thus also increasing your retention.

Phase four: the larger business of 350-plus people

Businesses at the bottom of this scale are still medium sized, but those at the top end are large. The organization is likely to have moved out of high, very fast growth and the focus will be on sustaining existing business and developing it, developing new products and services, and making the most of the resources. Mergers and acquisitions may be taking place. Recruitment will be focused on replacing roles and recruiting at a slower rate, although some organizations here will still be in high-growth mode. Any organization with more than 150 hires a year will need a dedicated central recruitment team or a strongly processed recruitment methodology rolled out across all line and staff managers and coordinated by HR or recruitment business partners. Capability will have grown across the business, systems and processes will have been put in place and long-term talent mapping and pipeline development along with employer branding will be the strong focus.

The costs of recruitment will be reduced as this is coordinated and spend minimized. Now may be the time to consider further investments in profiling and assessment methods to improve recruiting decisions, streamlining of recruitment processes through the introduction of an outsourced provider or an internal recruitment team who source directly, therefore reducing your reliance on agencies, reserving them for difficult or business-critical hires, and further L&D to support retention.

Key danger areas are: putting cost first in your choice of outsourcer or internal team, which may ultimately lead to failure on their part and be a business risk for the organization; failing to build long-term talent pipelines (through university relationships and sponsorships and through longer-term conversations with skilled staff); focusing only on the here and now because the existing system isn't broken and doesn't need urgent fixing; and failing to invest in people, creating a longer-term retention drain.

Advice here is to really maximize your investment in recruitment. Develop your recruitment strategy. Identify and profile your high performers so you can benchmark and develop others towards that benchmark. Segment your market and look at the demographic for your skill needs and its pipeline. Pay close attention to reward, diversity, equal pay, exit interviews, employer brand and career planning opportunities for staff. Ensure you have the best systems and track capability in recruiting decisions to improve them through better assessment. Place considerable emphasis on developing your own people and succession planning. Set targets for retention among your line managers and the HR team and also for internal promotions – say, 80:20 for the latter. Make recruitment and retention a key business objective and measure of all managers. Develop a culture of excellence along with an employer brand that really stands out as aspirational.

In this chapter we have touched on the key issues around recruitment costs, the implications for your business of both the real and hidden costs of poor recruitment, and given some brief advice on how to minimize loss at each stage of the development process of an organization. Each of the chapters in the book looks at these key issues in much more detail. The next chapter starts with an overview of two core contributing factors mentioned already in this section: retention and engagement.

Engagement and retention

03

The converse of expensive and poor recruitment as discussed in the previous chapter is, of course, good recruitment practice and having the right people in the right jobs at the right time. Jim Collins, in *Good to Great*, suggests that the best companies focus on getting the right people in the right roles. Those people then go on to decide where the company should be going and how it can get there.

Organizations can place strong emphasis on recruitment but still not make the most of the talent available to them. In isolation good recruitment is a great start – but that is all it is. A recruiting team can only deliver as much competitive advantage into a business as an organization can sustain and nurture.

This chapter looks at the engagement process in the early stages of recruitment and then how to retain people. It takes a big-picture overview at this point; some of the topics are dealt with in much more detail in ensuing chapters.

The engagement process is crucial to the employer brand. How you relate to and engage with potential recruits can have far-reaching consequences for both the brand and your capacity to attract and hire the best people. It is said that if someone has a bad experience with a shop or a brand, they will tell 10 people, and if they have a good experience they will tell one; recruiting and the recruiting process can work in the same way. It makes little difference if you are a local employer with a poor reputation or a multinational brand.

Engagement

Engagement with your potential talent

Engagement starts when a potential recruit gets to know of an organization or business; and it lasts forever, long after the recruit has left.

The employment life cycle

Figure 3.1 shows the process of engagement between an organization and a potential recruit. It shows how important it is to keep up the initial engagement during the critical first 90 days. In Figure 3.2 we can see how this process continues during the period of employment and how engagement can be increased and employees retained through the use of new roles, interesting projects and job-enrichment schemes.

Your capacity to attract people to apply for jobs with you will depend upon:

- your reputation as an employer;
- the perception of your brand, business or service;
- conditions of employment – hours, flexibility, pay, prospects, location of work;
- job content.

FIGURE 3.1 The joining life cycle

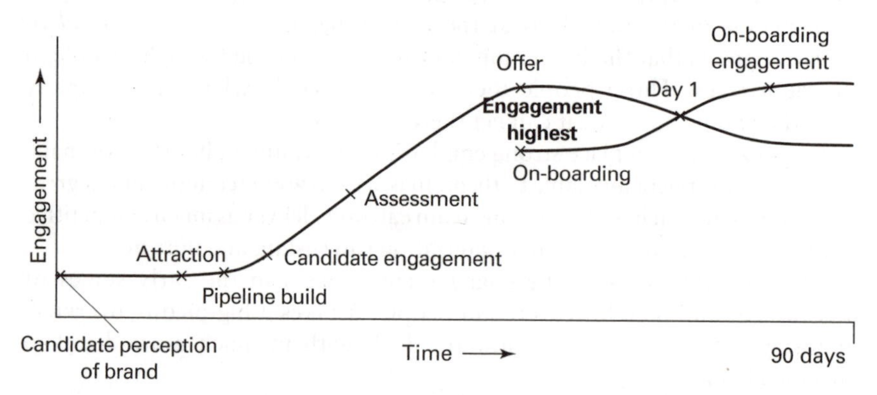

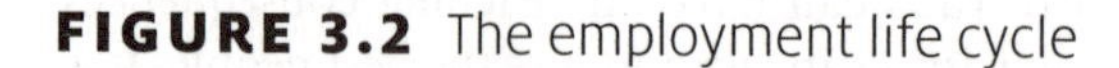

FIGURE 3.2 The employment life cycle

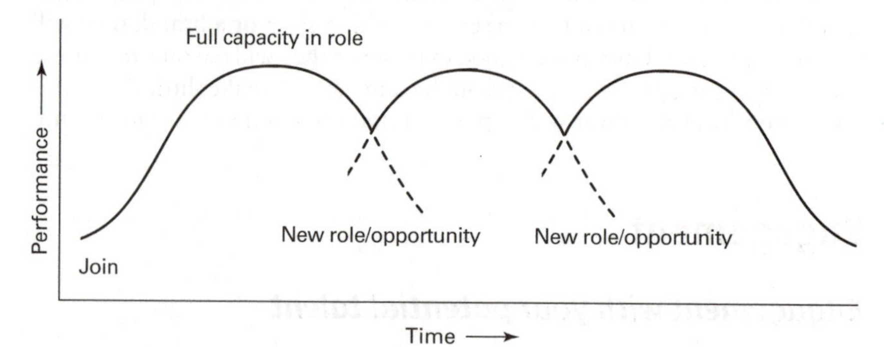

To get the very best choice of people, you'll need to satisfy or meet all of the needs above – unless you are in an area of high labour supply. Even if this is the case, to gain the best competitive edge you'll still want to attract the best people to work for you, despite the large choice. In this instance you need to be paying particular attention to your assessment process. In any labour market much will be gained from aiming to becoming an employer of choice.

Employer of choice

Pre-attraction

Engaging with your target audience means becoming an employer of choice in your chosen segment. Identifying, getting to know and delivering what your target market wants is half the challenge in becoming an employer of choice. Some examples are:

- *The Times* Graduate Recruitment Awards for the most appealing organization in each category for new graduates to join: in 2009 it was companies like PwC for accountancy qualifications, Oxfam in the not-for-profit sector and Procter & Gamble for sales and marketing.
- In Australia the Equal Opportunity for Women in the Workplace Agency has recognized the company Westaff for introducing grandparent leave for people who have been employed for more than three years.
- Many retailers offer a range of employment working patterns to suit working mothers in their shops, using 16–18-year-olds to take over their roles at weekends and in school holidays. This benefits all groups: a good labour supply for the business, good results for the community with a wider range of people employed, good experience for young people in their first job, and good for the working mothers who might otherwise have to pay for childcare.

For these employers, being an employer of choice means offering the potential supply of candidates something they find of value. Twenty years ago it was thought that offering a day's pay for a day's labour would be enough, and often it was. Now, in today's competitive economy, getting the best candidates is as competitive a role as selling to the company's customers. One of the ways to do that is to develop your brand.

Employer branding

The concept of employer branding was developed some years ago. Your brand is who you are and who you represent. It's what people identify with you when they hear your name, and it's how you are recognized. A strong brand will mean that the best talent will find a path to your door. When people join you they already understand and share your values. They buy into your vision and goals.

A brand is not just your logo or your advertising; it is the heart and lifeblood of who you are. Experts talk about brands with 'smashability' – the capacity to break a part off the tangible item and still recognize the brand. Kit Kat, Lego and Coca-Cola are brands that with just a fragment could be recognized as themselves. In recessionary times household brands have learned that if they stop spending on their brand development they will lose brand loyalty. Every time someone changes job we are asking them to 'switch brands' in effect. It's no different from going into the supermarket and seeing a rival brand to your normal favourite on offer for you to try it. A job advertisement or a headhunter is doing the same task. They are tempting the employee to consider switching brands. If the individual responds to the advertisement and applies for the job or agrees to an initial meeting with the headhunter, they are sampling a new brand.

As an employer you'll hope that when people see your advertising or engage with you, they already have a good idea of what your business might be like to work for. As a local employer it will be helpful for you to combine your employer branding with your local marketing policy and strategy. Supporting local events and helping with fundraising are not only good to do but they also send a message about who you are, the kinds of contracts you draw up for staff, the way you behave if you have to lay people off, the pay you offer, the length of time people stay with you. All these find their way around a community and will contribute to your brand. Developing a clear statement about that and making it an intrinsic part of everything you do means your brand will be of value to prospective employees.

However, it is just as easily damaged.

CASE STUDY

I have been made aware of a shop that has in its contract of employment that should the shop assistant (note: shop assistant, not CEO) leave they are not allowed to seek employment in a competitive shop within a 10-mile radius of their previous employer. The shop has such a bad reputation that it now struggles to recruit staff. It is a small market and word gets around.

The brand reputation of any organization, even in a tight labour market where demand outstrips supply, is important.

As employees, contractors or temps move companies more frequently in the workplace today, their perceptions of potential and past employers are really important. This is relevant not only for direct employers, of course, but also for recruitment agencies employing temporary staff. The major agencies may well have thousands of staff working for them globally directly – but thirty times as many may be going out to work for them every day. Their brand is as key as a direct employer as it is an agency employer.

Employees search for companies to work for that meet their needs: a brand that aligns with their values and requirements. This can be seen very clearly when it comes to meeting the employment needs of Generation Y. The *Guardian*'s annual survey of graduates in 2008 reported that two-thirds of today's graduates need to feel happy about a company's ethical record before applying for a job with it. One-third of this group defined ethical as including the company's approach towards its staff. We all have common needs at various levels and all of us will find satisfaction of those needs in different ways. The culture of the organization will meet our needs but may meet them in different ways to suit our own personality and brand.

Brands meet our needs

For example, employers such as John Lewis, Marks & Spencer and the NHS will meet the same needs for us as Google, a technology start-up or a small design agency – but each will meet them in entirely different ways. They will appeal to different types of potential employees. Their brand name immediately paints a picture.

John Lewis, Marks & Spencer

Likely to conform; safe and secure. All staff in each of these companies will wear some kind of uniform. Working environment is a large fit-for-purpose building that customers visit. Neither of these employers is likely to be dramatically hit by an economic climate and need to reduce their workforce significantly. People work for them because they value what they do and the way it makes them feel. These companies offer structured, clear career paths, security and the feeling of working for a leading brand that does meaningful work.

Google, a technology start-up or a small design agency

Perhaps 'cool' to some people, these businesses too will have a uniform – mainly based around not having a uniform. Less secure (arguably not Google) and subject more to the vagaries of the markets, so much less secure. Housed in a futuristic modern building or a funky loft. People will work for them because of the brand, the culture and how it makes them feel: leading edge with autonomy and freedom.

All brands can meet people's needs but the core differentiator for an employer brand is how it meets those needs and how it communicates that.

Guarding your brand

With the proliferation of online sites such as www.glassdoor.com where you can read about potential employers, the brand guardians will increasingly become your employees, former employees (take good care of how people leave, not just how they join), suppliers and anyone else who touches your business. You cannot stop them saying what they want but you can do your best to make it positive by making sure you are a great place to work.

Branding to develop a recruitment pipeline

A great brand will help with developing your pipeline of talent. Until recently most organizations simply used recruitment agencies to find the candidates they need for roles, placed advertisements directly and recruited 'in the moment'. Good candidates who were not employed were not communicated with further or held in mind for future roles.

Increasingly, however, companies can see the value in creating and retaining databases of good people, many of whom will have been fully assessed, for future roles. The next stage on from this is to create a community of people who have shown an interest in your brand and to communicate regularly with them, helping them feel part of the business and treating them as any other stakeholder in the organization. As the capacity to communicate cleverly, which is to say individually but also collectively, develops, the opportunity will grow to make regular touch points with potential candidates.

This can range from alerting them to new roles in their area of expertise, reminding them if they have not applied that a deadline is approaching, telling them about new developments in the business or learning and development opportunities, through to running 'drop-ins' for people who might be thinking about a career move. Not only will this potentially engage the candidate, it can also be passed on to their friends and colleagues, thus building your network and candidate pipeline for very little investment.

For large organizations this means a heavy investment in web-based systems to manage the process and a team to run the communications. However a cost–benefit analysis over a period of time will show that a reduction in agency fees and direct advertising through an increase in direct hires through building communities and pipelines will pay back the investment. Increasing the proportion of direct permanent hires you are able to make will reduce your recruitment costs over a period of years. This then leaves you a good budget to engage consultants in specialist sectors and headhunters to source scarce and critical candidates for you.

For each of these hires it means taking the long view – starting a conversation a couple of years before a hire point.

CASE STUDY

One IT recruitment consultancy started talking to a candidate for their sales director role five years before he took it up. In those five years he gained overseas experience and developed his own skills. The business went through a number of changes itself but it kept talking and both parties eventually reached the point when they were ready to make the move.

As you recruit for roles, retain people's details (taking care, of course, over data protection and ensuring you comply with current legislation), ideally in an applicant tracking system with a database attached so that the first thing you do once you have a recruitment specification is to search your existing contacts. Not only can this bring a cost advantage but it also means a candidate unsuitable for one role is offered another to apply for. Even if they are unsuccessful they feel they are being kept informed of other options.

Customer relationship management

You can develop this approach further through the use of a customer relationship management (CRM) system. Organizations are quick to develop CRM systems for their clients, but the same strong principles can be applied to possible employees. Keep potential candidates engaged by letting them know what is happening within the business to maintain their enthusiasm and interest. This is a real opportunity to differentiate as an employer and build a relationship with people who may have the skills you would value and wish to hire. Every time a new role appears on the careers section of your website, there is no reason why registered candidates showing an interest in relevant areas of your business should not receive an alert suggesting they check out the website for the new role. This means developing the careers section of your website like a job board. If your strategy is to recruit many candidates directly and you recruit enough people annually to make that worthwhile, then it will be a good investment in development.

Attracting new candidates

Your method of attraction will vary and there is more 'how-to' detail in Chapter Eight. Here we are concerned with engagement of the candidate so that the quality of the attraction is key. Attraction may mean:

- advertisements – digital or press;
- posters;
- flyers;
- local job centre adverts;
- internal employee referral schemes;
- liaison with universities/schools;
- headhunting;
- recruitment agencies;
- word of mouth.

It is the initial attraction strategy that will draw candidates in, but to keep them truly engaged it is the rest of the process to which you must pay attention. The candidate's experience of you as an employer of choice will be determined by how you deal with them through the recruitment process. Even if you don't wish to hire them, you would also not want to lose them as a customer or lose the opportunity to hire them at some point in the future – when they have gained more skills, perhaps, or when your business has developed. At the least you'll want them to tell their friends (and, with the advent of social networking, maybe the rest of the world) that they had a good experience of dealing with you.

Acknowledging the application

There is little worse for a candidate than sending off an application for a job, particularly if it is one that they are really keen on or if they really need work, and then hearing nothing back. Making sure this is not the case is an easy way to show yourself as a little bit different in how you deal with people. It's common when you are expecting high demand to jot a quick reply, either manually or automatically, saying 'Thanks and if you don't hear from us, assume we're not interested.' This at least does acknowledge the application but can be very impersonal and does nothing to build your brand. Figures 3.3 and 3.4 give examples of other approaches you could try. Both are designed to be culturally appropriate to different types of organization. You'll notice how both letters offer to keep applicants informed of anything that might come up for which they may be suitable, thereby developing the pipeline we have discussed.

Rejecting candidates

It is equally important that any rejections are handled well and in keeping with the overall look and feel of the rest of your recruitment process. There is no good or easy way of rejecting a candidate but if you are to reject someone at whatever stage, ensure you do it as quickly as you can – although not so quickly that it looks like you have not given it any thought. Offer as

FIGURE 3.3 Application acknowledgement: informal

Dear

Thanks so much for taking the trouble to apply for the job with us. We're really pleased that it looks like a role you'd be interested in and hope you'd also feel that we're a great company to work for. Check out our website for some reviews of our restaurant or venture onto tripadvisor for some really unbiased feedback – last time we looked we were pretty happy with it.

We've quite a few applications to look through so it may take us a little while to get back to you but we commit to doing so within two weeks at the latest. If at this point we can't offer you a first stage interview, we'll write and let you know. Please don't think that it's because we might never use your skills; it'll just be that right now we may have other candidates who match the brief better. We'd really urge you to keep an eye on the website for suitable roles for you as they come up and will always be pleased to hear from you. Equally, we'll keep an eye open at this end and let you know if we feel there is something you could apply for.

Once again, thanks for your interest – we really value that and if we are able to invite you for a first informal meeting, we'll really look forward to meeting you.

Best regards

much support and alternative direction as you can, perhaps suggesting they keep an eye on the website for future roles, or suggest some alternatives. Always hold in mind that although they may not have been right for this role, they may be perfect for others coming up and even if they are not right for the business you want them to leave the process feeling fairly treated and positive about your organization.

FIGURE 3.4 Application acknowledgement: formal

Dear

Thank you very much for your application to us for the role you identified as suiting your skills and experience. We really appreciate the time and effort you have made in putting together your application and look forward to looking through it in detail shortly, as part of our selection process.

We do need to tell you that we have had quite a large response to this role and will therefore not be able to invite for first interview all potential applicants who meet our requirements. If we do wish to invite you to first stage we will let you know within two weeks but will make sure we are in touch with you to let you know the outcome of our selection procedures either way.

If at this point we cannot invite you in for interview, please do keep looking for opportunities with us which may suit your skill set. We too will keep your details 'live' – which means that if we have another role that is suitable we would let you know so you could apply for that too if you wish.

Once again, thank you for your interest in our organization. We hope very much to be able to meet with you in the near future once we have reviewed the applications, but should this not be possible we wish you success in your next career move and hope to meet with you at some point in the future.

Yours sincerely

CASE STUDY

Graham Palfery-Smith, a non-executive director of a range of recruitment companies and with 30 years' experience of recruitment across 26 countries, suggests that the candidates you reject can be your strongest engagement tool. He explains that in his experience those candidates will tell other people about their experience and even if they were not offered a role, if they had a positive experience they will still be brand ambassadors for your business.

Assessment

Assessing your candidates can also be a powerful engagement tool. Each organization will use a range of methods for assessment. Candidates will often value a more stretching and challenging assessment process and this will also mean typically that a better hiring decision is made. The process itself will vary but most will include at least some form of face-to-face interview.

Interview or assessment invitations

This is an opportunity to be flexible and accommodating to the candidate – developing a perception of the organization and how it might be to work there. A dogmatic approach will suggest that the organization is more interested in its own needs and less concerned about the candidate's. Recruiting different types of candidates for different roles means a different approach. A recent graduate may be offered a couple of times for assessment, but with a more senior and scarce skill, more flexibility will be needed, such as video conferences or initial telephone calls to decide whether to move to the next stage. In the public sector it is likely that you will have one particular day that you will use for interviews, offering little flexibility. This can seem confusing and inflexible to applicants coming from outside the public sector. Whichever your approach is, it is important to remember that each of them builds a picture of the organization you belong to.

The interview itself

There is more detail on how to be an effective interviewer and on developing a sound assessment process in Chapter Nine. This section focuses on using an interview as an engagement tool.

You want your candidate to leave feeling they have been treated well, had a good experience and will commend both the process and the organization to their friends and colleagues. Reputation management, especially online, is a key part of the engagement jigsaw; forward-thinking companies are looking at how they manage their online reputation. One bad experience at an interview or assessment centre can quickly find its way to a wide range of readers via Twitter or Facebook. Equally, a good experience can work in your favour.

CASE STUDY

Following a good interview, a candidate was offered a role with one of the major broadcasters. They tabled a question online on Twitter asking whether current employees would recommend the broadcaster as an employer. Internal recruiters saw this and thought about how they might intervene, worrying that they might lose this key hire. They took a deep breath and decided not to and sat and waited to see what the response was. With relief they saw the business doing the work for them: there was an overwhelming consensus that this was a good organization to work for, and the candidate joined.

This will increasingly be the case. As already suggested, decisions like this may well be made more and more in the open domain rather than simply paying attention to 'significant others' round one's own kitchen table. In general, if a business pays attention to its people, treats them fairly and is open and honest with them, meeting their needs and listening to them, then feedback will be good and fair. Treating the interview as the beginning of this process of fair and reliable behaviour adds to the engagement picture.

It is important to remember a few key things:

- The candidate will remember how you start and end the meeting. Ensure your greeting is warm and welcoming and the ending is similarly so.
- You don't have to 'sell' the organization if you don't feel the candidate meets the needs of the role but it is important to spend visible time answering the candidate's questions and telling them something about the job.
- Maintain their self-esteem – even if they do not answer questions well, try not to make this obvious. It is helpful for the candidate to walk away feeling they have done okay.
- But avoid over-managing their self-esteem – in other words, avoid having them leave feeling they have nailed the job only to find that they are rejected the next day and have no idea why.

- Generally candidates like to feel they have been stretched at an interview but not made to feel inadequate, so by all means make the interview challenging – but not too much!

The best way of interviewing is to run a planned series of job-related questions. This also gives the candidate a good experience and will increase engagement.

CASE STUDY

In a time of scarce skills when the telecommunications industry was in high growth and good candidates were hard to find, one of the telcos ran an assessment centre for both potential salespeople and senior managers. All candidates were invited to lunch and a presentation either at the beginning or end of their centre to sell them the opportunity they had applied or been approached for. This simple investment made the conversion ratio of offer to acceptance much higher than might ordinarily be expected in such a market and arguably – along with the high bar of recruitment – helped secure really good people, enabling the business to hit its targets.

Negotiating the offer

How this stage is managed can have either a strong positive or negative impact on engagement. Candidates who are disappointed with an offer will often walk away from a recruitment process with a sour taste in their mouth.

For some specific 'how-to's on this, turn to Chapter Ten, which offers some tips on how to negotiate packages and make good offers as well as rejecting those candidates you don't want to progress with.

You will not be able to hire absolutely everyone you want to. Some candidates will simply want too much from a role or a package for you to meet their needs. Even when this is the case, you do want them to have a good candidate experience. Focusing on engaging them in the recruitment process with your organization, rather than simply thinking about how you may wish to assess them, will make an overall difference to your employer brand.

Many of the candidates you offer (80–90 per cent if you are doing your job well) will go on to join you.

On-boarding

Going back to Figure 3.1, you can see the point at which the offer of employment is made. At this point the engagement of the candidate is at its highest and it is then important to maintain that level throughout the on-boarding process, which starts as soon as you have decided to offer someone a job.

There may be some readers who feel that it is unnecessary to focus too much on this detail. Most of your employees will be grateful enough to have a job. Indeed, in some labour markets and in some economic climates, the competition for skills is not so high. However, a lack of focus on finding the best people can mean that there is an opportunity cost in running your business with the best possible people as engaged as they can be and therefore delivering to their highest potential. At least you'll get the best people in your area or labour market beating a path to your door, reducing your costs of recruitment – so everyone will win.

Organizations that do not focus on on-boarding miss an opportunity to reassure the prospective employee that they have made the right choice. Add to this the potential backdrop that the candidate's existing employer may well be trying to keep them by offering them a new role or a pay increase, and it becomes even more important for the offer process to be as engaging as the role.

We have addressed how engagement can impact your capacity to bring the right people on board, and how this starts prior to hiring, carrying on through the process. At the beginning of this chapter we also said how important retaining your people is, in order that the business can focus on hiring new talent where it is needed.

Retention

The Corporate Leadership Council's 2004 Engagement survey defined retention as a combination of 'rational' and 'emotional' commitment, with focus on the job, the team, the manager and the organization. Both of these forms of commitment together produce both 'discretionary effort' – where someone is prepared to 'go the extra mile', leading to improved performance – and 'intent to stay' – defined as not looking for another role, actively or cursorily, leading to overall retention.

CASE STUDY

An ongoing project by Randstad (one of the world's largest staffing businesses) to increase retention in its businesses (although they already significantly outperform the wider recruitment marketplace) has identified through their own research six pillars of success that drive retention and engagement: recruitment, on-boarding, career development, reward, management and culture. Hala

Collins, UK human resources director, who has already led a highly successful project in one of the operating companies to reduce staff turnover, is keen to apply the learning from that and other group companies across the rest of the group. 'Identifying the six pillars, analysing our practice under them and then applying each of the best practices across the group will lead to us hitting our retention targets. There are pockets of excellent practice across each of our group companies. We need to make sure this knowledge is available to all.'

Once you have recruited your candidates, retaining this talent becomes a really important business driver. Companies that have a limited labour market, geographically based, perhaps, or skills shortage need to pay particular attention to this if they are to retain the capacity to compete. Figure 3.5 shows six retention drivers.

Many people believe that individuals leaving a business – labour turnover – is a fact of running a business and is inevitable. Some turnover is not only inevitable, it is also desirable, but by not paying attention to it a business will waste money and opportunity. High attrition costs significant profit.

It's important to get the balance between retention and turnover right. Jack Welch, CEO of GE, famously commented that he 'sacked the bottom 10 per cent each year'. There is, of course, real value in new thinking and fresh people coming into the business.

This will not be the case for most businesses, however, and retaining people has a number of advantages:

- reduced cost of recruitment;
- less disruption to teams;
- reduced costs of induction for replacement people;
- retention of knowledge and capability in the business;
- shared cohesive sense of ownership within the organization;
- internally promoted staff can often be more successful than external hires;
- hard to replace scarce skills.

With focused effort and energy and an effective programme, Sun Microsystems reduced its turnover from 35 per cent to 18 per cent. Here are some ideas to consider if you want to reduce yours.

Setting labour turnover KPIs

Turnover figures vary enormously from industry and organization to sector and location. Table 3.1 shows the 2010 labour turnover survey data from the CIPD, outlining some of the differences. Comparing your business with others in a similar situation can provide a helpful benchmark.

FIGURE 3.5 Key drivers for retention

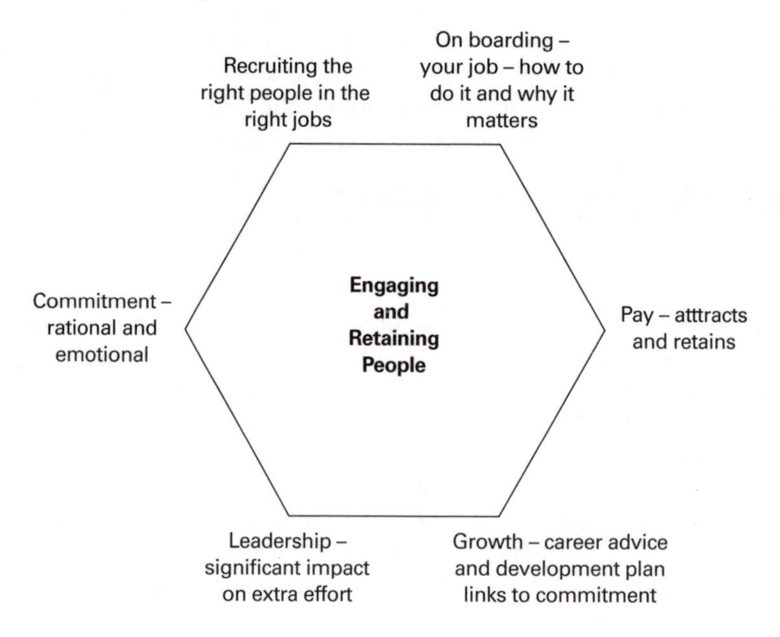

TABLE 3.1 CIPD Resourcing and Talent Planning Survey 2010

Median rate of labour turnover %				
2010	2009	2008	2007	2006
13.5	15.7	17.3	18.1	18.3

If you find that your organization's turnover is 20 per cent and your competitor's is 15 per cent, then you will need to identify why. If yours is below your sector's benchmark, then it may also be helpful to try and identify what you are doing right. Try and identify what is working or not, through surveys or focus groups. It's as important to know what you're doing well as it is to know what you're not doing or doing badly. However, if your turnover is higher than the benchmark, you will want to try and improve it. To do this you'll need to understand first more about what is happening and where, and secondly what is driving the turnover.

Gathering more data

The second stage is to identify where pockets of challenge or success are happening. This means breaking the data down in more detail to find out how particular groups in your organization are behaving. Most organizations will find it useful to look at some or all of the data on why people leave as it may throw up specific issues:

- Women don't return after maternity in the way the business might hope.
- Young people stay less than two years.
- There is a high incidence of leavers before one year is up.
- The numbers of leavers from poor performance has increased steadily over the last three years.

Use exit interviews to determine reasons for leaving. An example of an exit interview can be found in Figure 3.6 and can easily be adapted to suit your needs. If you have a large organization, it will be helpful to make this as quantitative as possible, while allowing space for qualitative information as well. A smaller organization can make more use of less quantitative data.

Once you have this information, you can begin to analyse some of the reasons for people leaving:

- It may be that the business has started managing poor performance rather better than in previous years and this has shown an increased turnover – which is a success. Clearly, the focus then needs to return to learning and development, management capability and recruitment, as all are interlinked.
- It may be that you have a high incidence of staff who leave within the first year, indicating a need to explore induction and recruitment much more fully. Are roles being 'oversold' at interview and are they really not as exciting in reality? Are you over-hiring for the roles, which is to say hiring a higher skill level than needed, or are you making such high demands on staff that they cannot deliver?

Whatever the outcome of your data analysis, you can learn 'what' but you also need to understand 'why'. Table 3.2 shows some varying reasons for this.

Internal factors

Data can be compared with internal factors. Obvious factors to consider are, for example, whether the business itself has experienced a downturn, a fast growth period, if career plans been put on hold, whether there has there been a change in management, a change in learning and development, a change in location or a range of other possibilities. Data will help identify specific reasons for leaving, enabling you to explore further what your organization can do to increase the emotional and rational commitment of your people.

FIGURE 3.6 Exit interview

<table>
<tr><th colspan="7">Exit interview</th></tr>
<tr><td colspan="3">Name:</td><td colspan="4"></td></tr>
<tr><td colspan="3">Department:</td><td colspan="4"></td></tr>
<tr><td colspan="3">Interviewer:</td><td colspan="4"></td></tr>
<tr><td colspan="3">Date:</td><td colspan="4"></td></tr>
<tr><td colspan="3">Length of service:</td><td colspan="4">Tick</td></tr>
<tr><td colspan="3">Under 6 months</td><td colspan="4"></td></tr>
<tr><td colspan="3">6 months–1 year</td><td colspan="4"></td></tr>
<tr><td colspan="3">1–5 years</td><td colspan="4"></td></tr>
<tr><td colspan="3">5 years plus</td><td colspan="4"></td></tr>
<tr><td colspan="3">Experience with X organization</td><td colspan="2">Yes</td><td colspan="2">No</td></tr>
<tr><td colspan="3">Would you work for X again in the future?</td><td colspan="2"></td><td colspan="2"></td></tr>
<tr><td colspan="3">If so, or if not, why?</td><td colspan="2"></td><td colspan="2"></td></tr>
<tr><td colspan="3">Would you recommend employment with X to a friend?</td><td colspan="2"></td><td colspan="2"></td></tr>
<tr><td colspan="3">What is your reason for leaving?</td><td colspan="2">Tick as they apply</td><td colspan="2"></td></tr>
<tr><td colspan="3"></td><td colspan="2">Work–life balance</td><td colspan="2">Leaving recruitment</td></tr>
<tr><td colspan="3"></td><td colspan="2">Salary</td><td colspan="2">Bonus/benefits</td></tr>
<tr><td colspan="3"></td><td colspan="2">Career development</td><td colspan="2">Manager</td></tr>
<tr><td colspan="3"></td><td colspan="2">Job content</td><td colspan="2">Better opportunity</td></tr>
<tr><td colspan="3"></td><td colspan="2">Personal/family reasons</td><td colspan="2">Other</td></tr>
<tr><td colspan="3">How satisfied are you with your overall work experience?</td><td colspan="2"></td><td colspan="2"></td></tr>
<tr><td>Extremely dissatisfied</td><td>Somewhat dissatisfied</td><td colspan="2">Neutral</td><td colspan="2">Somewhat satisfied</td><td>Extremely satisfied</td></tr>
<tr><td></td><td></td><td colspan="2"></td><td colspan="2"></td><td></td></tr>
<tr><td colspan="2">How satisfied are you with the way you have been managed?</td><td colspan="5"></td></tr>
<tr><td>Extremely dissatisfied</td><td>Somewhat dissatisfied</td><td colspan="2">Neutral</td><td colspan="2">Somewhat satisfied</td><td>Extremely satisfied</td></tr>
<tr><td></td><td></td><td colspan="2"></td><td colspan="2"></td><td></td></tr>
<tr><td colspan="3">What suggestions do you have for ways to improve X?</td><td colspan="4"></td></tr>
<tr><td colspan="3">What are the main things you liked about X?</td><td colspan="4"></td></tr>
<tr><td colspan="3">What are the main things you disliked about X and what would you do to change them?</td><td colspan="4"></td></tr>
<tr><td colspan="3">Any other comments?</td><td colspan="4"></td></tr>
</table>

TABLE 3.2 Leaver's metrics

Leaver's metrics
Number of people leaving in less than 1 year
Number of women leaving
Number of men leaving
Number of people leaving with over an hour's journey
Number of women not returning after maternity leave
Number of managers leaving
Demographically split data analysis, eg 16–25year olds, 25–40 year olds and post 40, for example
Numbers of shop floor/shop workers leaving (or quantified to suit your business)
Trends in turnover over 3–5 years
Voluntary leavers
Leavers from poor performance
Leavers from redundancy

CASE STUDY

Jack Gratton, CEO of Major Players, the leading marketing recruitment agency and winner of the *Sunday Times* Best Companies to Work For award, says although their staff turnover has traditionally been extremely low (12 per cent in an industry that often sees 70 per cent), their use of exit interviews has proved valuable in assessing reasons for leaving. 'All staff who leave us do so for a myriad of reasons (returning home to Australia, going back into the marketing industry, having a baby, sometimes to branch out on their own), but almost none of them leaves to go to a competitor. Recruitment can be a hard industry to work in and we also make sure it's great fun and rewarding . We are very proud that if people leave us it's precisely because they want to move out of recruitment or for personal reasons, very rarely anything else.'

External factors

Data can also be compared with external factors to see if the economic cycle is impacting retention. It may be that competitors coming into the market are also affecting it. For example, in an economic downturn it is highly likely in some sectors that the number of leavers from redundancy will increase as well as leavers through poor performance. Those sectors that experience a drop in demand for their services may well require a higher level of capability from their people in order to stay competitive than might otherwise be the case. Staff who were able to meet performance demands in a buoyant market may well not be able to do so in a more challenging market.

Equally, immediately after a recessionary period, staff who have remained in their jobs and not wanted to move will now start to do so – in other words, post recession there will be an increased turnover of staff. This is a key time to plan a new retention strategy.

Once you have collated the data, you can see why people are leaving and make some decisions about what steps to take to change this. It may be that you need to change a range of elements or just one. Many organizations find that their recruitment process is at fault, others their management capability

L'Oréal wanted to increase the retention of the staff they recruited by improving the on-boarding in the business, linking it even more closely to learning and development to ensure a seamless transfer from hire to induction.

CASE STUDY

L'Oréal developed a programme called FIT – Full Integration Track – which kicks off before new recruits join the business (L'Oréal hire some 200 experienced staff a year and some 30 graduates). The recruitment manager stays with them through induction, providing a 'fuzzy line' between recruitment and when they start. Managing candidates effectively has always been a cornerstone belief of Alex Snelling, at the time L'Oréal's recruitment director. The result has been a certainty now that if staff do leave after a few months (increasingly rare), they are leaving for the right reasons. 'We are not always going to get it absolutely right. We have a very strong culture here at L'Oréal which most of us love but which occasionally does not suit people. At least now we know we have given new joiners every possible assistance into the business,' says Snelling.

Key retention drivers

I will now explore in a little more detail the key retention drivers indicated in Figure 3.5:

- recruitment;
- on-boarding;
- growth and development;
- pay and benefits;
- leadership;
- commitment to people.

Below you'll find checklists for each area, which you can use to analyse your own performance. Aim to have something in place for each of the checklisted areas to improve retaining your people.

Recruitment

There is strong evidence to show that the more information a prospective employee can get about a role and the more experience they have of it, the greater the chance they have of matching their needs, and those of the employer, to the role. Some organizations have prospective employees come into the office for half a day to observe the role or have a try at it, both to see how they might do in the role and, as importantly, to see whether they like the role. Table 3.3 shows a recruitment checklist.

On-boarding

This part of the retention process focuses on bringing the new joiner over the threshold into the new business. It answers the questions 'What is my job, how do I do it and how does it fit into the bigger business picture?', allowing the new joiner to get up and running quickly so that their change of role is less stressful. As soon as this is realized, candidates will relax into the role and the chance of them leaving after a few days or a week is reduced. If this happens often, clearly it means there is something wrong with either the recruitment phase or the beginning of the on-boarding. Both of these activities also mean that it's best value for the business as the sooner someone is operational, the sooner they will add value to the business. Table 3.4 shows an on-boarding checklist.

Growth and development

Your organization might use a range of frameworks to ensure you have strong development plans in place. For many people this is one of the key

TABLE 3.3 Recruitment checklist

Activity	Tick
Clear role specification/job description	
Candidate has balanced view of the organization, its strengths and weaknesses	
Candidate has met people doing their role in the business or had a chance to try the role out beforehand	
Candidate ideally has experience of doing the role before in a similar environment	
The salary and benefits package reflects the value of the role	
The candidate understands the value of the role and where it fits in the business, and feels important to the organization	
Candidate understands and shares the values of the organization	
Candidate has met and formed a relationship with their direct manager before offer stage	
The assessment process is valid for the role	
The offer process suits the style of the organization and is congruent	

drivers of work – the capacity to develop, improve and 'get on'. The framework doesn't have to be complicated. For a small business it might be straightforward. For some businesses, offering career progression may be difficult. The opportunities become more limited as people progress through the business. Think instead about new skills, new opportunities for learning, opportunities to move across rather than up. Ford famously offered a learning and development budget for each individual of £200 to be spent on anything they liked – it didn't have to be work related. You could consider doing the same with vouchers to the local college of adult education or offering an individual budget for relevant development for their role.

CASE STUDY

My own father left school at 14, swept floors in a factory for a short while, joined a new factory (it saw the potential in his floor sweeping, I guess!), which decided to offer him training as a draughtsman. This he became, and won awards for, becoming one of the leading coal-cutting machine designers. He continued to be developed by the business and ended this part of his career at 60 as technical director of the same firm he started with at 15. This same firm also supported him through a year off for a heart operation in his forties.

TABLE 3.4 On-boarding checklist

Activity	Tick
New joiner meets all the people they will be working with in an informal way quickly	
New joiner understands the importance of their role to the organization (follows on from recruitment but needs re-emphasizing)	
New joiner learns about the organizational vision and strategy – ideally from a senior manager but the content is most important	
New joiner is very clear on what their role is and what is expected of them within the first few days and on an ongoing basis	
New joiner is given all the tools and techniques necessary to be able to do their role in an appropriate time frame	
New joiner has a buddy or mentor allocated as they join so they have an immediate colleague or friend, ideally outside their immediate department	
The whole organization or department is aware of the new person and joins them in a welcome coffee, tea or short event	
New joiner is made aware that someone cares about them as a person in the organization – their team, their buddy or others	
Everything they were told in the recruitment phase is true and valid	
New joiner spends time with their manager in the first week looking at their first month and thereafter considering their career development	

Other options to support a clear career development programme are to offer a number of training days per year for in-house or externally run courses, to be chosen and agreed with a manager as part of a planned development programme. Shadowing, planned reading, mentoring, action learning sets, discussion groups, quality circles, and project teams (working on exciting projects) are all also good ways of increasing learning towards career development.

Most importantly, people need to know what they are working towards, what they need to do to get there and that they are supported. Frameworks like Investors in People can help businesses that would not currently describe themselves as learning organizations develop a framework of development – and they offer a recognized award as well.

Internal promotion data

It's important to be able to track targets for and monitor internal promotions and progression. Again it may be desirable to have an injection of new talent in senior managers or at board level, but when a business has to hire all its senior staff and MD/CEO from outside the business, then it is not succession planning effectively. A target of 70–80 per cent internal promotions for senior roles throughout the business is realistic and has many benefits, not least of which is that people feel that they can see something to aim for and that their aim has its roots in reality. It also means that much of the know-how gained at senior level is retained within the business rather than walking off to your competitors. However, there has recently been a raft of chief executive appointments made externally in well-known high-street names, leading investors to ask questions of those businesses' non-executive directors about their succession planning.

Consider setting some targets for the proportion of internal promotions, and talent map your organization to see where potential future leaders are. Work out how to identify them and develop career and development pathways for them. Table 3.5 shows a checklist for career development.

TABLE 3.5 Career development checklist

Activity	Tick
All staff have personal development plans as a result of an appraisal process	
The organization has a clearly defined career development pathway	
People know what they have to do to be promoted or to move in the direction they want; this is written down and agreed	
Learning and development are part of the culture of the business	
Making mistakes is okay – and trying new things is encouraged and not frowned on	
There is a mechanism in place to avoid 'over-promotion'	
There is a target for promoting people internally	
Talent is 'mapped' through the organization via the appraisal process and high potential identified	
Extra-talented individuals have an opportunity to fast-track through the process	

Pay and benefits

The key leverage point of pay and benefits is to attract and retain. Many organizations fall into the trap of attracting but not retaining through their pay policies.

Reward is an art and a specialization in itself and there is not the space to go into it in great detail here. There is unlikely to be a 'perfect' system. Every system has inherent tensions between satisfying all stakeholders from shareholders to board directors to managers and staff. We have moved on from the days of Frederick Taylor's 'scientific management', which introduced piece work. However, reward does remain one of the key drivers. Herzberg's motivation theory tells us that pay is not an intrinsic motivator but not being paid enough is an intrinsic demotivator. Salespeople are more likely to be more motivated by performance-related pay and reward than others. In 2010, when the vast majority of salespeople had experienced low earnings the previous year, pay became their overwhelming concern. Ordinarily it would factor highly in importance but not override every other issue.

The Corporate Leadership Council's 2004 Engagement survey again shows that while pay itself (or satisfaction with total compensation) produces only a 9 per cent increase in effort, it can provide a 21 per cent increase in employees' intention to stay. Many employees often feel they need to leave an organization to keep their pay in line with that of others, which can create unnecessary staff turnover.

Reward is not straightforward, however, as the next case study shows.

CASE STUDY

In my own first management role, a more experienced manager who used to be a production manager in the manufacturing industry told me of the factory he used to work in. At this point, before studying organizational behaviour, I naively saw it as straightforward that pay should be linked to performance and that the more you paid people, they harder they would work. He explained how the shop-floor workers were paid a basic salary and then a bonus on performance. Each week the bonus would be calculated and 'chips' issued, which the workers could exchange for pay in the following week's pay packet. Most of the men kept the chips in their lockers until Christmas so their wives would not question them on why they had more money some weeks than others – they figured it was better to give their wife the same money in their pay packet each week to avoid 'grief', as once their wives saw a possibility of them earning more they would expect it each week.

In general, a reward system should reward the behaviours it seeks to encourage, just as the one in the manufacturing plant did. However, one can never quite account for people's behaviours. But when designing a reward system comprising pay, benefits and bonus, a good sense check is to ask what kind of behaviours it will reward. Most importantly, does the reward system seem fair? Fairness is key in designing pay and benefits systems. Table 3.6 shows a checklist.

Leadership

Leaders and managers provide a key role in gaining people's commitment to the business, the role and the team. If a person feels their manager has their interests at heart, is good at helping them develop and provides clear, helpful feedback, is interested in developing their career and is great in supporting when there are problems, then this manager will be a main factor in that employee staying with the business. The converse is equally true. There is a strong argument that people join companies but leave leaders.

TABLE 3.6 Pay and benefits checklist

Activity	Tick
The business has a clear strategy for pay positioning, eg it doesn't pay the best but is still aspirational because of other factors	
The system is fair, both internally and externally	
The system is considered in its entirety; includes not only pay, benefits and bonus but also location, respected company name, career plans, L&D opportunities, sabbaticals, flexible working patterns, etc	
In developing team or individual bonuses it fits with the company ethos and the behaviours you want to reward	
Continual benchmarking takes place with competitors, especially in a scarce-skills market	
Rewards can also be fast-tracked to match the fast-track system	
This links in with any talent-mapping process in the business – those individuals recognized as highly talented can access higher rewards	
The pay and benefits system rewards merit and potential, not length of service in undue proportions	

One of the ways, therefore, to increase retention is to invest in leadership development, enabling managers to work more successfully with their teams, forming a strong bond (with the necessary boundaries) and an emotional commitment to and from each other.

A further way is to link a manager's bonus and pay plan with their capacity to retain good staff. If retention is seen as a key issue by the whole business, reward should align itself with this goal. A manager's/leader's checklist is shown in Table 3.7.

Commitment to people

CIPD research (Managing Employee Careers survey 2003) shows that while talking to people twice a year about their career is important (this links to growth and development, of course), giving people a 'voice' in the business is equally important – if not more so. You might consider a range of consultation mechanisms: listening lunches with senior managers, breakfast feedback chats, 'round tables' made up of people across a range of departments, employee engagement surveys followed by workshops, etc, company meetings, creating as much job security as possible, offering flexibility in working patterns, and not creating a culture of 'presenteeism'.

TABLE 3.7 Manager's/leader's checklist

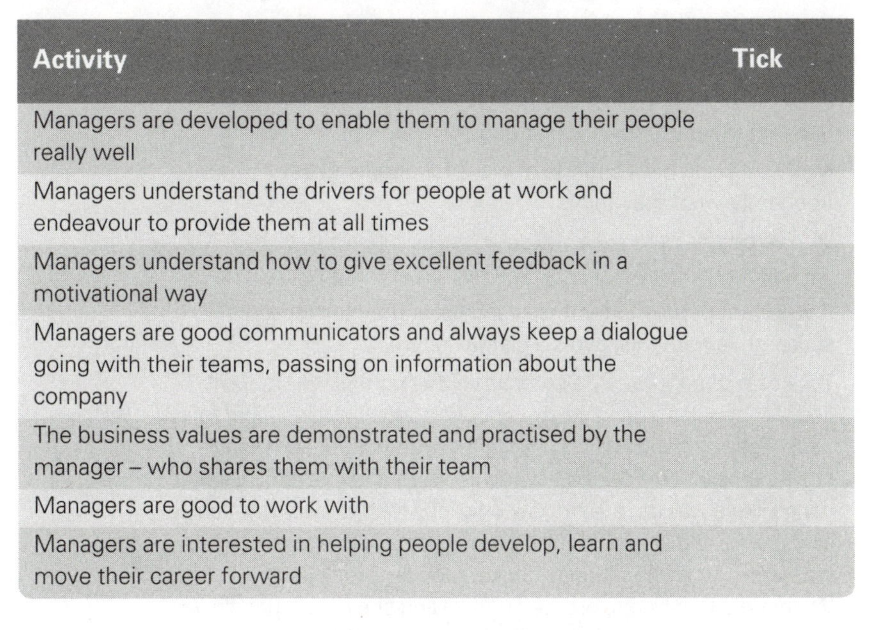

Activity	Tick
Managers are developed to enable them to manage their people really well	
Managers understand the drivers for people at work and endeavour to provide them at all times	
Managers understand how to give excellent feedback in a motivational way	
Managers are good communicators and always keep a dialogue going with their teams, passing on information about the company	
The business values are demonstrated and practised by the manager – who shares them with their team	
Managers are good to work with	
Managers are interested in helping people develop, learn and move their career forward	

The major shift in our working lives over the last 20 years has been the demise of a 'job for life', which makes helping people think about careers all the more important.

We don't join firms forever. We are in charge of our own careers. The old paternalistic relationship in which your firm would look after you is dwindling and exists less in the newer industries. Organizations need a new space to operate away from the old paternalism, adult to adult, where everyone understands the importance of what they do and all play a part in the organizational community, whose sands often shift. It moves away from the idea of employees as children who have to be looked after and more towards the idea of a partnership, perhaps a step on from the ideal of employee as customer suggested before. Table 3.8 has a checklist of some ideas for how to show commitment to your people. This is by no means an exhaustive list but designed to get you started.

TABLE 3.8 Commitment to people

Activity	Tick
Values will be a strong driver and come from the top; know what your values are – who you want to be and how to make it so	
Emotional commitment is four times as effective at driving performance as rational commitment (CCL 2004); but secure rational needs (reward, etc) first	
Ensure the business keeps its promises – and does what it says it will	
See that the business has a strong commitment to diversity	
Make sure you have a range of ways for people to say frequently what they think	
Involve people in running the business as much as you can; ask big questions and get people working on important projects	
If you want people to try things and fail and try things and succeed, reward this; avoid a blame culture	
Take care of people; large companies that do this well make it easy for people to be at work: in-house shops/coffee shops/ food/ travel agencies/counsellors/dry cleaners/doctors/occupational health; smaller companies have to be more creative and invest in things like duvet days, extra day's holiday for birthdays, birthday cards, cake and singing, publicly recognizing achievement, massages on Fridays, Friday drinks, Monday breakfasts, Valentine's Day treats, etc; be creative and show your people you care; small things cost little money and mean a lot	

Through these elements of retention your organization can ensure it is reducing the number of people leaving your business, so you can do the kind of recruitment you want to develop your business rather than spending a great deal of effort replacing people.

The key messages of this chapter are to use retention and engagement as real weapons in your war for talent. The more you are able to drive choice around whom you retain, the more you are able to shape the talent within the business. Low staff turnover is gained by paying attention to all the elements of retention and having a strategy in place to address them all. This is a continuous process as the external landscape is ever changing and any strategy needs to address both internal and external factors. Engaging people before, through and up to the on-boarding point means you'll increase the efficiency of your hiring process. Get it right more often and both of these areas will lead to greater performance. There is a strong link between engagement and profit, as the Great Place to Work Institute has discovered. The next chapter is about providing all of the elements of a great place to work that we've not already explored here.

Creating a great place to work

04

Great Place to Work is a trademarked name of an institute both in the USA (founded in 1980) and in the UK (founded in 2001), which researches and measures what makes an organization a great place to work. It runs the *Sunday Times* Best Companies to Work For employee engagement survey in the UK and a range of other surveys. It has concluded that particular aspects of an organization have the potential to make it 'a great place to work'. Some are directly in line with the six drivers we explored in the previous chapter.

I look briefly at each of the areas identified by them, exploring what they comprise from my own knowledge and experience. The areas are:

- vision and purpose;
- leadership;
- strategy;
- communication;
- career development;
- learning opportunities;
- community;
- culture;
- people strategy.

Vision and purpose

Creating a great place to work is similar to creating any great environment where people can thrive and get what they need. It's like creating a great country with a real sense of possibility and opportunity.

We all need to see how anything might make our lives easier, more successful, more fun and richer in the widest sense. We all need to be convinced of how in the first instance it helps us survive and then how in the second instance it helps us grow. In other words, we need vision and a sense of direction. If we don't understand the vision and where we are going, we cannot sign up. If your business doesn't have a vision, a story, a picture of the future, you will find it hard to retain the people you have and attract the people you want.

Intrinsically linked with the vision is the purpose of the organization. What is it there for? What is the business called on to achieve? What 'big' question can the business engage itself with to create meaning to our work?

Leadership

> The very essence of leadership is that you have to have vision. You can't blow an uncertain trumpet.
>
> Theodore M Hesburgh

The vision and the motivational environment must be developed by the leaders within the business. Strong, clear leadership is crucial to building a vision and therefore for success. To follow a vision, people have to know who to follow and why they are following them. In leadership development courses, people are often asked to identify well-known leaders and decide why they are or were successful. The common denominator is often strength and determination.

To recruit the best people, all layers of an organization need to be strong leaders and be able to articulate the vision. In a competition for the best people, it is often the business that can paint the brightest picture that will win.

CASE STUDY

Sue Evans of DS Connections, a talent strategy business, reports: 'Recruiting a UK finance director for a client, we offered a top candidate with a great background and skills – but he had two offers. I could see he was genuinely torn between the two. We were a little ahead in the game but he was still at final stages with the other company, which put us at a disadvantage. My recruiter was feeling nervous that he hadn't met us for a while. I arranged for him to meet the global HR director a couple of days after he had had both offers in. She really sold him on the big picture of the business and his career opportunity, and he made the decision to join that day. He's done really well with this client, been very successful and it's been a great move for him. He might not have joined if we hadn't been able to tell him a great story at the right time for him.'

Strategy

> The best executive is the one who has sense enough to pick good men to do what he wants done and self-restraint to keep from meddling with them while they do it.
>
> Theodore Roosevelt

Roosevelt is, then, in agreement with Jim Collins, whom we looked at in the previous chapter. As with your vision, to attract the best people you'll also need a strategy that makes sense. You'll need it to be clear and accessible to everyone in the organization – yet few people in organizations typically understand what the strategy is. There can be a sense that the strategy is for senior management to know and do, but all levels of people within the business can contribute to the strategy in their role.

To make your business a great place to work, be clear with everyone about your strategy and how they can play their part in making it happen.

Ask all your hiring managers and your recruiters to tell you what the business strategy is. If they cannot, they cannot hope to sell it to people they are recruiting. In an uneven labour market those candidates will simply go elsewhere.

Communication

If you are not communicating about these elements of your business, then it is likely you are also under-communicating in general.

Communication plans invade all you do and have a direct and indirect impact on recruitment and your capacity to hire the best talent. They will comprise:

- investor relations (the share price and how the analysts view the business);
- employer branding (how the organization is positioned internally and externally);
- internal communications (how informed everyone working in the business feels, how well they understand the values);
- suppliers (how you are perceived by all suppliers – and, of course, hiring suppliers particularly: do you pay on time, do you haggle excessively over fees, are you fair in your behaviours?).

And as communication is one of those dark arts, it's so easy to get it wrong. Like interviewing, as it's simply about talking, we all think we can do it well.

Career development

In my experience, some of the most challenging organizations to headhunt from are the larger ones, not because they have the best jobs, pay and benefits but because they are great at helping people to manage their careers. Every person knows what their next career move is and how they are to work towards it; some companies have career managers who are line managers, not HR, and who look after people's careers a step down from themselves, maybe in another division. Others have sophisticated mentoring schemes, and more again run career development programmes and offer coaching from qualified coaches across the business.

Whichever way it is done, there is an emphasis on developing people's careers both within the business and outside it, which headhunters find challenging to argue against.

Learning opportunities

Alongside career development, of course, sits learning.

According to many writers, learning is one of top five things that people value about a workplace. There are many reasons to invest in learning and development. People who learn and develop tend to do a better job and become more capable in their existing role. They also develop towards a different role or take on more responsibility, which means the organization not only has a wider choice of resources but also stands a better chance of retaining that individual.

Clearly, the capacity for people to grow and develop is a key motivator and will help greatly in improving your retention, particularly if you are finding people are leaving to develop their career – so both the section above on career development and this one go hand in hand. Great places to work look after both helping people to develop their career (which does not always have to be upwards all the time) and helping them learn new skills and take new directions.

If people can get growth and progression where they are, they have no need to seek it outside the business.

Community

Maslow's hierarchy of needs (Figure 4.1) shows clearly that once we have satisfied our physiological needs through our salary and our security needs through believing we will still have a job next month, our next most important set of needs is that of belonging.

Organizations contribute to this simply by providing workplaces and teams. However, how they function will make a difference to how people feel working there. If they really enjoy working with their colleagues and trust both them and their managers, this will contribute strongly to a feeling of belonging. Recognition for jobs well done, opportunities to make a wider contribution outside the day job and the chance to make real friends,

FIGURE 4.1 Maslow's hierarchy of needs

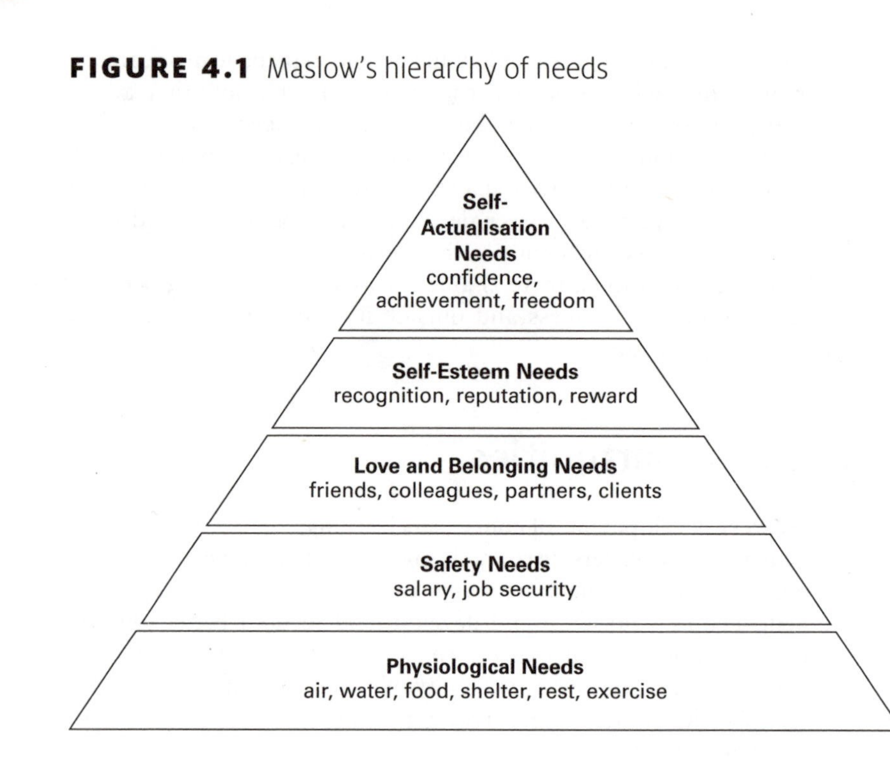

coupled with the knowledge that someone cares about you at work – these make a real difference here. At a more personal level, a *Fortune* study in 2007 showed that 22 per cent of couples who have a relationship at work go on to get married. More people meet their partner(s) at work these days than at college or school, which were previously the favourites; anecdotal evidence suggests that 15–20 per cent of couples meet at work.

Businesses have a huge opportunity therefore to create a real sense of community within their business: a sense of recognition and belonging that goes hand in hand with the employer brand.

Culture

This is where personal fit to a business is all-important. If you find an organization you feel at home in, where it feels like you have worked there forever, it's like meeting your life partner. It just feels right.

Not every organization will feel right to everyone, as we discussed in the previous chapter, but the culture of a place can do more to bind people together than anything else. It won't do so in isolation, though. A business with no career development or learning, vision or communication will struggle, however strong its culture.

The definition of culture could be 'how we do things around here'. This is made up of a series of often unspoken codes of behaviour and actions.

Anyone new has to assimilate these, but where there is a culture match, they do so quickly and feel comfortable with them. The on-boarding aspect of recruitment plays an important role here: if new people are unconsciously kept out of the culture for long they will not feel part of it and may leave quite quickly. Some companies will be proud if people who join either leave quickly or stay a long time: they see it as a matter of cultural fit. They may want to look more closely at their recruitment process.

People strategy

This last aspect deals with everything to do with people. It will often be called an HR strategy and can too often focus on what 'HR' does, how it is organized and what it wants to achieve. Great places to work genuinely put their people at the heart of their organization and recognize that without people, and good plans for them, they will be not be a successful business. The best businesses put how their people feel about working for them at the heart of their people strategy. They know that if people are emotionally engaged, they'll stay.

This look at what makes a great place to work concludes the first section of this book, which has focused on getting everything in place in your business to be successful at recruiting the best people. I've looked at the recruitment environment and how to place recruitment at the heart of your business. I've examined the costs involved in getting recruitment wrong – and equally the massive benefits of engaging and retaining your people (without which recruitment just becomes a black cost hole that people fall through) and how to make your place a great place to work. The next section is full of go-to practical advice on recruiting top talent that is right for you.

PART TWO
Making great recruitment happen

05 Elements for successful recruitment

This chapter heralds the start of the second section. This section provides all of the 'how-to' guidance you might need to recruit well for your organization. It starts with a list of 'must-do's and then takes us through the recruitment process, looking at best practice.

This first chapter focuses on the key elements you'll need in place to make recruitment work at its best for you and your business. Many of the elements are covered in other chapters in more depth, and if you are reading this book cover to cover you will already have touched on some of them in the chapter on engagement and retention.

The first, and most important, element is being emotionally engaged with recruitment itself. If someone truly engaged with an organization needs to be both 'rationally' and 'emotionally' engaged (according to CLC), then the same is true of the act of recruitment.

What follows is a checklist of elements you need to consider and put in place to be successful in recruiting the right people into the right roles to meet your business objectives. You may not be unsuccessful if you do not include each of these elements but you will stand the greatest chance of success if you do.

You might want to conduct a situational analysis against your recruiting activity. Decide which elements can be improved and work out which of those might contribute 'quick wins' and which might provide a large gain for a small amount of effort. The Pareto principle of 20 per cent of the effort can mean a gain of 80 per cent. A critical analysis of your recruitment may show that you never re-evaluate roles as they arise as people leave and also never evaluate existing people's capability to do those roles. Just by changing this process, you can decrease your recruitment costs and increase retention very quickly and simply.

TABLE 5.1 The elements of successful recruitment

Role evaluation
People evaluation
Strategy
Position in the business
Passion
Focus
Business buy-in
Supplier relationships
Process
Attraction
Assessment
Speed, cost, quality balance
Budgeting
Reward

Elements for success

Table 5.1 shows each of the elements briefly. The rest of the chapter provides more detail on each and asks questions to help you think about each of the areas and how to make them work best for you.

Element checklist

Role evaluation

Questions to consider:

- How do we know this role needs doing?
- If it's because 'someone was doing it before', where's the thought process that leads to replacing this automatically? Sense check the role.
- What actually needs doing?
- In what way can it best be done?
- Where is it best located (geographically and organizationally)?
- What sort of value does this role bring to the organization?
- What sort of salary and seniority should this role command?
- How does this compare with the market and our chosen market positioning?

So far, this is quite a rational process. It can become less effective when it takes on an emotional perspective, so it's helpful to have an objective perspective, either someone externally or an HR person if you have that function.

Once you have asked the questions about the role itself, you may then have come up with a different role, decided to share the role in the team, move it to another team or outsource it as a few of the options. This may mean that there is no need to recruit or that the recruitment is different from that first thought about. If you do end up with a new or existing role to fill, the next stage will be to draw up a role specification and a person specification, examples of which you can find in Chapter Seven. Assuming this is done, you'll then move to the next element: that of evaluating the people for the role, both those you currently have and those you don't.

People evaluation

Questions to consider:

- When do we need this role filled?
- If urgently, can this role be resourced with a freelancer or interim prior to permanent placement?
- For a long-term permanent role, who do we have already who could do this role (succession planning) now, in six to nine months' time with development, or in two years time?
- If we have someone, what development is needed?
- Do we need to recruit externally?
- How do we ensure that we manage both internal and any external recruitment concurrently?
- What assessment process do we need to put in place for this role?

You may have a succession planning process already in place in your business. If not, it would be helpful to put one in place – which means having the answers to some of these questions at your fingertips.

There is sometimes an opportunity to develop someone by adding stretching, and motivating, projects to their portfolio. Avoid the temptation to save money by 'dumping' activities on to someone. For development, they need to be from a more senior person's role – and interesting.

Many organizations find that by improving their assessment processes they can increase the applicant's chances of success by a considerable amount. You don't have to be a multinational to take assessment seriously. In a smaller business there will be a higher proportional cost if you don't get it right. Avoid the assumption that you need a couple of chatty interviews with a few people, and consider instead the sums involved in getting it wrong.

So you know what people you need. Your recruitment strategy is the next element of success.

Strategy

Questions to consider:

- How do we resource the work to meet our business goals?
- How important to us is the resourcing/recruitment function internally?
- What are the risks and costs of not meeting our hiring needs?
- What is our market positioning? High/low payers?
- How can our culture support our resourcing needs?
- What blend of flexible/permanent/outsourced resources do we need?
- Will we buy in the skills we need or develop them ourselves?
- What are the benefits and risks of each?
- Where and what is our labour supply?
- If there isn't one, how do we create one?
- What mix of internal and external hiring do we need/can we manage?
- How do we manage the resourcing function?
- What processes do we need internally?
- How do we manage the efficiency–effectiveness balance?

It is clear from this checklist that in order to develop a strategy, you need first to decide what your business goals are and where you are in relation to both your internal set-up and your external markets.

You'll need to decide which the highest driver is: recruitment or cost. Clearly you'll be looking for a balance of the two, but very new businesses are likely to see cost as a key driver, while fast-growing funded businesses are likely to see recruitment as the biggest driver (the opportunity cost of not growing and losing out to the competition being key). Larger businesses are likely to see top talent and best value as their main drivers.

Once you have this decision in place, you are in a position to begin to develop your strategy.

Recruitment's place in the organizational structure

Questions to consider:

- How critical a role does recruitment play in the development of this business?
- How hard is it to find great candidates?
- How much recruitment do we plan to do this year (doubling in size makes it strategically critical)?
- How is our employer brand perceived?
- How important is it for us to be developing a talent pipeline?

- Which part of the business will fail if recruitment does not hit its targets?
- What stops us from recruiting well, to time and to budget?

Where you position recruitment in your business organizationally will depend upon the role it needs to play for you. If you consider it to be the most important element in your business to overall success, then recruitment needs to sit at board level. If, however, your business is in a steady state of growth in line with inflation and you have little labour turnover and a ready supply of candidates, recruitment can probably be handled by HR.

Wherever you choose to site it, it is important that is has influence and perceived value across the business.

Passion

Points to consider:

- You either love or hate recruitment.
- Staff your recruiting team with people who'd rather be elsewhere and you'll get poor results.
- Passion is a critical element in the most successful recruitment teams.

For too many organizations, recruitment is a function tucked in a back room or something managers do when they have nothing else to do. Although we have made great strides in this area in the last 10 years with the advent of recruitment process outsourcing and focused internal recruitment teams, recruitment can still be left languishing with people who have 'better' things to do. If recruitment is not a priority for your business and it has low impact on the business when roles are not filled, this may be less important. But for any business that has talent at the top of its agenda, placing recruitment in the hands of experts who love their job or empowering managers to do it well will bring best results.

At the very least, recruitment has to have influence. Meeting a great person who can contribute to the growth or health of the organization and driving that through are the hallmark of a great recruiter, whether they be the MD themselves, a line manager or an internal professional recruiter.

Focus

Points to consider:

- Ideally give your recruiters nothing else to do.
- If someone has many different tasks, they are likely not to do any of them very well if they are responsible for implementation as well as strategy.

Often organizations give recruitment responsibility to people who have other roles and responsibilities. Of course, hiring managers need to do their own recruitment and make their own hiring decisions, but their key focus should be on doing their day job and making hiring decisions, not running the entire branding and attraction process. Where they are spending much of their time recruiting, this should only really be when they are in high-growth mode and need to spend a high percentage of their time interviewing or assessing.

The process of recruitment strategy development and implementation should sit outside the line and ideally with someone who does nothing else. If you are a small business, then make sure that whoever you ask to do the recruitment sees it as really important and a critical part of their role when recruitment is taking place. Above all, avoid seeing recruitment and your recruitment suppliers as an irritant, or you won't get the quality of people you need. Moreover, a good recruitment consultancy can act as your internal recruitment team.

If you have an internal recruitment function or team, then getting buy-in from your clients, the business and its leaders is crucial to your success.

Business buy-in for internal recruitment teams

Points to note:

- Prioritize building sustainable relationships with hiring managers.
- Take the trouble to understand their needs.
- Make it your business to understand and support them.
- Understand that time is crucial to them, so add value in every way: role and people specification development, assessment advice and management, supplier briefings, CV screening, appointment arrangements straight into diaries, feedback provision through to offer management.
- Remember that without them you don't have a role!
- Deliver to time.
- If you cannot deliver to them directly, find someone who can – and fast.
- Deliver great qualified candidates.
- Follow the process right the way through.
- Provide advice and guidance all the way through the process.
- Support and develop your hiring manager's interviewing skills and how the role is presented to increase candidate buy-in.
- Ensure your offer-to-acceptance ratio is high.
- Above all, work in partnership with them.

Most internal recruitment functions will have some suppliers. They may be recruitment agencies, job boards, local press, radio, advertising agencies, social media. The relationship with these suppliers will also make a key difference to how successful your recruitment function is. Although most agencies are highly professional, if you treat them badly they will struggle to market you really well to their best candidates.

Supplier relationships

Points to note:

- Above all, work in partnership with them.
- Recognize they have other clients and you need to work for their attention.
- Avoid cutting rates to the bone – it won't deliver best candidates, so is a false economy for key roles.
- Ensure they understand each role and what's required – this will save you time as they can then really add value through the screening process.
- Make communication with suppliers your priority – this may not always be directly, of course, but making their job easier will be valued and again drive the best candidates to your door. Things than matter here are: feedback on CVs, ease at making interview arrangements, feedback after interview. Treat your suppliers as trusted advisors and they will behave like them.
- The more you use your suppliers to deliver, the more you can focus on the bigger picture.
- Ensure they are able to provide metrics about each stage of the process for you so you can report into the business on hiring effectiveness, cost per hire, time from brief to start date, attraction methods, etc.

Process

Questions to consider:

- Is my process fit for purpose?
- What are my metrics?
- Does the process meet the needs of my business?
- Does it meet the needs of my candidate base?
- Does it meet the needs of my suppliers?
- Is it as simple as possible?
- Is it as cost effective as possible?
- Does it maximize the opportunity of a successful hire?
- Is it fast?

These may seem obvious questions but often the process can be so unwieldy that in a short labour market, candidates have gone elsewhere before the your business has even reacted to their CV.

Start by mapping your process out. Then decide what metrics you need. Get some benchmarking if you can from other companies and see how yours compares. Critically evaluate each element of the process. Do we need to do this? How could we do it better? Who else could do this? Where are the bottlenecks? What can we cut out? Where is there duplication? And so on until you have stress tested each element. Continue to work on your process, remembering that it may be different for different roles and parts of the business. See it as a living thing that should be constantly changed in light of the market and external conditions.

A large part of your process will be attraction; this is very susceptible to market shift.

CASE STUDY

Maria Traynor from a large US financial services organization explains: 'My organization has been on a design and development path for the past two years, trying to create a "best-practice" approach to recruiting. Our organization is decentralized with six main offices to support the various business units plus various call centre and sales locations throughout the USA. Our talent acquisition team is considered a shared service, which means that a recruiter could physically be located in Georgia recruiting for positions in Arizona. Recruiters are also expected to act as back-up for vacations and other absences. To this end we have been fine-tuning recruitment policies and developing common practices with both the process and our applicant tracking system. The goal is a seamless and transparent recruitment experience for our hiring managers and a shared level of knowledge for our recruiters. Is it a best practice? Since that is a subjective term, I don't know how to answer. Is it meeting our organization's goals right now? The answer is yes. However, since organizations are ever changing, so must the talent acquisition model being used, so we've allowed room for change.'

The point Maria makes about the capacity to flex and change as the market demands is an important one to hold on to when designing recruitment processes.

Attraction

Questions to consider:

- What labour market are we in?
- How important is attraction to us?

- Are we getting the candidate supply we need?
- Is the candidate quality sufficient?
- How much is our attraction costing?
- What is our attraction strategy for different types of roles?
- What is our employer branding?
- What is our market positioning?

In a market of candidate oversupply, it may be challenging to manage response as there are more candidates on the market. The use of the internet now makes it easy for a candidate to apply for a role without much thought or effort – which means increased effort on the organization's part to manage and process those applications. This swings the emphasis back into the process element of recruiting. It is worth remembering the points made in acknowledging and rejecting candidates here.

In a short labour market where skills are in short supply, more effort will be needed to attract the right candidates, and resources will need to be focused in this area. The capacity to be creative and also have a good 'story' for potential candidates will be the keys to success here.

A successful attraction strategy needs to be followed through by a strong emphasis on assessment.

Assessment

Questions to consider:

- What do people need to be able to do, know and behave like to be successful in this role?
- How can we find out in our assessment process whether they are?
- Balance the assessment process with candidate needs.
- Balance it with the importance of the role to the business.
- Balance the costs of assessment (time and process) with the need to hire certain roles at speed.
- Ensure your assessment is valid, is recognized by the British Psychological Society and won't prejudice certain candidate groups. Avoid the cheap online ones that require no training to administer, as they are unlikely to produce a more useful result than an interview and could be considered very poor practice as well as expensive.
- Make your assessments fit for purpose; this means choosing each assessment for job groups separately. Different roles will require different methods.

If your focus is on getting people into roles quickly, this is the area that can often let a process down. We have already identified the high costs of re-recruiting a role and getting a hiring decision wrong. As candidates become more skilled in job hunting (typically, candidates will attend far more job interviews and have far more jobs than they did 20 years ago), organizations need to become more skilled in assessing.

Speed, cost, quality balance

Questions to consider:

- What is most important:
  - speed of hiring?
  - low cost of hiring?
  - quality of the candidates?

Figure 5.1 shows the balance between speed, cost and quality. It is the recruiter's job to decide how to balance these three elements. This will vary from business to business and role to role. Each role needs to be decided on its own merits but most organizations will have a broad framework of objectives within which to work.

The need is to recruit at speed, while managing the cost and quality balance. This does not mean that picking the first candidate you are able to dredge up at speed is top of the list of key elements. Different roles will clearly take different amounts of time to resource. A temp needed by 9 am can be provided by a good staffing provider when they've been called at 8 am that day. A CEO will take a shade longer but need not take as long as executive headhunters might have you believe. Some roles will need briefing out to suppliers at higher cost but may be resourced more quickly that way when speed is the top driver.

FIGURE 5.1 The balancing act

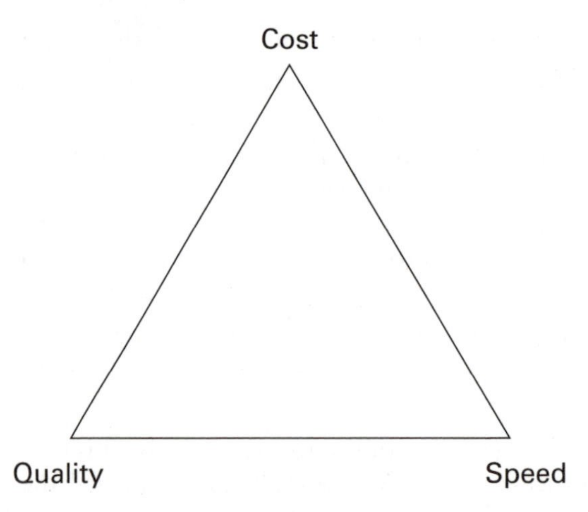

SOURCE: *The Professional Recruiter's Handbook*

Use the resources and suppliers you have, holding your three drivers in mind, and deliver your roles as fast as you can without compromising on quality any more than you need to. Use your passion and focus to increase the speed and quality while managing the cost effectively.

This applies not only to profit-generating companies. Service delivery in not-for-profit businesses can experience just the same level of risk in reducing costs above everything else. A lack of public sector service workers, coupled with a reluctance to pay for and focus on the hiring of these roles, can lead to serious deficiencies on service delivery, with far-reaching consequences for the service provider.

Budgeting

Questions to consider:

- How many hires this year?
- Cost per head of recruitment last year?
- Benchmarked cost of recruitment across your industry?
- Use of internal recruitment incentive schemes?
- Use of internal promotions?
- Recruitment model: insource, outsource or agencies?
- Involvement of procurement?
- How is recruitment managed?
- Recruitment control?
- Direct vs indirect hires?

Although we've already covered the area of cost versus value and speed, delivering a recruitment budget is challenging.

CASE STUDY

A software client I worked with years ago found that as they were growing very quickly to meet customer demand, their recruitment costs were spiralling. In fact, they were finding that any profit they might be making month on month was being eaten up rather more than it should have been by recruiting fees. They decided to centralize recruitment and treat it as a service to the line managers, with recruitment being a profit centre and shifting the bulk of the recruitment to direct from agency-led. Today this is commonplace but then it was an innovative model. They reduced their spend by over 35 per cent and the time taken in hiring managers considerably. This strategy is now relatively commonplace.

Costs will always need to reflect the business objectives of the organization. They will be higher in organizations where key skills are crucial and scarce. Having a clear picture of your likely recruitment costs at the beginning of the financial year and then delivering on them in the most cost-effective way will be an important part of the financial director's budget management. The costs of recruitment and decreased retention can soon put a strain on any good recruitment budget.

Reward

Questions to consider:

- What do you want people to do/how do you want them to behave?
- Why do you want people to work for you?
- What do you want to be known for in your business in relation to reward?
- How does how you reward reflect your client base and their expectations?
- How can you work with trade unions positively to ensure that reward works for all?

Reward needs to be linked to your business objectives in the same way that your strategy is. If your strategy is to offer best prices, then clearly your pay rates will need careful control, often through the implementation of the minimum wage. If your strategy is to offer best service, then you may need to offer some form of performance-related pay. Reward (which includes all reward, not just pay) will reflect both the brand of the employer and its market positioning.

Equally, the reward needs to reflect the behaviours you want from staff. If you want them to be innovative, then there should be some form of reward (not necessarily financial) for trying new ideas. If you want to reward staff through a meritocracy, then rewarding simple length of service or inflationary pay awards will not be the right answer.

Of course, the topic of reward is a specialist one and this book does not aim to offer specialist advice, more a series of thoughts to enable you to identify whether you have considered some of the options and issues.

All of the topics discussed in brief in this chapter are the key elements of world-class recruitment. If you use this chapter only to assess your recruitment practices and processes, you will still have focused on the most important aspects. For a more detailed explanation of many of these areas, and tools and techniques to help you further, read on.

06

Developing a successful recruitment and talent strategy

This chapter deals with the thinking behind who to hire and how to hire them to reach your business goals. It also considers briefly the importance of developing a wider talent strategy for not only incoming but also existing staff.

Just as with those wider business goals, whatever the size of your business, to be successful you'll need some form of strategy. As with most things, if you don't know where you are going, you have no idea where you'll end up. If you don't know how you're going to hire the people you want, or who they are, it's not so likely to work. You may have a business plan that outlines resourcing plans for the next year or three or you may be running your own business and hoping to wind down and be thinking about recruiting someone to do more work so that you can relax more. The scale is less relevant. The key is working out how to achieve what you want.

A strategy is a systematic overall plan outlining how you are going to achieve your objectives. Before exploring how to develop a strategy it's worth lingering briefly on the consequences of not having one.

Not having a recruitment strategy means the following:

- Your business cannot meet its orders and loses customers.
- You cannot deliver your newly won care contract and lives are put at risk.

- You don't have enough drivers to deliver your product, so you have to outsource it at a high cost, losing money to meet client need.
- Lack of a permanent recruitment plan and action means you consistently hire expensive freelance labour, which not only ratchets your costs of employment up but also loses the intellectual capital built up in the business through recent projects.
- Qualified staff in your market are scarce, but because there is no plan to recruit junior staff and train them, you lose market share.
- You are attracting staff to your roles but no one takes your jobs because you haven't thought through how to position yourselves. You didn't realize it was their decision as well as yours.
- You can attract local unskilled labour but really struggle with the scarce skills needed to sell and market your product. Through your expertise in staffing up with local labour you are now overstaffed but with a lack of sales.
- You can see there is a real market opportunity in one area but you miss the chance of addressing it as you have not hired the right people.
- You start offices in three new countries abroad and open the roles up to people from the UK on secondment, flying them out quickly because the clients want immediate action that you have promised and new incoming staff are typically on three months' notice.
- You cannot take a holiday this year because you don't have any support.
- You simply cannot attract the staff you need.
- Retention is poor because you over-promise in the roles when you hire people, so the role expectations are not met.

As if the consequences above were not bad enough, add in the issues of retention, assessment and engagement, and the list increases still further:

Lack of retention, assessment and engagement means the following:

- The people you hire do not work out in their roles because your assessment process doesn't pick up numeracy issues.
- Graduates do not stay because they find the role does not meet their intellectual needs.
- Little attention is paid to the culture of the organization and as a consequence people don't really buy into the business. The business 'lacks soul'. This impacts performance.
- There is scant attention paid to developing people in their careers, so people leave to find a career elsewhere.
- Reward doesn't meet the market needs and so staff are lured to competitors for more pay.

- There are no training or learning opportunities, so people cannot develop or feel the business has their interests at heart.
- People do not feel cared about as people and will leave.
- Some people are over-promoted and then struggle.

And there are many more reasons to have a talent and recruitment strategy in place. In the same way as you would not leave to chance the ordering of raw materials for your factory to deliver your customers' orders, neither should you leave your hiring or talent development to chance. Without some control over the talent you have and bring into your business, you will have no control over your business and whether it can deliver on your organizational objectives or goals.

You may be running a small business or you may be an HR director in a larger business or a student of human resources. You may feel that a strategy is far too complicated or indeed unnecessary for your needs, but the following case studies and the subsequent guidelines and ideas in the next section are relevant to everyone. How you apply them to suit your particular situation will be your decision and choice, of course. Even a small business needs a plan. A recruitment or talent strategy builds and develops in a staged process. This process may vary a little but this next section outlines the stages to work through to develop a hiring strategy for your business.

Talent and recruitment strategy development

Steps in brief:

Stage one: situational analysis – Where am I now?

Stage two: business mission or vision, objectives and goals – Where do I want to be?

Stage three: gap analysis – What is the difference between where I am and where I want to be?

Stage four: strategy development: a plan based on the findings from the previous stages and the capability of the business – How am I going to reach my goals?

Each stage will now be explored in a little more detail, providing a 'how-to' guide for you to work through.

Stage one: situational analysis

Who am I? What is my business? What are the raw facts about the business?

Here you may just want to note down the business you are in, the number of people employed in the business, your retention rates and any specific characteristics of the business.

You can, of course, go into more detail and do a situational analysis using a SWOT analysis (see Figure 6.1). Develop this in direct relation to your recruitment and talent strategy.

The SWOT analysis originated at Stanford Research Institute in the 1960s. It was developed from research funded by *Fortune* 500 companies as a way to discover why corporate planning failed. So it was used 'after the event' as an evaluative tool. Now it is used in all sorts of situations but primarily as an analytical tool:

S = strengths;

W = weaknesses;

O = opportunities;

T = threats.

Figure 6.1 shows how to set out a SWOT.

In this context a strength is a particular skill or distinctive competence that you have within your organization in relation to recruitment or talent. Strengths may include having a good name in the market, paying above market rate or low staff turnover, for example.

FIGURE 6.1 SWOT analysis

S	**W**
• Good internal recruitment team with good business relationships • Excellent candidate engagement • Great business story to sell	• Location hard for many candidates to reach • Slow process for technical staff • Poor interviewing skills • High attrition
O	**T**
• Good name/brand in market • Market expanding • Global business expanding	• Competitors starting up offering higher salaries • Skills scarce

A weakness is anything likely to stop you achieving – it could be a lack of knowledge, support, skills, experience or process.

An opportunity is any aspect of the external environment that could be good for you and help you achieve your business objectives. This might be an event that results in increased demand, such as the Olympics or other sporting event. The effect of the European Year of Culture in Liverpool has created investment and been long lasting.

A threat is anything in the external environment that could hinder you in achieving your objectives. This might be a competitor, for example, or the economic environment. A threat to one organization could of course be an opportunity for another.

You may need to find information to complete your SWOT. Other people in the business may need to contribute, you may need to seek other opinions and you may need to do some external research. Data to populate your SWOT will include both internal and external factors you have identified as relevant and important to the business's overall goals and objectives. Some of them may be drawn from the analysis you did on retention and attrition. First, let's consider what external factors you may need to include and perhaps research.

Broad external factors and research

External factors research will include considering the wider external environment as well as the external labour market: the things that might happen and will impact you but that you cannot directly control. To do this you can either simply list the sorts of things which are likely to have an impact – perhaps competitor employers in your local market, supply of part-time workers, labour supply in your sector – or you can also do a PESTLEC analysis to take a more 'belt and braces' approach. This is a tool that enables you to look outside your business into your market sector, and beyond, to check out what influences might be around to adversely or otherwise affect your sector. PESTLEC is shown in Table 6.1.

PESTLEC stands for different aspects of our world. Ask yourself how this element will impact your business and its recruitment in the future. What impact might this have and how can you maximize its opportunity or minimize its threat?

Labour market external research

You may want to do some more specific market research linked to the labour market you are working within. This may be a geographic area, it may be a town, county or city or rural area. Equally it may be a specific skill set such as data capability and knowledge or manufacturing resource planning or retail management. Or you may have a combination of these, as in the example below. Clearly assessing what is relevant to you is the most important. It may be as simple as finding out the most cost-effective way to recruit people in your area. Here are some further ideas:

TABLE 6.1 PESTLEC analysis

P = political	What is the political landscape and how will this impact recruitment in your business?
E = economic	How is the economy faring? What are the supply and demand for your labour market like? What are the economic factors in your local area?
S = sociological	How does the way we live impact recruitment in your business? Will this mean an over- or under-supply of particular types of people? What is the demographic landscape?
T = technological	How can technology be used to deliver for your customers and how will this impact your hiring needs? How can you use technology to help you in your recruitment?
L = legal	Are there any upcoming or new laws you need to know about?
E = environmental	Increasingly important: how does your local environment impact your staffing?
C = cultural	What external cultural factors bear on your talent and recruitment strategy?

- Some general labour market research. How is the unemployment in your area? Your area might be geographic or a specialist skill or a range of both, creating different labour segments you need to look at. Vodafone, or any other technology company, for example, has a range of segments in a regional area, such as a local segment for unskilled staff near to Newbury. If Vodafone expands past a certain point it will have used all the available local labour within travelling distance and may have to find alternative strategies. This is something a London-based business does not have to contend with – but they have other challenges. Equally, Vodafone will then have roles for specialist technical and sales and marketing staff, which they need to attract nationally or even Europe-wide and provide attractive opportunities in terms of work, reward and lifestyle.
- Completing a benchmarked salary and bonus survey to see how your pay rates, benefits and bonuses relate to your market. This will help you work out how your reward strategy relates to the external labour market and therefore whether this is a strength or weakness. There is a range of salary surveys in the market available free or if you are a CIPD member you can access their reports free too. Add to this some primary research with your suppliers or the job centre to validate the secondary findings (these go out of date so quickly). You can see a candidate-rich market turn to candidate-short in as little as three months.

- Talk to your suppliers about how they perceive the recruitment market to be right now in relation to the talent you need. Are you in a candidate-short or -rich market? Ask them how they perceive your business – is it an organization they find easy or hard to present to prospective candidates? Either way, why? Try to understand the key selling features of your business and how they relate to competing employers. Developing some unique selling points (USPs) will really help when it comes to building an attraction strategy. This will also tell you whether you need to develop some USPs.
- If you are a larger business and meet your competitors at networking events or local gatherings, ask them how they are finding the labour market and what they are doing with their talent management.

Once you have collated all the external market information, you'll move on to internal data. You'll see that much of the key to a good strategy lies in having good management information and data to work with. The stronger your available metrics are to work with, the better your strategy will be as it will be developed in the light of good information on what is happening now in your business. Once you can see which of these are most important you'll know which to include in your SWOT. Table 6.2 shows a series of metrics that will help you determine your organization's strengths and weaknesses. From these you'll be able to add the findings into the SWOT.

Completing your SWOT

Pick out the key points from both the internal and external factors to include on your SWOT analysis. Choose anything that looks unusual or has a high impact, either good or bad, to place in the one-page analysis as these will be opportunities for improvement or consolidation of strengths.

Sometimes it's hard to be objective about this, so you may want to get your findings sense checked before you deliver your strategy as a result of them. If you are a resourcing manager, ask your hiring managers to give their opinion and even complete their own mini SWOT. Anyone with a 'helicopter view' of the business will be quite well placed to complete this exercise.

Once you are happy you have completed the SWOT, you can then see at a glance what kind of shape you are in as an organization and, most importantly, what shape your recruitment is in. Ask yourself the following questions:

- Do you have more strengths than weaknesses?
- Do you have more opportunities than threats?
- How important are each of the strengths and weaknesses and opportunities and threats?
- Can you match any of the strengths to the opportunities?
- Can you convert any of the weaknesses to strengths?

TABLE 6.2 Recruitment metrics

Recruiter workload	How many roles is one recruiter, recruitment manager, HR or each line manager handling?
Time to recruit	Length of time taken from requisition sign-off to candidate acceptance of offer. Break this down into job types or departments, which may tell you that particular roles are hard to fill or particular managers are hard to recruit for – for whatever reason. Many companies set a goal of 30 days for an offer to go out to the right candidate, which should be achievable for most mid-range and junior roles. Senior role requiring a headhunt may take longer. It is useful to organize an escalation process for roles that exceed minimum standards.
Cost per hire	The total costs of recruitment (excluding labour) divided by the number of people hired.
Direct sourcing analysis	Where your candidates come from; the percentage who come from each of the sourcing channels you use, from headhunting at one end of the spectrum to job boards and your website at the other. This will help you make good decisions about advertising and labour spend.
Agency sourcing analysis	Where your candidates come from but this time in relation to third-party recruitment agencies.
Internal/external candidate hires	The proportion of internal and external hires. This can also be split down into promoted hires and non-promoted. Promotion may have its own target – say 75%+ to create a good balance of incoming fresh talent at a senior level but still allow promotional and career development opportunities for employees. Non-promotions would support decreasing the leavers target if people have an opportunity to move location for personal reasons or are in a role where they no longer enjoy a particular task.
Diversity and inclusion	Monitoring of candidates from under-represented backgrounds both on shortlist submission and hires.
Employee referral	Number of employees referred internally – a key way to increase good-quality candidates is to pay an internal 'bounty' for placed candidates who pass their probationary period.
First-interview-to-hire ratio	Number of first interviews it takes to make a hire. This helps you work out how much pipeline and activity you need to make the number of hires you currently have. If you know it takes 10 interviews to make a hire and your team has 10 roles to fill and they only organize three interviews a week, you can work out it will take eight months to fill all 10 roles – which leads to the next important data collection.

Lost/gained revenue	If a role stays vacant for eight months, how much revenue has been lost from or could have been gained for the business in this period? If negligible, then the question of need for the role arises. Ask line managers: 'What is the cost of not hiring this person?'
Second-interview-to-offer ratio	How many people are falling at the second-interview hurdle? Could more be done to weed out unsuitable candidates at or prior to first interview? Is the second interview a more senior hirer – what can they feed back up the chain?
Offer-to-acceptance ratio	How many people reject an offer of employment with your business? If the recruiter is doing their job and you have a strong process, this should be very few regardless of your salary structures. Very few businesses offer the very best salaries in the market and many offer less than the market rate. If you pay mid-range salaries, you'll need to do recruitment really well to compensate. There are several really straightforward things to do to help this – you can find more detail in Chapter Seven.
Labour turnover	Annualized number of times you turn your labour. The metric around people who leave within the first year is of particular relevance here – anyone who leaves within a year in general terms (this may be higher in some markets like call centres or the media industry) is not a recruitment success. Focus needs to go on where the early leavers come from – are they focused in one area of the business, are they supplied through one source: external, internal, agency or direct; what can be learned about them? A further useful distinction is to find out what your industry norm is; not so that you can be complacent but more so that you can understand how you relate to your competitors.
Retention data	As outlined in Chapter Three – there will be some useful data here on how, why and who stays with the organization. If you can identify who will stay, it may make sense to include this group in your strategy. Time for new hires to become productive. This links to the effectiveness of your on-boarding programmes – this book links this closely to the effectiveness of recruitment.

You need now to consider the business goals and objectives before the final stage of developing your recruitment strategy.

CASE STUDY

UNESCO engaged a firm of consultants to conduct a strategic review of its recruiting practices against its overall objectives in 2009 to evaluate to what degree it was achieving the strategic goals set out in its 2003 strategic review of people policy. The review concluded that much good work was being done and the policy delivered but made some recommendations around strengthening the proactive nature of recruitment: reaching out to good people in candidate communities to increase the quality of hires, improving the time to hire from inception, making more of internal talent available and increasing progress in working with people in their probationary period to ensure strong on-boarding.

Any organization conducting such a strategic analysis and review is likely to find areas to improve and often they sit within exactly these areas: the core areas of retention (internal recruitment and career development), time to hire (efficiency of the process) and better quality of people and of on-boarding.

You'll formulate your goals as a result of your analysis and in line with the overall business objectives of your organization. Say your business is good at getting people to accept your offers of employment but finds it hard to get them to come along for interview – what might that suggest in terms of goals? Say your business has a turnover of 70 per cent, your industry norm is 30 per cent and half of those exits are performance related – what does that suggest about where the focus of your goals might lie?

Stage two: setting objectives and goals

Any starting point for recruitment goals will be the overall business mission or vision, objectives and goals. There is little value in setting goals that do not support the overall vision or strategy of your organization. If the goal of your organization is to expand globally, your recruitment strategy will need to reflect this. If the goal of your organization is to maintain its position as a thought leader in life sciences, this too will inform your recruitment strategy. The two cornerstones of your strategy will be the make-up of your labour force (who to hire) and your recruitment methodology (how to hire them).

Alongside the objectives, you need to understand any further goals, employer branding or positioning your business has decided upon or adopted.

- Where does the business position its reward programme?
- What are the values of the business?

- What is important for the business around employee branding?
- How does the organization view recruitment, retention and engagement?

If your organization views recruitment as 'irritating', then your strategy may include some educative efforts. If it positions its reward strategy lower than other competitors, it will need to develop some other USPs to compensate for this. If the business has no stated values and doesn't know what it's in business for (why everyone gets out of bed in the morning to go to work other than to collect a pay cheque), it will need to find out before you can develop a hiring strategy. If it wants to enter and be placed high up the Great Company to Work For listings, take part in awards and sees people and their development as crucial to the success of the business, then it will really need to focus to achieve this.

So, what are your goals? What do you want to achieve? Here are some examples:

- Achieve 200 high-quality hires by the end of the year.
- Save 20 per cent from the recruitment budget compared with last year.
- Reduce the number of temps or freelancers in favour of permanent staff.
- Increase the number of fixed-term contracts.
- Improve the retention rate from 60 per cent to 45 per cent in two years.
- Increase the diversity of applicants from external sources by 25 per cent by the end of the year.
- Increase the number of hired applicants generated through internal referral scheme by 50 per cent.
- Improve the offer-to-acceptance ratio from 60 per cent to 85 per cent after July.
- Reduce the number of employees leaving before one year by 25 per cent by the end of the year.
- Improve the predictive sourcing of candidates to reduce the advertising spend by 15 per cent this year.

You'll have noticed that these goals are SMARTER goals. This is to say they have a range of characteristics as follows:

S = specific;

M = measurable;

A = agreed;

R = realistic;

T = time bound;

E = enjoyable;

R = recorded.

Without making goals conform to something like this you can easily end up at the end of the process not really sure if you have reached your goals or not. 'Improve retention' or 'reduce time to hire' may sound like a good plan, but when you get to the end of the project what does that really mean? Reduce by one? Improve by 500? So make sure your goals are measured as well as something you can get others bought into achieving – and make them enjoyable to stand the best chance of success.

You may have found that you have a large number of people leaving the role within the first six months. Their reason for leaving may be that they don't like the role or they didn't really understand what it involved. This may lead you to develop a hiring and assessment strategy that enables them to develop a clear picture of the role before they start. It may mean you accepting a lower interview-to-hire ratio but for a longer-term gain of longevity of service. The costs of losing people after a six-month period are high, much higher than assessing people more fully, which includes elements of them experiencing the role. Even if this takes longer and dissuades more applicants, it may still pay off longer term.

The areas to focus on for your goals are the ones that are causing the greatest pain to your organization or likely to afford the greatest benefit, either financially or in results.

Take the time now to work out what you really want to achieve with recruitment and talent in your business. Very often we are so busy getting people on board and being reactive that there is little time to sit down and plan our actions. To be in control of this it's really important to take a step back and look at the big picture. Only too often new resourcing managers or directors come into a business and are pushed to deliver immediate results so that they never actually take the time to consider the overall goals and strategy; their focus never moves from delivering the day to day. While this may not always cost them their job, it might cost the business its competitive talent edge and a higher retention rate.

Once you have determined your goals, make sure that you get buy-in across the business for them, that they are truly in line with the overall business strategy and that they will serve the interests of the business as well as your own. Assuming you have now done this, your goals and your situational analysis are complete, so the third stage is to determine the difference between where you are now and where you want to be – your 'gap'.

Stage three: gap analysis

You'll use your SWOT and your goals to determine the measurable difference. You can see a gap pictorially displayed in Figure 6.2, in this case in relation to retention. Your gap may vary and you may have more than one. Your gaps could relate to any of the internal metrics outlined earlier. Sometimes your biggest gap can provide the greatest quick wins. At other times a large gap may not be having a great impact on the business, so it's important to remember that it's not just the size of the gap that matters, it's the impact that the gap is having on the business as a whole.

FIGURE 6.2 Gap analysis: labour turnover rate

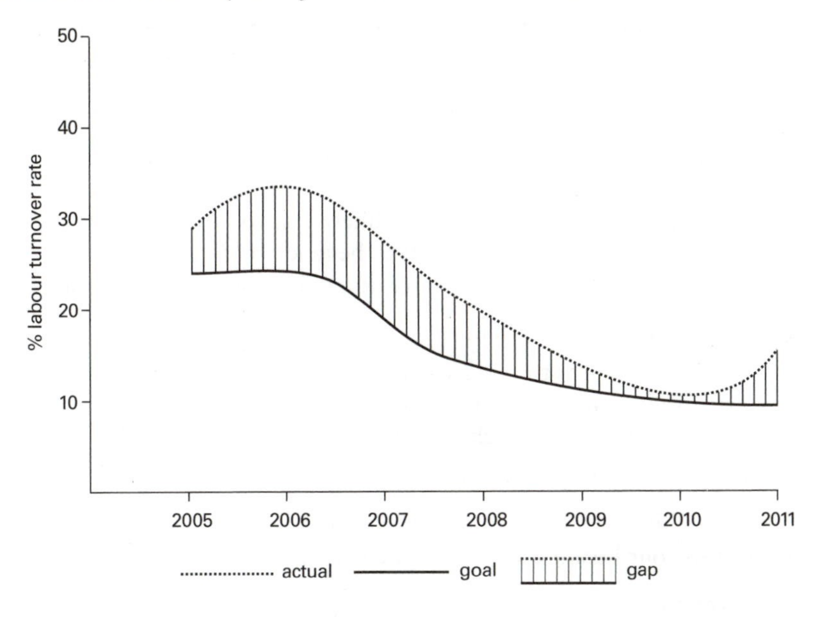

CASE STUDY

A large organization was losing more staff than it wanted to and decided to gather data over six months relating to leavers' reasons for leaving. These were captured at exit interviews conducted by the HR team. It found that 75 per cent of the reasons for leaving were represented by four factors, two of which involved career progression and development. The business decided to put some simple measures in place to reduce leaving for career progression as a primary reason. Every employee had a career conversation with their manager every six months and was encouraged to be able to articulate their career goals. Career coaches were used to help define career paths in general and people were encouraged to think about work as a career rather than just a job.

Once you have identified your gap, then you can begin to define your strategy. Part of this may be making a business case for investment into a particular aspect of recruitment or retention you want to improve.

Let's say you have a general gap in your retention.

Retention gap

Your current retention is 35 per cent. Your competitor's retention is 26 per cent. You may decide that you want this year to reduce your retention to 30 per cent, with a view to further reducing it the following year to 25 per cent, which is more in line with your competitors.

Work out what this gap represents in terms of lost profit. This will support a business case for funding activities, which you can demonstrate will move you towards the goal. It's unlikely just to fall of its own accord and will need a focused business effort to be made by all stakeholders.

Your business case for reducing retention might look something like this:

- Average salary of £40,000.
- Takes four months to replace someone, have them work their notice, start with you and get them up to acceptable performance in the role (some roles will take much longer).
- Cost per head of loss is £13,300.
- 2,000 employees and a turnover of 36 per cent.
- Cost to your business of £9.5m each year.

Your competitor:

- Average salary of £40,000.
- Takes four months to replace someone, have them work their notice, start with you and get them up to acceptable performance in the role (some roles will take much longer).
- Cost per head of loss is £13,300.
- 2,000 employees and a turnover of 26 per cent.
- Cost to your business of £6.5m each year.

Difference in competitive advantage:

- They have £3m more available to spend on R&D to improve their products and services.
- £3m to enter new markets to gain competitive advantage.
- £3m more they could pay their staff.
- £3m more for swish new offices.
- £3m more for learning and development.
- £3m more profit to return to the shareholders.

This business case delivers a good argument for investing in further resources to increase retention.

A further example may be found in the time it takes for you to recruit someone; an extra month could cost the business dearly.

Business case for reducing time to hire:

- Average productivity worth £60,000 a year.

- Takes three months currently for roles to be filled and the person to start. While they are absent, productivity in that space is reduced to £10,000 a year.
- Cost of lost productivity is £12,500 in three months.
- If time to hire were reduced to two months it would reduce the lost productivity to £8,300 per person, a saving per person of £4,200.
- Assuming 100 hires per year, this is a bottom-line saving of £42,000 a year.

A potential case for investment but not as strong as retention.

Once you have worked out your gaps and your business cases, it's time to complete your four-stage process and develop your strategy.

Stage four: strategy design and development

This is as simple as asking: 'What are my options for achieving the result (my goal or objective) that I want?'

Your goals may be simple – how to hire one person – or they could be complex – how to deliver best-value just-in-time recruitment to a major brand. You could be facing any of the challenges below.

Fledgling business

You are about to hire your first real employee. Up to now you've managed with the founders working long hours, their partners pitching in where they can, favours borrowed from friends and some part-time labour from the local job centre when you needed it – although it wasn't always possible to get anyone good. Recently you have become busier. You have decided to take the plunge and hire someone full time to look after the office, take enquiries while you are out with customers and manage some of the projects.

You don't want to make a mistake because some of the temporary labour forgot to pass on messages from time to time and you nearly lost a big customer. So you need to be very sure to hire the right person.

What are your options?

Small business

You have 120 people and are in a fast-growing market. You've also just secured some funding to double in size over the next six months and negotiated a lease on another floor in your offices in a large town in the north of the country. You have been in business for three years, so you have grown pretty quickly. You are in the service business in quite a competitive market and you win good business because you have developed a new process that enables you to deliver in a much faster way and compete on a cost basis. You are not the only business in the large town, of course, and unemployment is low. Some of the skills you need are pretty scarce around you.

You need to make sure you expand fast enough to satisfy the investors and take advantage of your new process before others catch you up. In short, you need speed.

What are your options?

Larger city company

You have 2,000 people based in a regional city and then a range of offices around the country. You are working in financial services. You have a low staff turnover in the city, surprisingly, but you are one of this city's largest employers. Much of your work is low skilled and a high proportion of it is customer and process oriented. Your skilled staff tend to stay with the business. Your business is not expanding more quickly than the market, although there have been a couple of mergers and acquisitions lately which have made the business grow. These are still being worked through, so you have been making some redundancies where there was duplication.

You have quite high turnover of staff in your customer services team and need to ensure you can replace these quickly and keep your staffing levels up without adversely impacting customer service.

What are your options?

Rural factory

You are based in a rural county and make a consumer food product, employing 300–600 people over the course of a year. Your head office is in London and this is where your marketing and sales functions are based. You are expanding gradually as you are very successful in licensing some of your products to other brands and this is proving very popular – and also solid, profitable business for you. Your business is very seasonal, which means that your labour needs fluctuate greatly and you employ double the number of people at certain points of the year that you do in others. Quite a lot of these people come back year after year but you are still left with 100 temporary staff to recruit locally in one month. This year a new employer, a large supermarket, has opened down the road, paying more than you do, and many of your temporary staff have taken part-time annual roles with them.

What are your options?

You'll notice that each of the cases above finishes by asking what the options are. It's important when developing your strategy to consider a range of options and then evaluate them rather than rushing quickly to a decision.

Whatever your goal, I recommend you develop at least two, and preferably three, possible strategies and then evaluate the best options against whatever criteria are relevant.

CASE STUDY

A public sector business was not meeting its hiring needs and was spending a lot of money failing to do so. The HR director decided on a strategy of refusing all job requisitions unless they were 'mission critical'. This led to an increase in achieving their hiring numbers and an improvement in the ratio of people required versus those hired.

The strategy alone may be a very good strategy in a downturn or consolidation phase and certainly made the numbers look stronger but does not support a business need for growth, and left this organization potentially poorly positioned to deal with the growth in demand for the business's services.

Strategic labour choices

Your people

You have a range of choices of who to hire, and on what basis, and most organizations use a blend of each of these choices:

- temporary labour;
- casual labour;
- freelances;
- external consultants;
- project workers;
- permanent labour;
- agency workers;
- fixed-term contracts;
- contractors;
- internships;
- apprenticeships;
- graduate trainees;
- part-time workers;
- full-time workers;
- job shares;
- interim staff;
- diversity of labour force;
- geographical spread;
- home/office based.

And this is not an exhaustive list. Once you have decided which jobs need doing, the next task is to decide what sort of labour is needed to do them. It is worth considering each of the different types of labour and the advantages and disadvantages of each. You can see this in Table 6.3.

TABLE 6.3 Strategic labour choices

Type of labour	Advantages	Disadvantages
Temporary labour: used to cover an absence in a permanent role or to deliver variable resourcing needs	Can call resource on or off when you want	May not always be available/lack of commitment
Casual labour: unskilled labour used on a daily basis	Able to keep cost base down	Quality may be less than ideal and availability hard to predict
Freelances: specialist short-term talent	Can call resource on or off when you want; talent you need may not be there when you need it	Can bring in skills you may not otherwise have access to
External consultants: experienced skilled staff engaged on a contract to achieve a certain aim	Can provide key skills that may not reside in the organization and provide an external perspective	Costs and output need managing carefully to provide value as costs will be high
Project workers: staff engaged to fulfil a specific project	Can allocate direct costs against an event or project	May not be able to staff project up with qualified staff at the right time
Permanent labour: people engaged on a long-term employment contract	Can rely on the availability of resource and building up emotional and intellectual capital in your workforce	Costs can be high, especially in a service business and there is a need to ensure there is enough work for all staff, to maximize use of resources
Agency workers: staff working directly through an employment agency and then subcontracted out	One point of contact and no need to manage the temporary workforce directly; no employment responsibilities; reduced costs and time	Few, if any, accept control of the workforce which lies with one agency rather than internally; risk associated with this

Fixed-term contracts: staff on a contract lasting for a fixed period of time; sometimes used as an alternative to permanent employment in some sectors	Can budget effectively	May reduce engagement of staff and therefore reduce value gained
Contractors: similar to the above but could be on a rolling contract instead of a fixed-term one	Can find scarce skills that may not otherwise be available for permanent hire; flexibility of workforce; direct project allocation of costs	Higher costs than permanent employees
Internships: unpaid work experience typically for graduates or young people	Inexpensive labour; allows you to assess someone before making them an offer; brings new blood into the business	Easy to abuse, especially if uninteresting tasks are allocated; can take a lot of time to do well and manage to the benefit of both parties
Graduate trainee schemes: graduates experiencing and working within different areas of an organization	Builds a useful talent pipeline for the future	Expensive to do well, as attracting and developing the best graduates can be costly – but good value for the right businesses
Apprenticeships: school leavers learn a skill or capability 'on-the job' and combine this with vocational education	Builds a useful talent pipeline for the future	Very few, except they need doing well to gain full advantage
Interims: senior staff on a short-term contract brought in to deliver a specific project	Brings new skills into the business; interims are often skilled turn-around people but will implement as well as recommend, which can be a limiting factor with some consultants	Expensive but can be value for money if the terms and deliverables of the project are agreed and clear

TABLE 6.3 continued

Type of labour	Advantages	Disadvantages
Full-time: generally means a 37.5 hour working week	Labour available when necessary; staff become skilled and a valuable part of the business proposition	None other than the same as permanent staff
Job shares: where two people share a full-time job	Can have a wider range of skills in one role; able to create a more diverse workforce through enabling better work–life balance	Can be challenging for the people sharing the role and can be more costly
Part-time: staff working a variation on the 37.5 hour week – can be any number of hours	Can deliver flexible working across a range of shifts if required; can create a more diverse workforce; able to resource more effectively from some sectors	Staff are not always available and the costs of employment and organization can be higher
Diversity: a wide range of people making up the workforce, from different backgrounds, sexual orientation, gender, race, ethnic group, religion	Evidence shows that a diverse workforce is more productive	None – in some areas and businesses can be challenging to achieve
Geographical spread	Can be easier to recruit a wide range of candidates as your capacity to attract is not restricted by possible higher costs or labour availability (eg London base only)	Costs of offices can be higher if not consolidated, but again not if in cheaper areas; can be harder to service smaller offices with central support functions
Office based/work from home/hot-desking	Greater choice of candidates as location less of a problem; works for knowledge-based more senior roles	Can be harder to manage a team or create a sense of team belonging

Your choices about what make-up of your labour force to consider and the levels of skills will also be determined by many of the external factors you already identified in your SWOT. If labour is short in your area, you may have fewer choices about how to employ your staff. Equally, if you have a good, strong employer brand, you may find you can choose your preferred employment method.

Charles Handy was the first to discuss the rise of the flexible worker in his book *The Future of Work* in 1984 and there has been a significant change in the last 20 years just as he predicted, with an end to both a career for life and an organization for life. The business of managing today's talent and workforce, as you can see from all the employment choices in Table 6.3, is far more complex and more of an art than it has ever been before. A hot topic, of course, is diversity. The global nature of many organizations and the diverse nature of our country mean that we have an opportunity to gain from creating diverse workforces that reflect the culture we live in today and help create value in the intellectual property of a business serving a wide client base.

CASE STUDY

Spencer King, communications director for Enterprise Rent-A-Car, emphasizes the importance of diversity in recruitment and how it can bring huge business benefits: 'Actively recruiting a diverse workforce has many tangible business outcomes. To have a workforce that reflects the community in which we do business allows us to better tailor our services and build trust and goodwill among our diverse range of customers and suppliers. A diverse workforce helps us understand our customers better, identify problems and engage with them. Some of the broader benefits of recruiting a diverse workforce that we have seen include: access to a wider range of resources, skills and ideas among our employees that we can tap into, improving staff retention, which leads to lower recruitment and training costs and increasing employee efficiency and lowering stress due to cross-functional teams, ie employees are capable of a variety of roles thanks to their different backgrounds and skill sets.

'Enterprise is able to recruit a diverse workforce successfully by employing an extremely broad-reaching recruitment strategy, recruiting from almost every UK university – marketing our programme at over 120 universities across the country. We don't demand that graduates have a specific degree grade or subject, as we believe that measuring against our core competencies through our interview and assessment centre process more accurately assesses a candidate's ability. By casting the widest possible recruitment net, we are able to recruit as fully diverse a workforce as possible.

'Our recruitment advertising campaign also includes specific efforts to target a diverse audience. For example, we advertise in several minority media, such as *Diversity Milkround*, *Where Women Want to Work*, graduate-women.com and *Real World*. We also profile a number of our minority employees on websites, demonstrating to potential candidates our equal opportunity recruitment culture, including the Target website.

'Attending diversity-focused recruitment fairs, including The Eastern Eye careers fairs in Edinburgh and Glasgow, the GRADES fair and the LGBT Careers Fair in London, for example, also provides great opportunities to attract and recruit diverse candidates.

'Enterprise's unique approach to recruitment has certainly been successful at attracting diverse candidates, with our management team currently at 35 per cent females and 17.5 per cent black and ethnic minority. We are confident that continuing to build a diverse and culturally competent workforce will ensure our organization's sustainability and future success.'

Whatever your goal and strategy, and the case above shows how Enterprise Rent-A-Car is making their strategy work brilliantly for them, it is time to consider how you might deliver it into the organization.

Strategic recruitment methods

How you see and treat recruitment will drive your choices of method. Many organizations see recruitment as a non-core part of the business and therefore best outsourced. Various management strategists will argue that any business should focus on its main business activity, its primary task, and outsource anything else it does to others for whom that activity is their primary task, like the staffing and logistics companies. Others will say that people have to be part of any primary task of a business and philosophically therefore need to be looked after by internal staff. This philosophical perspective leads to challenging decision making around what to do about recruitment and can explain some of the constantly shifting sands between outsourcing and insourcing recruitment in many organizations. A recent study showed 18 per cent of organizations insourcing from an outsourced contract and a similar number outsourcing from an insourced contract, although this is also the hallmark of a new market, of course, where the 'ideal' is still being worked on and discovered.

Insource/outsource

One of the first choices to be made is whether to manage your recruitment internally, whether to outsource it or a combination of both. Outsourcing could mean anything from contracting to use a local recruitment agency for all your recruitment through to a full recruitment process outsourcing (RPO) contract on a global basis, including offshoring. Insourcing means managing all of your recruitment within the business, employing your own staff and either recruiting directly using a range of methods or using a range of agency suppliers contracted via a preferred suppliers list or on an ad hoc basis as needs demand. A hybrid model will mean a combination of both methods as recruitment is not 'one size fits all'.

The advantages and disadvantages of each of the methods are outlined below and your choice will be driven by a range of factors.

Insource specialist recruitment team who recruit directly

Some companies see this as the only strategy to adopt and it's widely used in the USA with 'corporate' recruiters making up the majority of the staffing industry. The strategy has been made easier by the advent of social networking and job sites, making reaching good candidates easier. The skill of attracting and securing them for your business is still critical, however. This can still be separate from managing and outsourcing your temporary or contracted labour.

Advantages: You have complete control over your recruitment needs and can deliver them more cost effectively. Cost is a major advantage. Everything can be controlled better in terms of your employer positioning to candidates. You will be sure, and can evidence, that you have covered all bases in the market for hard-to-find roles. Internal moves can also be handled through this team with ease.

Disadvantages: It puts all your eggs in one basket and does not give you any flexibility. Furthermore, if you cut off all relationships with the agencies it might be hard to remake them. It's also quite an internally inflexible solution as whenever you hit a downturn in recruitment you will have a group of underemployed staff 'on the bench'. Equally, if the recruitment needs become too much to handle, then you'll have to contract in additional resources. For more specialist roles you will have a generalist working on them, which may make them less effective.

Works well when: You have a large number of lowish-level homogeneous roles that need constantly replenishing as the turnover is relatively high (maybe a call centre environment, for example). You have a reasonably steady state in your recruitment with a stable number of job requisitions live at any one time. You have enough critical mass to have a spread of background and experience in your resourcing team, who can handle all roles in the different aspects of your business. So if you need a technical architect you do have a recruiter who has some expertise in technical recruitment; if you are operating on a global platform you also have some linguists. Works well when your focus is on cost and speed.

Insource through a central recruitment team who manage the agencies

This means you have a smaller in-house recruitment team who do not recruit directly for themselves but manage a series of agencies to provide the candidate supply and the candidate servicing. The recruitment team chooses the agencies and either allows them to deal directly with the line managers or takes a more centralized approach and manages all of the recruitment from a central hub. Administrators are used to book interviews, and account managers to deal with the hiring managers, screen CVs and support hiring decisions.

Advantages: Almost the best of both worlds, where you have a dedicated knowledgeable resource who can drive the process and make sure it happens, while accessing the best specialist recruiters in the market to deliver on key roles. The internal team plugs the gap between the agency and the hiring managers. In a larger organization it will be best to have a central hub controlling it all, in a smaller one maybe just one person overseeing the whole process. In a very small business this may be one of the partners, business owners or HR. Internal moves can be handled through this team assuming a central resource, making best use of internal labour and potentially reducing retention.

Disadvantages: Expensive, as you'll not only be paying internal people to manage the process but also agency fees, which you may not be able to get at an advantageous rate if you are unable to deliver volume to the supplier.

Works well when: Your focus is on speed and quality of recruitment rather than cost. You may be on a fast-growth trajectory or in a competitive market for scarce skills, requiring a combination of specialist know-how and internal coordination to get the best people as fast as you can.

Insource through HR business partners

HR business partners working in your business sectors as support to your senior managers and their teams. Typically an HR business partner will handle a general task list and will not be specialist in any one area, managing anything from learning needs and reward through to absence and policy. There may or may not be a centralized HR function made up of experts for them to refer to. They act as a first-line support.

Advantages: They have a really good overview of the business area, its culture and its people. They will be able to advise on internal redeployment better than others and support the hiring managers in deciding what role is needed – perhaps better than a more separated central recruitment manager. An HR person with a recruitment background would be ideal here.

Disadvantages: HR people are by their own admission sometimes generally less interested in recruitment, hence the advent of dedicated recruitment teams. Today recruitment is a career in itself and a skilled part of HR, due in part to the skills shortage but also the different skills a recruiter needs.

Works well when: There is a low need for recruitment in a division and the HR manager has, or is able to build, a small number of relationships with good agencies to deliver on an ad hoc basis, allowing their own role to focus on advice and coordination rather than driving candidate attraction.

Outsource temporary labour only

A business puts all of its temporary labour supply with one agency. That agency is responsible for the supply of all temporary labour, both supplying the labour and employing the people concerned, taking away all of the administration around employment and candidate supply. The business simply has to report on candidates who are not working satisfactorily. The client and the business will work out metrics to assess performance. Most often this will be around fulfilment rates: the number of roles filled at any one time; as close to 100 per cent as possible is the objective.

Advantages: Two clear advantages – cash flow for the client and time and effort savings in recruitment. The agency will cash flow the payroll of staff, saving around six weeks, depending upon contractual agreements. Staffing is done by the contracted agency, not internal employees. The risk around fulfilment is handed over to the agency, which means the client has to be very sure the agency can deliver in the way they need. Administrative or production line roles are ideally suited to this situation, as often lack of staff at this level does not constitute high risk (except in care situations) to the organization, whereas a lack of development or senior staff could do.

Disadvantages: For a large client it is hard to think of many. The costs can be higher, but marginally so when considering the cost of finance and time. The main disadvantage is where the client does not have confidence in their supplier. If you are not convinced an agency will deliver your needs, then do not progress with them. There is also a possible risk around culture and values – the staff employed by the agency need to fit into your organization and work to your agenda and 'the way we do things around here'.

Works well when: You have a large number of temporary staff in your business. This could be a council contracting out its care workers and social workers, locums provided to hospital trusts, administrators and secretarial staff provided to a large private sector business, housing officers in the public sector, workmen on a building site, and so on.

Outsource temporary and permanent labour up to a certain salary

This is similar to the example above except permanent roles are included in the contract. This may or may not involve professional employees and that will depend upon where you set your salary banding. If set at £27,000 in London (obviously there will be regional and country variations here), it will preclude most professional staff and certainly all senior ones.

Advantages: This locates all general permanent staff under one supplier and will bring some additional cost advantages.

Disadvantages: The supplier may not be best placed to recruit permanent staff and it places all of the risk with them. You may wish to spread your risk. Additionally it is also, while similar, a slightly different skill set, so you will want to ensure that your supplier can evidence delivering on both.

Works well when: Your supplier is trusted and can evidence delivering both types of employee and can generate candidates successfully at these levels.

Outsource all recruitment except board and next level down

Working still with the outsource model, this may involve a range of suppliers or one supplier. Some of the larger staffing businesses have acquired professional staffing firms to be able to offer a 'one-stop shop' service. In this instance they will broadly be able to fulfil any role you need to recruit for, using their specialist teams for the more senior or specialist roles. Most of those do not play actively in the search space, however, and you will need to engage a specialist headhunter who knows their market for board level and potentially also the next level down. Salary is a good way of delineating contracts.

Advantages: All the previous advantages of bringing all the recruitment under one roof.

Disadvantages: All the disadvantages of bringing all the recruitment under one roof. A way of managing the risk is to set a contractual timescale for delivery of candidates against a specification. At that point if the agency has not supplied, the client may well go elsewhere.

Works well when: A supplier is set up to deliver the majority of the roles your business needs to hire. Roles that may be mission critical or executive level can be left out of the contract.

Shared service model either internal, outsourced or offshored

A range of organizations (local authorities, for example) or branches chooses to share a central resource service (which may or may not be outsourced), delivering both HR and recruitment.

Advantages: Cost saving and the capacity to recruit experts in certain fields such as reward and L&D rather than a range of generalists.

Disadvantages: It is harder for staff in the team to be close to and understand the businesses they service really well, as they do not work within them, so it can be challenging to support them most effectively.

Works well when: There is some homogeneity of need for roles in the different areas and where the central resource team have made an effort to get to know all of the different business areas so that they can direct candidates well.

Hybrid model – any combination or variation on the methods already discussed

Many companies will have unique needs and one size may not fit all.

Advantage: You can tailor the solution to the specific needs of the business.

Disadvantage: It won't be tried and tested, and most aspects will need to be developed from scratch.

Works well when: You are a large business where investment can pay back or a small one that needs flexibility.

Table 6.4 is a blank evaluation template that enables you to compare and score the different options. You fill in the criteria for your business down the left-hand side in place of the examples shown, and then Table 6.5 shows how this might be scored and a decision taken. It does not consider all your strategic options but it does consider the majority, and again this can be tailored to the ones you are considering.

TABLE 6.4 Evaluating strategic choices for your business – blank template

Factor	Insource specialist recruitment team who recruit directly	Insource through a central recruitment team who manage the agencies	Insource through HR business partners	Outsource temporary labour only	Outsource temporary and permanent labour up to a certain salary	Outsource all recruitment except board and next level down	Shared service model either internally outsourced or offshored
Number of hires per annum (internal transfers and external new hires) – this is about sheer scale							
Number of locations and geographical spread – UK/Europe/global or one office in one town?							
Level and type of roles 80:20. If 80 per cent of your roles are of one type							

TABLE 6.4 continued

Factor	Insource specialist recruitment team who recruit directly	Insource through a central recruitment team who manage the agencies	Insource through HR business partners	Outsource temporary labour only	Outsource temporary and permanent labour up to a certain salary	Outsource all recruitment except board and next level down	Shared service model either internally outsourced or offshored
Candidate market – whether your candidates in each of your markets are in short or good supply							
Employer brand – how you are perceived in the market – can be determined by how many applications you receive							
Importance of cost in relation to quality, cost and speed							

Competence of the business to hire in current situation – can be determined by your ratio of offers to acceptances	
Competence of the business to hire all roles needed within the necessary time frame – can be determined by those roles not offered within 6 weeks of the requisition being raised	
Organization used to outsource	
Total score	

TABLE 6.5 Evaluating strategic choices for your business – completed example

Factor	Insource specialist recruitment team who recruit directly	Insource through a central recruitment team who manage the agencies	Insource through HR business partners	Outsource temporary labour only	Outsource temporary and permanent labour up to a certain salary	Outsource all recruitment except board and next level down	Shared service model
450 permanent roles and 200 temporary roles	4	4	4	5	4	2	1
3 global locations	2	5 (in each location)	2	5 (at some locations)	4	2	1
A strong spread	5	5	1	5	2	4	1
Mostly candidate-short especially in some specialist technical areas	2	4	1	5	4	2	1
Halfway up the *Sunday Times* Best Companies to Work For league table	5	5	3	2	2	2	1

Speed crucial as delivery to clients paramount and margins good	4	5	1	4	4	3	1
Good	5	5	4	5	5	4	1
Poor	4	5	2	5	3	3	1
Yes	3	3	1	5	4	4	1
Total score	34	36	17	41	32	26	9

Factors in choosing your recruitment strategy

The choices of strategy (of which these are a few of the main ones) can be assessed in relation to the factors in your organization. List your factors in relation to these solutions and then score them on a scale of 1 to 5, where 1 does not meet the need at all and 5 meets it perfectly. You can then add up the scores for each of the solutions. While a very rough and ready approach, it does give you some indication of how to further your thinking.

You'll see from Table 6.5 that this company may therefore choose a hybrid strategy of outsourcing its temporary labour and having a dedicated in-house recruitment team who manages agencies. However, the score for a direct recruitment team hiring directly is also high, so another approach might be to combine the three:

- Outsource the temporary labour flow – assuming you can find a staffing agency happy to handle 100 roles.
- Set up an internal recruitment team working under a recruitment director or manager.
- Have this team do a blend of direct hiring (like an internal agency) and indirect where they manage recruitment agencies to deliver candidates. You might choose the agencies to help on the really hard-to-fill roles where they will have specialist market knowledge. This way you are also putting your best resources on your toughest but most important opportunities.

If, however, your situation is not like our fictitious company above and you have a smaller or larger number of roles, then your strategy will clearly change. Let's look at when each of the solutions might suit a specific situation.

Outsourcing

More and more global companies are turning to global staffing companies in the first instance for their temporary labour supply, employing a high percentage of their labour through a third party. This has a number of clear advantages, the overriding one being cash flow: companies gain on average a six-week cash flow advantage of paying staff along with the removal of all of the administration, organization and risk associated with managing the workforce. In many cases it also removes the need for training, support and management of staff as this is also done by the staffing company. If staff are out in the field and in roles where continuous development and mandatory training are required, the staffing agency delivers this as an added-value service. To fulfil the requirements of the contract, the staffing agencies will all contract among themselves, creating in effect a one-stop shop for staffing within the business. Services will be delivered generally through an in-house approach, with staff from the agency sitting in the client offices and acting as one of the client businesses. When suppliers change, those staff are then often transferred under present employment conditions ('TUPE'd') over to the new supplier. Smaller outsourced providers also offer nimble web-centric approaches, however, as can be seen in the next case from recruitment outsourcing specialists PPS.

CASE STUDY

Housing association Peabody's temporary recruitment process was not meeting the organization's needs. A master vendor agreement was in place, which charged a fixed fee per hour for each temporary worker placed within the organization irrespective of the role. Requirements for lower-skilled and lower-paid workers were satisfied but Peabody experienced difficulty in sourcing temporary workers in professional roles. As a result, in many instances temporary workers were being supplied without the necessary experience and skills for the role. Vital contract support functions such as management information were provided through manual spreadsheets and it was clear that Peabody was not getting the most out of a recruitment partner.

Offering a combined permanent and temporary recruitment solution, PPS's innovative web-centric approach to recruitment has improved the situation.

The features of PPS's recruitment software allows permanent vacancies and temporary assignments to be requested online by hiring managers. The roles are predefined from an establishment list developed and maintained by Peabody. Recruitment suppliers are able to load temporary candidates' CVs on to the PPS software system and permanent candidates apply to positions directly via an application form linked to Peabody's website. PPS's direct sourcing methodology, using Boolean and X-ray search techniques, gives Peabody access to a more targeted response to their requirements and minimizes the risk that high percentage-based fees are paid to recruitment agencies for candidates that can be sourced online. Where advertising is required it is predominantly online. Whether temporary or permanent, PPS's recruitment specialists conduct competency-based sifting and telephone screening interviews. This has been found to save time for hiring managers and internal HR, while ensuring only the best available candidates are invited for face-to-face interview at Peabody. Permanent time to hire has tumbled from an average of 70 days to just 35.

Although this service is predominantly seen in the staffing sectors currently, there is also a growing move towards treating the hire of permanent staff in the same way, albeit having them still employed by the business. The challenge of this approach for these roles is that more senior permanent hires are often less easily replaced, creating competitive advantage for the business when they are supplied and creating risk when they are not. The risks of a generalist supplier not being able to provide a specialist staff member are higher than with general staffing, so there can be a reluctance among businesses to put their professional and specialist recruitment into the same supplier contract.

Increasingly, however, the top players in this sector are adding professional services firms to their businesses. Adecco, Randstad and Hays, the three largest global recruitment businesses, all have strong professional services offerings in some of their markets and certainly within the UK. Rolling your professional permanent recruitment in with your staffing will work if there are enough strong and capable recruiters in the various professional aspects of your business you will need to hire for.

Choosing your outsourcer

As well as the procurement team clearly looking at best price or value along with contractual terms, the business and HR need to look at supply capability so you know exactly what you are signing up for. First, do an analysis of each of the roles you hire and check to see if these can be supplied from your staffing provider. Check not only that they have a specialist business but how many staff work in that business, who else they supply and what breadth of roles they recruit for. Clearly, on top of this you need to ensure they are financed appropriately, able to take on the level of risk and can pay their (your) staff on time and without problem, so do your due diligence as well.

Perhaps one of the most important things when choosing an outsourcer is to make sure you choose one that shares your business's values and organizational culture so you can work in partnership together

CASE STUDY

According to Stephen Gilbert, client services director EMEA at recruitment process outsourcing and talent management specialist Ochre House, too many RPO providers have grown complacent in the mature markets of the USA and UK and have come to rely on standard 'one size fits all' offerings. And while this approach is unlikely to satisfy the growing demands of the next generation of outsourcing projects in these countries, it is almost certain to fail in the emerging markets of EMEA. At the same time, organizations may need to come to terms with the idea that handing over the reins to a partner is not an admission of defeat or a loss of control but the best use of available resources. The starting point for all this will be a rigorous selection procedure that must leave the buyer with complete faith in their outsourcing partner because, in the words of Ian Ruddy, European people services director for telecoms giant Telefónica, 'The day you have to take the contract out of the drawer is the day you don't have a partnership any more.'

Very often the quest for greater savings masks the need for a team who truly understand your business drivers. It's crucial to have staff managing your contract who can get alongside the business and culturally fit your business really well. Often the success of the contracted arrangement will depend upon it. Explore the values of the business in some detail before buying on price and ensure they are aligned with yours, as are the staff that they propose to deploy within your business. There is a presumption when buying recruitment services that it is a transactional purchase. At the lower levels this may be true, but recruiters are human like anyone else, they are not machines. They need motivation and passion for their client and the role. In a market where candidates are in short supply and your procurement of those scarce candidates is crucial to you achieving your business objectives, the quality and ability, over and above what you are paying for them, of the recruiters you engage with will determine your success. In other words, you get what you pay for and the risk assessment in your decision making must reflect this.

Offshoring

To this end you may consider offshoring your recruitment processes a little high risk, but with enough care and attention it can be highly successful, either internally or outsourced.

CASE STUDY

Carol Hammond, a shared services implementation expert, talks about a high-tech systems integrator/outsourcer client she works with who successfully implemented shared offshored services.

'We worked in a fast-moving, competitive environment and had already implemented HR shared services, which were fully embedded and working well. A need to keep up with demand and save further costs meant a review recommended offshoring for over 70 HR processes, including recruitment and exit, to our HR team in India.

'After discussion and evaluation of current process, we agreed to split recruitment processes so that some elements stayed onshore (for local legislation, time or cost reasons), while the majority of the activity moved offshore (rule-driven, transactional, repeatable processes). These included much of the day-to-day administration involved and we also designed an operating level agreement to sit behind the service level agreement and an audit process so that we could properly monitor and measure performance.

'As we got to know the HR team in India, we saw we had a team who were capable of doing more than we originally envisaged, so we agreed to transfer more complex processes and call handling over to India, which was seen at the time as quite a radical step. The India team handled all incoming calls for recruitment, including liaising with agencies and prospective employees. Only queries were escalated back to the UK.

'The launch went very well. Post transfer, our biggest frustrations were nothing to do with the people or the processes, but MIS and technology. We had to develop the processes to manage this and provide more training for the team in India.

'In India the change was seen as positive, with more interesting work coming into the team. There were some challenges to minimize risk of attrition through team morale as some of the work was seen as transactional. However, we did see the cost savings achieved and improved process speed and efficiency as a direct result of the transfer of work.'

How to be successful with outsourcing

As the previous case study shows, this is a partnership. However much you have delegated all activity and risk to the staffing organization, it will only be successful if both parties play their part in making it so. The day contracts are signed there must be utmost commitment on both sides for it to work. If the client signs an advantageous contract and sits back smiling, waiting to see if the agency will deliver, it will almost be certain to fail. So the day after contracts are signed, work should start laying the foundations to make the relationship work well.

The day the outsource team takes over is the most important day in the business and how they are introduced and welcomed into the business will have a strong impact on the relationship they have with the business long term. How this is transitioned needs to depend upon what the business is used to and has been doing before. You'll need to on-board your outsourcer as carefully as a new recruit.

Insourcing

Increasingly organizations are considering bringing all of the recruitment in-house.

CASE STUDY

Penny Davis, HR director at Balfour Beatty Workplace, has chosen to develop an in-house agency approach. She has recruited someone from the recruitment agency sector to develop an in-house agency. She believes in empowering managers to deliver and be accountable for their own performance and hiring decisions but also giving them help by offering a cost-advantageous (through a not-for-profit internal agency) solution within the business to compete against the traditional suppliers in that market. It's early days but there are already strong signs that the managers are appreciating the value gained.

Delivering your strategy into the business

Whichever strategy you choose, a service needs to be delivered into the business. It needs to give advice and deliver the right people into the right roles for them at the right time within budget. If this means physically walking around the office to take a job brief or follow up a set of CVs for interview, then so be it. Delivering a service does not mean sending out long complicated forms for managers to complete and then further hoops for them to jump through in order to be allowed to hire people; it means making 'buying' easy. We would be unlikely to take our business to anyone who made it hard to buy.

To this end the service needs to be proactive as well as reactive. The hallmark of a good team is that they are finding good people in the market and bringing them both to the attention of the business and marketing the business to those individuals – not simply filling the role they have on their desk. So the recruitment team can contribute over and above any cost-per-hire saving by finding and attracting the best people in the market and identifying a space for them where they can contribute. This is delivering real recruitment value-add and may make the difference between the company beating the competition and achieving its goals or not.

If you have a dedicated recruitment team, consider organizing them like an external recruitment consultancy. If it is staffed and remunerated like a recruitment agency it may well deliver high value back into your business. The staffing industry is very good at filling jobs and working to purpose with a sense of urgency, and people with a broader HR background are unlikely to be interested in working in that way.

In the next chapter the concept of the fit-for-purpose process touched on above is developed. Having a great strategy, good intentions and a drive to succeed will take you a long way – but without a robust process which makes it easy but also 'safe' for the business to hire, you may yet be unsuccessful.

A recruiting process fit for purpose

07

It was said by my first boss, the late Peter Lloyd, that good recruitment is 'like a hot knife through butter' and while there will be many roles for which it feels more like sawing through a redwood or pushing treacle uphill, there is much truth in this. When you get the process and the mix right it's actually not that hard and will feel easy and smooth.

CASE STUDY

Gerry Wyatt founded and runs a successful job board called graduate-jobs.com, used by many of the leading graduate recruiters. So he knows a lot about recruiting. He'd agree it's probably more true to say he is an expert in attraction, but like many smaller businesses he doesn't have to recruit too often. Recently he was looking for a (graduate) marketing assistant, crafted a great ad and received a huge response – everyone in the world wants a job blogging and hanging out on Facebook for a living. He read a wide range and quantity of CVs and interviewed several people over a couple of weeks and hadn't found anyone with the passion he needed. Then a new CV dropped into his in-box on Friday. It was perfect. The candidate was contacted for a telephone interview over the weekend, interviewed in the offices on Monday, sense checked with a telephone interview with another team member on Tuesday, completed some assessed tasks overnight, had a final interview in the office to meet the team on Wednesday, was offered and accepted the job by the end of the week. He started the following week.

Your process will be one of the differences between success and failure and the focus needs to be on making your process run smoothly so it can take the hills and dips with ease. This chapter takes a broad look at the recruitment process from requisition sign-off to offer letter generation and everything in between. Little time is spent on individual requirements of different applicant tracking systems or talent platforms on the market, but the part a system has to play in success is considered.

The chapter starts by looking at the objectives of a recruitment process and then takes a role from inception to completion through the process, putting some tools alongside which you can adopt or adapt for your own business. You'll need to ensure the process you have in your business fits within the legal framework you are operating in, of course, and more can be found on this in Chapter Nine. It will also need to blend the internal goals of the business with the external labour market and environment it is working within, as Figure 7.1 shows. There is little point in having a perfect process that does not cater for your business needs or the needs of your likely candidate community.

Like the case study above, your process should be as easy as possible and avoid creating too many hoops to go through. It must meet the market needs and you need to be clear what each step adds to the process. It's a good idea to critically re-evaluate your process every few months.

FIGURE 7.1 The recruitment process relationship

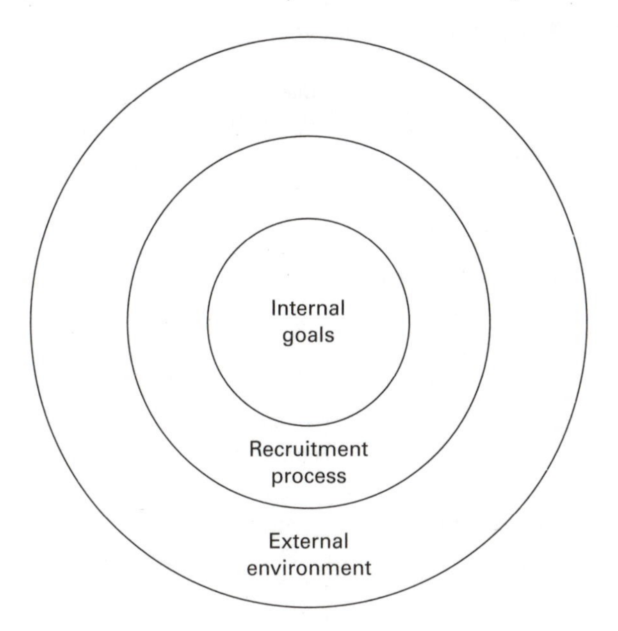

There are three aspects to the process:

- whether it delivers sufficient information for you to decide if the person has the competences to do the role;
- whether it presents a good enough picture of your organization for the qualified candidate to be inclined to join your business;
- whether it needs to make it easy for the organization to recruit someone if there is an agreed business need.

There also needs to be a good process to plan the resourcing, and a sign-off process that works commercially and for the financial director.

In general your 'big-picture' recruitment process will look like Figure 7.2. You can start anywhere in the process but you need always to go in a clockwise direction:

Client acquisition: in this case identifying a role you need to fill;

Client strategy: how you propose to go about filling that role and determining the specifications;

Candidate attraction: using internal and external attraction mechanisms;

Candidate management: managing the candidate through to offer and start date.

FIGURE 7.2 The recruitment cycle

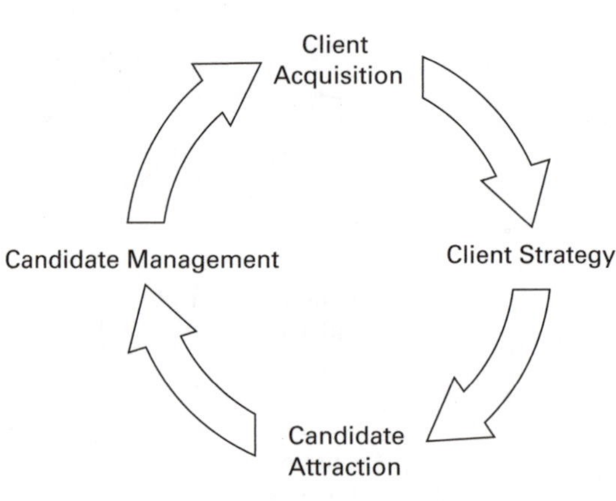

SOURCE: *The Professional Recruiter's Handbook*

Business plan

Most hiring needs are generated from the business plan. Someone leaves and they need replacing, or the plan needs rethinking, or a new account is won, or there is a plan to start a new division, or to develop or market new products or services.

What not to do

This might be as good a place to start as any. Most of us learn through mistakes, so looking at others' mistakes can help us be forewarned. If you only read this part of the chapter it'll give some good headline top tips. Top mistakes are:

- making it complicated with multiple sign-offs for each stage of the hiring process;
- not exploring each potential job requisition thoroughly to see if the tasks can be done another way;
- ignoring your internal talent pool;
- not aligning the recruitment process with the business culture and values;
- trying to run recruitment on the back of a cigarette packet;
- conversely, spending so long measuring what you are doing you take your eye off the main objective;
- not having job requisitions signed off;
- having no centrally organized supplier management process, creating extra cost;
- creating too unwieldy a centralized bureaucratic process;
- not training managers in how to recruit and interview;
- not maximizing your existing employee networks to attract talent;
- ignoring succession planning;
- not bothering with assessment;
- hiring on gut feel or desperation.

And this is by no means an exhaustive list.

Objectives of any recruitment process

There is no 'one size fits all' process that everyone should immediately adopt. Like any process, there are systems and processes which you could apply to make it the most streamlined and efficient. Lean manufacturing processes, for example, a philosophy developed in the 1990s by Toyota, focuses on the elimination of waste, thus creating greater customer value at the end of the supply chain.

'Fit for purpose' means a system that suits your business. A large multinational will clearly have different needs from a smaller growing business on one site.. It makes no difference what size or type of business you are, this is about getting the process right for your business and making it work for you.

With any process you'll have the tension and balance between being effective and getting results – 'doing the right things' – and making sure they are done efficiently – 'doing things right'. The tension between these may well come back initially to the business goals. If the business goals are to grow at almost any cost, to take market share in a short time, then your process will be different from that of an organization that is more mature and is looking continually for the lean efficiency gains from its process.

Equally, of course, your process needs to be able to adjust easily to the shifts in the external labour market and internal goals, so it is important not to design your process in such a rigid way that it cannot be adjusted readily to market and organizational changes. So the process needs to be robust and nimble at the same time. This may be a simple as shifting slightly some of the checks and balances in the system. When costs are an issue and labour is plentiful, there may be an additional layer of sign-offs for new hires; for example, a headcount freeze for permanent staff may need to be part of a process for a while or the introduction of new assessment processes, which of course need to be included in your recruitment process.

Figure 7.3 expands on the recruitment cycle depicted in Figure 7.2, showing a simple recruitment process. Many of the individual steps, like recruitment briefed through to candidate shortlist submitted, have a further series of steps inherent in each, which are covered later in the chapter.

The overall process

This will need some kind of system or method to hold it all together. Whatever type you choose, the first task is to make sure everyone understands and works to the agreed process. This is not always as easy as it sounds, particularly if you have a business with line managers used to 'doing their own thing', using agencies they have individual relationships with and making their own decisions in a vacuum once they have their requisition signed off.

The first thing to ensure is that any system or process you choose is robust and works well, while remaining as simple as possible with lots of performance checks along the way.

FIGURE 7.3 A simple recruitment process

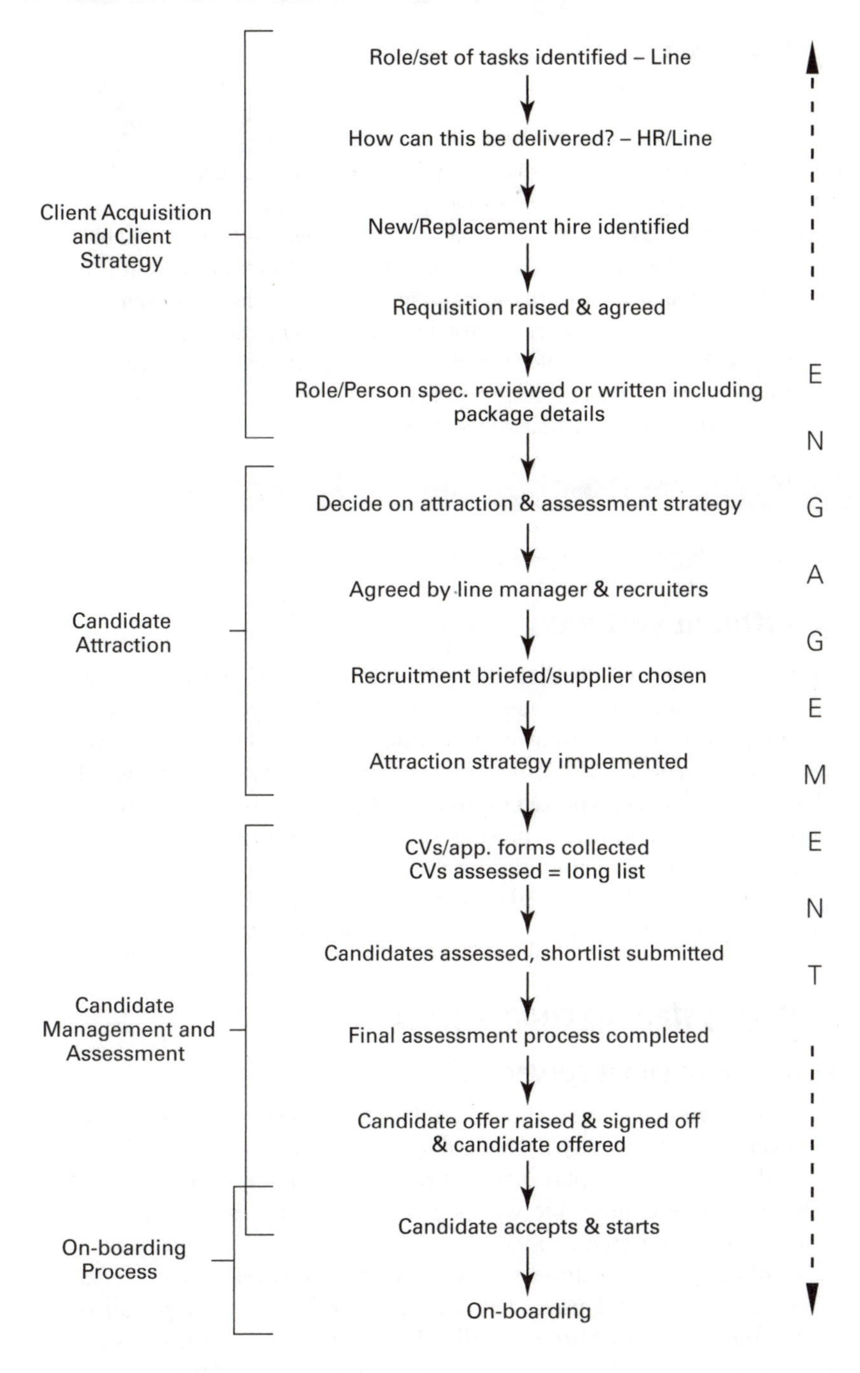

CASE STUDY

As Graham Palfery-Smith says, the most important role of a manager is to select, develop and keep good people, but the focus needs to be on doing this rather than attracting the talent in the first place. He suggests the recruitment industry has been slow to develop ways to streamline recruitment processes, with one or two exceptions, and the opportunity now is to make it more efficient in terms of how it goes about recruiting, giving the manager firstly more candidate choice and secondly more time to devote to their core task of selection, development and retention.

Graham has 30 years' recruitment experience across 26 countries and has worked with a wide range of recruiting businesses. He now spends his time as a non-executive director of a range of businesses in and around recruitment.

Recruitment systems

Should you decide one of these is appropriate for your business, you will need to do an evaluation of them to see what will suit you. Choose one that fits your process rather than one around which you have to work, but ensure that you choose a specifically designed recruitment one rather than a package which has been bolted on to an HR package as an afterthought. In general, you should consider linking your choice of system to your overall business objectives. Are you looking for volume recruitment, does it satisfy your reporting requirements like bringing the cost per hire down? Will it track and log jobs which go over the time-to-hire benchmark?

Types of system to choose from

Web-based or client server

This decision will be governed to some degree by the size and complexity of your business and your own particular needs. If you are a multinational, your IT department will play a strong role in the choice of your system and it will need to be compatible with other systems and may well sit on the existing client server environment.

A small business may choose to use a web-based server where you pay for the service you get and use. This is an advantage as you'll get all of the updates and upgrades automatically. It will almost certainly result in a lower cost but you will have to work with what the system provides instead of tailoring it very closely to your own needs. So the output of this type of system needs to be looked at more carefully before you buy.

Other considerations

How established is the vendor? Do they have a track record and reference accounts like your business? Check out their service record and history. Meet the team who will be looking after you. Are they enthusiastic and do they always get back to you? Are they value for money? Is this a small enthusiastic team with a few clients for whom you will be an important new addition or are they creaking at the seams with their new client base?

No system

Of course, if your need to recruit is occasional, say no more than 20 roles a year, then there is no need to invest in a specific recruitment system. Use of a good spreadsheet and letter templates will be sufficient, coupled with a scanner for roles that attract posted applications – or even a good paper-based tracking system. There are still plenty of organizations that have these.

Data Protection Act

Whichever one you choose, your system will need to hold the whole process from start to finish and it will also need to be compliant with the Data Protection Act 1998 if you are operating in the UK. This Act is intended to ensure that personal information is handled properly. The Act gives individuals the right to know what information is held about them and imposes criminal penalties on recruiters who use the information unlawfully. You'll need to ensure you understand how this system relates to what you are doing and be aware that an applicant can request to see any file on them at any point, including notes made at interview.

A simple recruitment process in detail

This section takes us through a piece of recruitment from start to finish, using best practice for an imaginary organization, Beech.co.uk. It is not a 'one size fits all' solution but contains most of the elements most businesses will need. I use the recruitment process from Figure 7.3.

Beech.co.uk

Beech.co.uk is a manufacturing business based in the Scottish Highlands with a sales and marketing office in Hertfordshire. All the products, primarily kitchens, are made out of beechwood and they also supply beech saplings for hedges and woods as well as the bluebells to go with them. They sell through a range of distribution channels. Made-to-order kitchens are sold through a major high street retailer, beech trees and saplings through garden centres and direct to local authorities and large estates, with planked timber being sold to builders' merchants. They are about to embark on marketing individual products, such as bread boards and turned bowls, to consumers online, manufacturing them in a new facility in Scotland. They will also sell planked wood online for craftspeople to make their own products. They employ 550 people in the manufacturing and forestry business in Scotland and 15 people in Hertfordshire. The sales team is based in Hertfordshire and manufacturing, product development, marketing, HR and finance in the Scottish office.

They are just about to recruit a new marketing manager to look after the online business – a new area for them, so they want someone who has strong experience of digital marketing and search engine optimization (SEO).

Stage one: business objectives

Beech's business objective for the year was to increase their profits. Their turnover was good and they employed a good number of people locally in Scotland. However, because they were selling their main product lines through wholesalers, their margins were very low. They wanted to squeeze more profit from the business so they could deliver value back to their shareholders, which a number of employees also were.

They looked at the products they were selling, their customers and their production facility to see where there might be an opportunity. They found there was a lot of waste in their wood from making the kitchens. Lots of offcuts were going for firewood. So they investigated with a range of craftspeople in Scotland the possibility of using the products to make high-quality, high-margin kitchen and home products in beech. They decided to sell directly to customers to keep the margin high, although they would also market them through their existing distributors where they could.

They didn't know anything about selling directly but realized the opportunity was to do so over the web and adopted that as their channel of choice.

Establish if there is a need for recruitment

Once the business strategy had been adopted, they realized they needed someone with, or a solution to developing, knowledge of internet selling and to help build a website. They also wanted to get themselves a high ranking on the search engines. They considered recruiting an agency to help them build the website but wanted control themselves. They then considered hiring a product manager for the new range but one of the directors was keen to take this project on and had done all of the feasibility study and established the relationships with the producers. The key tasks and knowledge that seemed to be needed were knowledge of internet marketing and e-commerce, how to build a good website (but not a programmer, as this would be outsourced, at least initially) and how to drive customers to that website.

How can this be delivered?

Beech has to decide here what key tasks need doing and how most effectively to get them done. In this part of the process it is important to consider:

- What needs doing?
- How important is this to the business?
- What is the impact to the business of not getting this done?
- What is the return on investment in this role likely to be?
- What options for getting this work done are there?

They decided to hire a digital marketing manager who would take responsibility for developing their digital marketing strategy and oversee and manage the development of their website, which would market their entire product range. The website would include articles about growing your own beechwood or hedge and making your own crafts as well as marketing the artisan (hand-made) kitchens and new range of home goods. The marketing manager would take charge of the whole distribution channel, building up a database of customers, developing their relationships with them and focusing on SEO plus social media to enable people to find them. They would engage a PR agency to get coverage in the homes and gardens press and this would be managed by one of the directors.

Sign-off on the brief

In Beech.co.uk this is relatively straightforward as they are a small business, but sign-off is an important part of good practice. In a larger organization it becomes key for both resource and cost control. In Figure 7.2 you'll see there are two key touch points where sign-off is suggested. The first is once the need for a hire is identified and the other once an offer is raised. As the time lag between the two can sometimes be quite long, it is useful to have this final check and balance in the process. Organizations may also wish to include a further one but this will depend upon the levels of complexity of the business. Often there are informal touch points as part of the assessment process, like a manager conducting a final interview. There is an example hiring requisition form in Table 7.1 and this can be used both at the beginning and end of the process to avoid duplication. Good sense says that the requisition needs to be agreed by the HR team, the hiring manager's line manager, to ensure they support the business case, and signed by whatever authority the business may confer.

A complete requisition

Part of this requisition (see Tables 7.2, 7.3, 7.4) needs to include a job specification and a person specification. Ideally no recruitment should take place until a requisition is signed, but this isn't an ideal world. Organizations may need to flex the requisition process to a degree to suit individual needs.

TABLE 7.1 Hiring requisition form

Beech.co.uk
Hiring requisition form
This form is to be used to support the recruiting process for the role below

General information	
Hiring manager	Today's date
Department	Team
Position information (attach the role and person specification)	
Job title	Broad outline of role
New/replacement/restructured?	If replacement, who replacing and why?
If restructured, how does role sit within team? (Attach organization chart if appropriate)	
If new, is it signed off in overall departmental hiring plan?	
Role information	
Permanent/contract/temporary	Full-time/part-time/fractional appointment
Hours of work	Salary and grade
Benefits	Holiday
Approvals	
Hiring manager (name)	Date
Department head (name)	Date
HR director (name)	Date
Board director (name)	Date
Offer made	£ offered, benefits, level in business
Date of offer	
Candidate's proposed start date	
Offer accepted	Yes/no (if no, reason for refusal)
Hiring manager (name)	Date
Department head (name)	Date
HR director (name)	Date
Board director (name)	Date

TABLE 7.2 Job description

Beech.co.uk
Job description

Job title	Online marketing manager
Location	Herts office
Reporting to	Marketing director
Basic function (summary of job)	To plan, manage and implement marketing services to include direct marketing and online marketing, in line with the marketing plan
Principal areas of activity (up to 12)	Plan, coordinate and implement customer retention and up- and cross-selling programmes to increase direct sales and customer loyalty Plan, coordinate and implement direct marketing and online marketing campaigns Manage and deliver the website and online marketing to develop brand name and market presence, and gain more customers Develop SEO to first page position for common searches Manage the design and production of all materials to support the direct marketing programmes Deliver all activities on time and on budget Liaise between internal departments regarding the implementation of all marketing programmes Manage and liaise with external agencies
Key measurements	Performance against targets and objectives Ability to deliver effective database/direct marketing, online marketing and SEO against agreed key dates and budgets Increase online business achieved against the business plan Effectiveness and quality of communications and interpersonal skills to achieve objectives
Direct reports (job titles)	Marketing assistant
Other relevant responsibility indicators (annual sales value, production value, quality/ assets controlled, budgets, etc)	Budget of £350k

Signed by .... Marketing director
Date: ....
Signed by .... Employee
Date ....

TABLE 7.3 Person specification

Beech.co.uk
Person specification

Job title	Online marketing manager
Location	Herts office
Reporting to	Marketing manager
Basic function (summary of job)	To plan, manage and implement marketing services to include direct marketing, online marketing and SEO, in line with the marketing plan
Key experience and qualifications	*Essential* Significant business-to-business marketing or experience of working with a recognized business brand, instigating and leading on a range of online marketing and brand development activities Market planning experience Strong online and SEO marketing experience and demonstrable results obtained Demonstrable results in running campaigns Ability to work with both technical and sales teams – bridging the gap Excellent analytical and research skills Good first degree, 2:1 minimum *Desirable* CIM qualification membership Business degree with marketing as a specialization or MBA Run project teams to deliver programmes Agency and supplier development and management Demonstrable knowledge of CRM systems
Personal skills	*Essential* Influencing and communications skills Presentation skills Team working and interpersonal skills Personally charismatic with good leadership skills
Candidate's motivations and aspirations	A candidate who is motivated by change, success, making a difference and moving a business forward. Creative and an ideas person Interested in developing their career by taking charge of all online marketing communications activities
Other relevant responsibility indicators (annual sales value, production value, quality/ assets controlled, budgets, etc)	Marketing assistant direct report Budget of £350k

Signed by .... Marketing director
Date: ....

TABLE 7.4 Combined job and person specification

Beech.co.uk
Job and person specification

Job title	Online marketing manager
Location	Herts office
Reporting to	Marketing manager
Basic function (summary of job)	To plan, manage and implement marketing services to include direct marketing, online marketing, telemarketing and field marketing programmes, in line with the marketing plan
Principal areas of activity (up to 12)	Plan, coordinate and implement customer retention and up- and cross-selling programmes to increase direct sales and customer loyalty Plan, coordinate and implement direct marketing and online marketing campaigns Manage and deliver the website and online marketing to develop brand name and market presence, and gain more customers Develop SEO to first page position for common searches Manage the design and production of all materials to support the direct marketing programmes Deliver all activities on time and on budget Liaise between internal departments regarding the implementation of all marketing programmes Manage and liaise with external agencies
Key experience and qualifications	*Essential* Significant business-to-business marketing or experience of working with a recognized business brand, instigating and leading on a range of online marketing and brand development activities Market planning experience Strong online and SEO marketing experience and demonstrable results obtained Demonstrable results in running campaigns Ability to work with both technical and sales teams – bridging the gap Excellent analytical and research skills Good first degree, 2:1 minimum *Desirable* CIM qualification membership Business degree with marketing as a specialization or MBA Run project teams to deliver programmes Agency and supplier development and management Demonstrable knowledge of CRM systems

Personal skills	*Essential* Influencing and communications skills Presentation skills Team working and interpersonal skills Personally charismatic with good leadership skills
Candidate's motivations and aspirations	A candidate who is motivated by change, success, making a difference and moving a business forward. Creative and an ideas person Interested in developing their career by taking charge of all marketing communications activities
Other relevant responsibility indicators	Marketing assistant direct report Budget of £350k

Signed by .... Marketing director
Date: ....

As part of the specifications, a reward package is drawn up and agreed.

Drawing up a reward package for a role

Ways to draw up a package:

- Look at what the commensurate salary in the business is currently.
- Benchmark the role against other roles in similar businesses.
- Decide what the role is worth to the business.
- Evaluate competitive hiring and decide how to position yourself in terms of package.

Pricing a role is rather like pricing a product. You'll need to decide which strategy you will adopt, and this is tied in with your employer branding. Are you the best payers in the market or do you offer other things in relation to reward such as career paths, career coaching, learning and development? Your package choices will reflect a balance of how important the role is to the business, what you'll need to pay in the open market and what behaviours you want this person to exhibit.

A reward package will involve:

- Salary, wage, daily or hourly rate. Generally speaking, you'll pay permanent employees an annual salary with or without provision for overtime, depending upon your employment contract. An employee paid weekly rather than monthly will earn a weekly rate for a number of hours worked. An interim manager or consultant is likely to work to a daily rate, which usually excludes expenses unless separately negotiated, and a temporary employee is likely to be paid by the hour for the services they deliver. Many of these employee rewards will be sensitive to the movement in the market and the smaller the level of pay (eg an hour as opposed to a year), the more price sensitive the rate will be.

- Bonus, commission or performance-related pay. A bonus will be dependent either on the discretion of a manager or on the achievement of certain measurable targets or objectives. The advantage of a discretionary bonus is that it may not be possible always to know what is an achievable target at an early stage in a project. The advantage of a clear set of targets is, of course, that it is clear to all what needs to be achieved and by when.
- A bonus can be paid on either an individual or a team basis. Both have their advantages and disadvantages. A team bonus needs very good performance management if the team is not to be working at the lowest common denominator, and can cause anguish if some team members do not pull their weight. However, where customer service by a team is required, the system can work well, as all will want to give great service to all customers, not just the individual's own.
- Commission is usually payable on sales and is generally expressed as a percentage of sales or revenue gained. A bonus may not be so directly related. Often a salesperson will have a threshold over which they have to sell in order to start earning commission. This threshold usually covers their costs of salary and employment and therefore means that once they reach a certain target they are beginning to make some profit for the business and are able to share in that profit. Often commission schemes are graduated so that as the revenue increases so does the proportion paid in commission.

Share option schemes

Some businesses, often new and smaller ones, offer share option schemes to employees, who hold them as long as they are employees. An expert is required to set these schemes up but often they are a substitute for some pay for people at a senior level when a business is founded. Many have been successful and Microsoft is a good example. By 2000 it had created approximately 10,000 millionaires through its success.

Holidays

Holidays are a benefit but there is also a statutory minimum requirement, which varies from country to country. In the UK currently it is 20 days plus bank holidays. Many employers, especially in the public sector, will offer more. In the USA and SE Asia the norm is between nine and 15 days' paid holiday plus 10 days' public holidays, yet one in four Americans get no paid leave at all. Holidays have grown as pay negotiations have taken place over the years, and time off in the UK was seen as better value for business than extra pay, whereas the opposite is true in the USA.

Benefits

In the UK if you have over five employees you must provide the opportunity to pay into a pension, although the business does not need to contribute to it. Otherwise in some roles a pension is seen as a marked benefit, although in most Western countries as the demographics change this is becoming a major issue for pension funds. Some pension funds are now closed.

Other benefits might include share purchase schemes at preferential rates, death in service insurance, life assurance, health insurance, permanent disability insurance, critical illness insurance, cars or car allowances and business-class travel. Some organizations also offer other benefits such as gym membership, preferential rates on mobile phones, courses in subjects of interest, events and socials, a cycle ride-to-work scheme, season ticket loans, sponsorship of courses, etc.

Some businesses now offer a flexible benefits scheme worth a certain value where employees can choose their benefits from a pot of options which may suit their lifestyle.

The ownership of benefits can be problematic and range from finance, HR or procurement, as all will have a hand in buying provisions. The challenge can occur when the emphasis ceases to be on adding value to an employee but more on saving costs for the business. It's important to remember what the benefits are there for and the value of them to people.

Additional benefits

An organization will design its benefit strategy to suit its own situation but primarily as a tool to enable the best people to both join and stay with an organization. Some businesses operate under particular circumstances and need to offer benefits to counteract or support those circumstances. Some may need to offer a relocation allowance. Some will offer taxis or transport to and from work. Some will offer uniform or business dress.

CASE STUDY

Fred and Mo are salespeople for an office furniture business. They both earn a basic salary of £26,000 with a £2,000 per month car allowance. They both have a threshold of £5,000 per month and a target of £12,500. Once they sell £5,000 they start to earn commission. Anything they sell over £5,000 they earn commission at 5 per cent. Once they sell over £12,500 they earn commission at 10 per cent. If they sell over £16,000 they earn commission at 20 per cent.

So their commission payments look like this:

Fred: sales in July £13,000; bonus payable £800;

Mo: sales in July £18,000; bonus payable £1,500.

This is a progressive commission scheme as it encourages salespeople to keep selling after they hit their targets. Some schemes will also pay a target achievement bonus for when staff hit their targets, of say £100.

Decide upon your attraction and assessment strategy

Once the role is designed and signed off, the next step is to work out:

- how to attract the candidates;
- how to assess which ones can do the job.

The following two chapters are devoted to both of these topics so here it is dealt with in outline only, but it includes a step-by-step approach to working with an agency successfully and recruiting in-house for yourself with no professional help, as well as a step-by-step approach to assessment, albeit in brief. First, the attraction strategy is explored.

Attraction

Options:

- Engage one or more recruitment agencies.
- Recruit in-house through print or online advertising.
- Use an internal referral scheme (not usually used as a stand-alone solution).

As a general rule, if the role is a straightforward one, where candidates are available and there is a low level of expertise needed in assessment, then a straightforward advertisement run internally would be a good cost-effective solution. For Beech this would mean any of the roles in the factory that would use the local labour market. It may be worth posting an initial advertisement in the local press for this role just in case there is someone available with the skills required and living locally.

However, this is unlikely to be successful in Beech's care. Once this local market has been explored fully through a possible local ad plus internal referrals, it is highly likely the business would need to turn to external support.

As this was a new type of role for Beech, it made sense to engage a couple of specialist recruitment agencies to do the work. They could be engaged on a contingency basis and only paid a fee if Beech hires a suitable candidate. The agency would advise on package and candidate availability. Beech knew that everyone is going digital and candidates would be in short supply.

Beech's location was also likely to be a problem. Most of the digital expertise is in London or other major cities and it will take some effort to get someone to move to the Highlands. The business feels it is crucial for this individual to be based in the main office as this is such an important venture.

An agency will do a great sales job on the candidates and weed out the ones who would not want to relocate. Beech decided to pay a good relocation package or even consider an initial contract followed by permanent employment to make sure for both sides that they had the right person.

The key to success was choosing the right suppliers.

Choosing and engaging with an agency supplier – a 10-step approach

This can be challenging, especially if it is an area new to the business or the hiring manager. Some sectors will be more sharing than others, so if you know people in other organizations like yours who hire this kind of role, ask for advice. But if you are starting from scratch, here are suggested ways of finding a good supplier.

1. **Identify a specialist recruiter** that works exclusively in the area you are hiring into. General recruiters are good if you have a range of roles and only want one point of contact, but for a specific hard-to-fill role a specialist will be the best.
2. **Identify a range of suppliers.** You could simply use any search engine. Type in 'recruit a digital online marketing manager' or 'specialist digital marketing recruiter' and see which suppliers come up. Bear in mind they are likely to be sponsored links or pay-per-click advertising, which in itself is not a recommendation.
3. **Choose your key suppliers.** It may be a good idea to choose three consultancies, one perhaps that is a known 'name' in recruitment and a couple of specialist ones that you like the look of, so they talk your language and seem both credible and experienced in their field. Check out their clients and more importantly the roles they are carrying to see whether they do recruit the kind of candidates you are looking for.
4. **Brief your suppliers.** In a candidate-short market, how you approach and brief a recruiter are important. If you have not worked with them before and if you are briefing them on a role that is a little out of the ordinary (the location for Beech makes it so), then you have to work hard to make it easy and appealing for them to work on. Avoid imagining that they will be thrilled to hear from

you and eager to help you with your role. They may say this but in reality they may not be able to help. Some good recruiters will say if they cannot help but others may not. This is one of the disadvantages of working on a contingent basis with an agency. If they do not want to work on your role they will not.

5. **Plan what to say in your briefing session.** Plan your approach, which will ideally be by phone. You are seeking to understand from them how they might help and then to engage them in your business and enthuse them about it so that they can effectively sell it on to their potential candidates. In essence they are your outsourced recruitment function.
6. **Checklist for briefing.** When you ring them, ask the following:
   - Tell me about how you work with your existing clients – what process do you follow?
   - What similar candidates have you placed where in the last three months?
   - What is the market like for these types of candidates at the moment?
   - What are the good candidates looking for from a role?
   - How many candidates do you seek to put forward for each role?
   - What sort of package do you think I will need to pay?
   - How quickly will you submit a shortlist?
   - What do you need to know from me to really attract the best candidates?

   Ask them how you can help them find the best people and what process will work best for them. The bane of recruiters' lives is lack of communication from the client – having to chase for feedback, not hearing and having to try and keep candidates happy. A client who is going to build a good relationship and return their calls, making it easy to work with them, is highly motivational.

   Bearing in mind the answers:

   - Send them a role specification for them to pass on to candidates.
   - Send them some details about your business. This needs to be a sales-oriented sheet about the business (in Beech's case the new business venture) and include all of the sales features of the role.
   - Tell them what it is like to work in the business, the culture, the values what the business is trying to achieve and the career opportunities.
   - Build a relationship with the consultant yourself. Often consultants will be motivated to deal with people who make an effort to get to know them, and how you sound and act will reflect the culture of your business back to the agency. It is all they will have to judge you by.

7. **Consider offering an exclusive option.** It may be worth offering one of the agencies an exclusive opportunity to fill your job, as they can then devote more energy to it than they might do if they know that three other agencies are working on it. Consider giving them a one-week start to present a shortlist and if you like the look of the shortlist keep it exclusive until you have conducted first interviews. You can always open it up again later.
8. **Agree fees.** Exclusivity means that you might also be able to negotiate the fees. Again this may affect how keen the agency is on working with you, so take care not to negotiate so hard that you find the agency does not work on your brief. Recruitment, like many other things, is about supply and demand and so if your candidates are in short supply it is likely you will have to pay a normal rate-card fee to ensure you are able to hire.
9. **Agree how you will work together.** Time frames and communication lines are important. Offer the agency an opportunity to speak to the hiring manager directly if that is not you, as the closer the recruiter is to the person who makes the decision, the easier it is for them.
10. **Receive CVs.** To have a good relationship, make sure you stick to what you agree. Get CVs back quickly and efficiently, give full and helpful feedback. Do what you say you will do and help the recruiter as much as you can so that they will be able to do their best work for you. Finally, you'll receive a shortlist of candidates and you'll manage this through as in the in-house model below.

Had Beech.co.uk chosen to recruit for the role in-house, the following would have been a good approach.

Recruiting for the role in-house – a five-step approach

Although this five-step process looks shorter, this does not mean it will be less work. In fact, it will either mean more work through doing everything yourself or that you may be without candidates at the end of all the work you do put in. There is no guarantee in recruitment that you will find what you need easily, and recruitment consultancies exist for that very reason. However, for some roles it may be worth going it alone, especially with the advent of online advertising, as the cost is low and you can always brief an agency afterwards should this not work. You'll have lost some time but sometimes this is worth the risk.

1. **Identify the media appropriate to your role.** Large companies will have a recruitment advertising agency to do this for them, but you can identify good media choices yourself just by exploring the media available online.

2. **Find a list to choose from.** In the same way as you found a supplier, you can also find the right media to use. The first decision is the choice between online or print. This choice will depend on the role you are hiring and the applicants you are seeking to attract. For the local labour market, local print-based advertising, a local recruitment agency or even a shop window will be the best method. For a more specialist approach or for senior executives, either online or a combination of print and online will work well. For a really senior role (usually handled by a search or selection firm) the *Sunday Times*, possibly plus one of the executive websites, will be a good combination. For an online presence, www.onrec.com offers a comprehensive list of online sites to choose from. Again use a search engine to identify the best ones by acting as if you are a job hunter for the role you have in mind. Notice also where the recruitment agencies for your type of role are advertising, as they will have proven it to be successful. The British Market Research Bureau shows that using the internet is the favoured job-hunting method for one in four UK adults, which is not as high as you might think, but for professional roles it is likely to be much higher. The most likely job hunter on the internet is 33 years old with 11 years' experience, according to the National Online Recruitment Audience Survey (NORAS).
3. **Choose one or more media.** Just as you might choose one agency to start with and see what the response is like, you can do the same with your choice of media. Most will charge around the £200 for a single advertisement, so it may be worthwhile drawing up a shortlist of three and going with the first one for a week and reviewing response before deciding if you need a further site or two. Many of the roles are aggregated now and jobseekers will do a general search rather than go to a specific job board. Evidence from research shows that most jobseekers are motivated by roles today rather than relationships with specific agencies or job boards or media, and many will find roles through agencies advertising them rather than from approaching the agency directly.
4. **Draw up your advertisement.** Consider the key selling points of the role. Why would someone want to join you and why would someone want the job? The golden rules of advertising are to put job title, salary and location in the ad to gain maximum response. You then say something exciting about the role (think about your audience), something about your company also and then something about the person. As you are in a candidate-short market, you'll want to make the ad as attractive as possible and not make it too hard to apply. When you are likely to gain a wide range of applicants you may want to make the application criteria more challenging to cut down the number of people applying. Figure 7.4 shows you an example of how the ad might read.
5. **Place your ad in the relevant media.**

FIGURE 7.4 Example advertisement

Digital Marketing Manager

Scottish Highlands £45,000

(relocation package/contract available)

This is an exciting opportunity to help us build a new area of our successful business from scratch. You'll be responsible for developing our e-commerce offering for our new product range which is already flying out of the door. You'll decide on the strategy and build a small team to implement it.

Ideally you'll have a strong track record of a successful e-commerce implementation and the know-how to get us in front of prospective clients too.

To tempt you up to the wonderful Highlands of Scotland we'll offer generous relocation and accommodation for the right person, as well as a fine malt.

Contact us today so we can chat it over.

Tel: 00000 000000

Creating a shortlist

Whichever method you choose, you'll hope to have CVs or application forms to assess. Your CVs will either come pre-screened from your agencies or you will need to screen them. If you are working with agencies, check what screening they have done. Some will have interviewed, all should have checked for the candidate's right to work in the UK and all should have explained the role and checked that the candidate both meets your criteria for hiring and is motivated towards the role. You can assume to a degree that anyone applying to an advertisement has some degree of motivation towards the role, otherwise they would not have applied. That said, be aware that some candidates will be testing the market, so you'll need to assess this again at or before the interview.

Decide on your shortlist criteria

As this is a specialist role and the location is an issue, lack of candidates is likely to be a greater problem that an over-supply. However, it is good practice to decide what you need someone to have. Focus on what you need them to be able to do, what you need them to know and what evidence you might be looking for rather than how many years' experience, as not only might this fall under the Age Discrimination Act 2006 or Equality Act 2010 but it might also mean you miss some good candidates who have done a lot in a short time. Having shortlist criteria simply makes it easier to decide who to hire.

For Beech.co.uk the criteria could be:

- Project managed an e-commerce site development from a marketing perspective.
- Has worked with one of the major digital suppliers or a smaller successful firm.
- Experience of managing a web development supplier.
- Broad background in general marketing and has moved into digital.
- Used to a high degree of personal responsibility in existing role.

For this role there are no hard and fast rules and sifting CVs depends on a level of personal judgement. Not all roles will require this. Some will simply mean screening on GCSEs or degree, others on the programming language used, and this can be done with volume by an applicant tracking system.

Assess the CVs

Create a long list of six or seven candidates. Don't be afraid to be flexible if someone stands out but doesn't meet one of your minimum requirements. If you are recruiting on behalf of someone else it's often a good idea to share a long list with them. They will feel they have had an element of choice without having to plough through 20 CVs. If they have chosen the people to interview, they will then be in a positive frame of mind to interview them. In Chapter Nine, on assessment, you'll find a useful CV evaluation tool.

Candidate shortlist submitted

From your long list you'll decide which three or four candidates you'll want to interview. It's worth doing a final check that these candidates meet the criteria as you'll be spending time with them and they with you.

Assessment process of shortlist

Beech.co.uk decide to use a three- to four-stage interview process and a psychometric test which their HR manager has used previously in other businesses. She wants to see how independent the candidate is likely to be but also how good at working in a team. It will be a fine balance for them to find someone who can work on their own without much supervision but knows how to manage the team of directors as well. If you have used a recruitment agency you trust, you may well choose to forgo the telephone interview and assume that they have already done this part of the assessment process along with the CV evaluation.

Telephone interview

In Beech's situation this is a chat to find out how the candidates sound on the phone, check a few details on their CV, but mostly to explore the relocation issue. It will not be a good use of time to bring someone up to the Highlands to find that they hadn't realized how long it took to get there and what the weather was like! Telephone interviews often need to be completed in the evening as candidates often struggle to speak to prospective employers during their working day.

First interview

This will take place in London. The interviewing team plan to fly down for the day and meet all the applicants. They hope to take a final two or so to a final stage. They'll do a competency-based interview and look at some of their work, so will need to set up interview facilities with internet access. If you are holding all your interviews on one day, ensure you allow enough space in between. Ideally, interview with more than one person. This allows for two opinions but also for one person to take notes and listen carefully and for the other to ask the questions.

Final interview

Beech plan to fly two candidates up to the Highlands for a final stage, as there is a chance one will reject the location. At this point they will spend a half day there meeting the rest of the team, having lunch together at the local pub and meeting the rest of the directors both formally (the candidate will be doing a presentation) and informally.

The final stage will be post offer, when the business will fly the candidate's family up for a long weekend to look at houses and let them get a feel for the place. They will not reject the second-choice candidate until this is done and the contract has been signed.

Final assessment process completed

At the end of the process the business should be in a good position to offer one first-choice candidate, with a second choice in the wings. In reality in a candidate-short environment, you may not have that luxury, so the assessment process is as much about you marketing the opportunity as it is about you assessing the candidates. Avoid leaning too heavily on the marketing, however, and ignoring the assessment. This is often where interviewing goes wrong. It's all too easy to fall into this trap, particularly with a candidate who looks great on paper and where you have a major problem to solve. It is perfectly possible to do both elements in one interview.

Choose the best candidate

Make them an offer verbally and then follow it up in writing. You'll need the offer authorized, of course, before making it.

Candidate is offered and accepts

As in all the best fairy stories, we hope the process turns out well in the end. Sadly, in recruitment it's not always the case. However, by managing the process well from start to finish you can increase your chances of success. One of the benefits of good recruitment consultants is that they are trained not to lose candidates at offer stage. They do 90 per cent of their work leading up to offer and to lose that work at the last hurdle for no reward is not profitable for them, so they will be paying close attention to their candidate right the way through the process. Bear in mind they may have the candidates interviewing elsewhere as well (especially if they have great in-demand skills), so it's worth checking this out with them. Equally, someone interviewing with you directly may also have other roles in the pipeline. Avoid making assumptions about this and check it out at first interview stage if not before.

But assuming your candidate loves the Scottish Highlands, you have your candidate. Now you'll need to focus on them joining you smoothly and on-boarding them well. In Beech's case it's also going to be about on-boarding the family as well as the individual, which can sometimes be even more of a challenge.

The next chapter looks in depth at the role attraction plays in your recruitment and tells you how to make yours the best possible. We've seen how challenging that can be in a candidate-short market, so this will be a focus of the chapter.

Attraction

08

If it is accepted that competitive advantage can be gained from people, then attracting the right kind of people towards the business is the cornerstone of great recruitment. In this chapter we cover in more detail how to brand yourself as an employer to ensure you attract the most able candidates, talent pipelining and ensuring that the attraction strategy delivers the applicant base needed. Your employer brand will provide a framework for good individual attraction plans to be successful.

Simon Barrow of People in Business and Tim Ambler of the London Business School first discussed the concept of an employer brand in an academic paper in 1990. Since then it has been picked up by most organizations and is now the centre of thinking around attracting talent. The employer brand is as much about the employee experience as it is about simply attracting them. Great brands attract great talent because of their name: brands like Virgin, Apple, Accenture, Sky, to name but a few, will attract applicants as they are aspirational places to work. Other brands will need to work much harder to become a brand at all and then be recognized as one. However, the brand then needs to live up to its reputation. Your people need to have a great experience working for you for your brand to be complete. A brand is about a whole, not just a graphic or logo or 'name'.

How to develop a great recruitment brand

There will be some good further reading out there on this topic but what follows is a checklist of ideas to start you thinking about both how to make your brand a great place to work and how to get that message out there to your target market.

Identify the business need

What do you need people to know or be able to do to deliver your product or service? What talent and skills do you need? Can you buy in those skills or do you need to develop them within your business? What might these skills and behaviours look like and how could you recognize them? A way to answer this is to profile your existing top performers, identify their skills, knowledge and attitudes, and then see where you might attract 'more of the same' from.

CASE STUDY

One of my clients identified a higher fallout of staff within the first year than they wanted. We engaged a trained analyst to use psychometric testing and meet their top performers, to identify the knowledge, skills and attitudes that were making them successful in the client's environment, along with their motivations to succeed. A new recruiting process was then developed to sharpen up their selection process. In the first six months the turnover from new starters (within a year of joining) was 10 per cent, down from 23 per cent.

Decide where and who your target candidate communities are

Once you know what candidates you are looking for, you can identify how to find them. Are they geographically available to you? Do you have to bring people into the area? If people are not available in your area, can you revisit the question of who you need and maybe develop some of the skills in house? These are very different questions and answers depending upon whether you are a rural or city business with more labour choices.

Get to know your target audience. Learn what is important to them, what their lifestyle is and how you can meet their needs. The different generations, ethnic groups, religions, personal situations, ages, genders, sexual orientations and education of any strong diverse workforce will all have different situations and motivators. Organizations will need to find ways of accommodating all the varying needs and wants of their employed population in the same way as it would its client base.

Decide what kind of employment experience you can offer

Just as a business might need to work out its unique sales proposition for its products and services, so does an employer brand need to decide the same, except in this case it is called an employee value proposition. This encapsulates the key desirable features that the audience you wish to attract will be interested in. Not only must it attract the audience you are looking for, it also needs to ring true to those people already employed in the business. So the brand needs to be truly lived, not just spoken, as your employees are likely to be the strongest brand advocates.

Think in terms of the employee experience – just as you might your customer experience. Follow this experience through from the very first contact with the company to the last experience with the organization and indeed what happens after that. People leaving your business will be ambassadors for you in the same way that people working there will be.

Involve everyone

This is not just an HR project. The value of a great brand is that it delivers a great employment experience for all stakeholders: existing and previous employees as well as prospective ones. The whole business needs to be involved in creating and living this brand, for they are really the brand architects. If part of the brand values is to make it easy for new employees to join and feel welcomed by the business, it takes everyone to want to make this happen.

Part of your recruitment strategy might be to promote internally. Internal promotions and sideways moves along a career trajectory are as much about employer brand as hiring people externally.

Measure your brand and its effectiveness

Understanding how your people and prospective employees view your business is crucial. Start by measuring what your brand is currently, both internally and externally. Internally you can do this by questionnaire, by running focus groups, or a combination of the two. Within this it could also be very useful to identify and measure 'moments of truth' – touch points in the employment process: the first day, for example, receiving regular constructive feedback, an appraisal or applying for a new role. How these key events are handled makes a tangible difference to how an employee feels about their employer brand.

Externally you can gain information from the type of applications people make to join you. If you have a large number of good unsolicited approaches for work, then it is likely you have a good brand. If you pay well but struggle to attract people, it will be either that your brand has a poor reputation or people don't know about it.

Once you have gathered the information, you can then take steps to change or hold on to your current brand – but this is not a short-term process. It may take five years to go from an average to brilliant employer brand. How much resource to put into this will be determined by the size of your business and the need to attract good people.

Communicate your brand

The final element is to ensure everyone knows what your employer brand is and what it stands for, both internally and externally. The recruitment process in itself communicates the brand loudly and clearly by the language used and the methods employed, as will the rest of the business processes you adopt.

Identifying your people needs

Once you have laid the foundations for good recruitment, you'll find it easier to attract talent. You next step is to work out how to do that for all of the roles you are hiring.

First, identify where your candidates will come from. Define what blend of experienced, trainee, full-time, part-time, skilled, unskilled, permanent, contract or temporary labour you'll be using. Most large organizations will have a blend of all of these and each of them will require a different approach to attract them.

Typical make-up of a large organization:

- Graduate trainees to build a long-term talent pipeline.
- Apprentices taken on to learn a particular skill or craft who also study alongside their work.
- Unskilled temporary part-time labour drawn from a student base. This may sometimes pull through into the graduate trainee attraction. Many of this group will regularly work temporarily. A temporary workforce can be both recruited and employed by the business or via an agency.
- Local unskilled labour, part time (people with families or caring for others or students) or full time. Permanent experienced hires.
- Skilled full- or part-time labour. Permanent experienced hires.
- Skill-short professional labour – permanent or contract. Full time or part time. Either employed directly through the business or through an agency.
- Interim staff – staff engaged on a short-term contract to manage a project with an end date, often where the main business has neither the skills nor the capacity to manage it themselves.
- Leadership team – usually permanent or very occasionally fractional (three or four days a week) appointments drawn from existing labour force or attracted externally.

Although you could use a different attraction method for each of these groups, many will overlap. Below are pointers on developing your capacity to attract people to work for your business and suggestions on what methods everyone needs to use.

Attraction methods

These can be categorized into broadly two types: direct and indirect. Direct attraction is using a clear and straightforward method of attracting candidates and will have a direct cause-and-effect relationship, such as running a press advertisement for a role. Indirect attraction is supporting activity that will contribute towards, but not directly lead to, the attraction of candidates – such as employer branding. We'll look at each of them in turn, identifying which methods will be useful under which circumstances, but in essence you need both. Table 8.1 shows a comprehensive range of different methods in each category.

To put your business in the best position to recruit staff at any one time, use as many of the indirect methods as you can as often as you can. Indirect activity supports the direct methods which are used when you have a specific staff need. The more pictures there are on the web of your employer brand winning awards, the more favourable press you receive, the better a profile you have, and the better the way you present yourself on the careers page of your website, the better response you'll have when you try and recruit directly. Indirect methods can be seen as the background to targeted recruitment campaigns to recruit specific staff at a specific time in a particular targeted way.

TABLE 8.1 Candidate attraction methods

Direct	Indirect
Large-scale advertising	Employer branding
Targeted advertising	Social networking
Employee referral scheme	Blogging
Headhunting	Winning awards
Contacting old applicants	Gaining national standards, eg Investors in People
Internal role advertising	Reputation management
Posters	Liaising with universities/local colleges
Flyers	Engagement activities
Recruitment agencies	Career page on website
Own web advertising	
Running apprentice or graduate trainee schemes	

A survey of 600 recruitment businesses by the selection and leadership experts DDI showed that the following recruitment interventions were the most successful:

- job boards and internet bulletins;
- permanent and temp recruitment agencies;
- college and school-to-work partnerships and internships (for college grads and school leavers);
- employee referrals, company websites and internal job postings.

In other words, a range of indirect and direct methods. The survey did not suggest that other methods were not useful but that these were the most likely to yield cost-effective results. Although you'll use a range of methods, ideally include the methods above.

The background, or indirect, methods are explored first. Identify how many of these your business is using now and if it's not many, make a plan to introduce them, perhaps not all at once but over a period of time.

Indirect candidate attraction methods

Social networking, blogging, own careers page

This section involves the use of the web as a background tool either to drive traffic to your own website where you'll have available vacancies posted or as a brand-building activity. Both social networking and blogging will have a positive impact on your search engine optimization (SEO). The more useful content you write both on and off your site can result in increased visits to your site.

Encourage your staff to blog about what is happening in the company. The chances are you'll have a clear policy on what can and what cannot be shared, but if not, have one developed or produce some guidelines, so staff can be clear about what they may write about and what they may not. Set up a LinkedIn group and an account in Twitter (a networking site more oriented towards social interaction) and develop followers and members of both so you can alert potential employees to new jobs as they arise. You can also develop your brand personality through how you use any of the social networking sites, creating a look and feel which will appeal to your applicant base.

A quick glance at LinkedIn, the main professional social networking site, shows how companies who are using the site connect with existing, future and past employees. There is an 'Ogilvy past, present and future' group, which is a corporate group clearly owned and managed by the business, with over 6,000 members. Infosys has a similarly large group owned and managed by itself and uses it to post jobs and also direct people to its website. The largest of the corporate employee groups is the HP group, which has over 43,000 members globally. This group is for ex- and current employees and runs a database of past employees.

P&G alumni have a group which links to their own alumni site, which accepts both the posting of alumnis' CVs for searching by recruiters and also the opportunity for recruiters to post roles to the site. This sort of initiative is a great opportunity to connect with candidates you have identified you want for your business. P&G candidates are often sought after in recognition of a great employer brand with a heavy emphasis on learning and development and career progression. Ex P&G'ers are recognized to be both valuable and able. When you are looking for ideas to develop your own employer brand you could explore how P&G do theirs. They have both great product brands and great employer brands.

You may worry there will be posts to the group which are unfavourable to the business, but if your business has great engagement, genuinely offers good career opportunities and a great working environment, and your recruitment works well, then there should be nothing to fear.

LinkedIn and Twitter both carry jobs in paid-for advertising. LinkedIn makes it easy for a prospective applicant to search the jobs but also to see who they might know who already works at that company and to read about the business. They can see how many recent promotions there have been and the latest news.

CASE STUDY

Some companies are using LinkedIn to develop their own resourcing and talent pools in a very structured and strategic way, as Mark Williams, aka 'Mr LinkedIn' and an expert on resourcing through social media, explains:

'A smart recruiting strategy is built around identifying top talent and building relationships with them, and LinkedIn is the ideal place to do it. The key stakeholders in this strategy are the senior directors for certain business functions and their buy-in and full cooperation have been key to making this work.

'Internal recruiters create or take over the LinkedIn profiles of senior managers and directors in the business. The profile has links to websites (recruitment pages and other pages) as well as embedded video and pdfs giving further information about the business and career opportunities, but they are careful not to make the profile appear too corporate. It still has the feel of a personal profile with full career history, etc, and information about the manager or director.

'They start building a strong network, connecting to other relevant users in their market/sector (including but not exclusively people the manager knows). They also join many relevant groups.

'Once a decent-size network has been established (this is an ongoing process), they begin to search for top talent. When an individual is found, the internal recruiter will undertake the following process:

- Send them an invitation to connect. Remember, this comes from a senior decision maker in a large company in their market – they are hardly likely to refuse!

- Once the invitation has been accepted, they contact the manager to ensure that this is someone that appears to be of interest.
- The new connection is contacted (apparently by the manager) and invited to meet for a coffee – no agenda, just a good chance to meet with someone in the market.
- The manager is informed where and what time they need to meet the prospect.
- This meeting is unlikely to result in an application. Remember, this is a proactive talent-pool-building exercise. But personal contact has been established.
- Recruiting staff maintain contact with the individual on an ongoing basis (frequency depends on several factors established at the coffee meeting).
- When a suitable vacancy arises a message is sent again to the individual, asking them if they would like to apply. If need be, a further coffee meeting is arranged with the manager but normally the individual agrees to an interview.

'This strategy is still in its early days and while no appointments have been made yet, recruiters are very encouraged by the quality and quantity of talent they now have access to. Only time will tell if this proves to be a valuable use of their time but they believe they now have a significant advantage over their competitors and a more effective and higher-quality talent pool than can be offered by recruitment agencies.'

Search engine optimization

Once the basic rules of advertisement writing have been paid attention to you'll also need to add SEO capability – this is the capacity of the ad to be picked up by a search engine and the advertisement consolidators like www.indeed.co.uk. Indeed lists all of the jobs advertised on all the job boards and has its own front-end search engine, so you can search against job type and location. A quick search here reveals jobs for CEOs and trainees alike. With the candidates going where the jobs are, today you'll need to make sure your job gets noticed and is at the top of the list. Another way of doing this is through Twitter.

CASE STUDY

Emma Kellaher of recruitment agency to the hospitality industry Caterek, explains: 'Twitter has helped us in the recruitment process by helping cut recruitment costs. Not only this but we have found Twitter to be especially appealing thanks to the audience it attracts. The advantage of Twitter is that it taps into the passive jobseeker market, and also allows you to connect with people you wouldn't normally be able to get in contact with. For example, we are following some CEOs, MDs and senior executives from some blue-chip companies who are key decision makers, and we can Twitter them at any time. Equally, we are being followed by some very senior candidates currently looking for work. I believe the advantage of using Twitter is not for direct recruiting but for building and maintaining a candidate and client community of your own that follows you, thus building the advisor relationship, which in turn adds value to our service and makes us their agency of choice.'

Your own careers page

The main online place to build your presence and say who you are is your own careers page of your website, although this is only useful if you are driving traffic to your site via external engines or your brand name – so this activity is all interlinked.

You can make your site as simple or as complicated as you like and examples range from a list of jobs to a comprehensive set of information about joining a particular company. The design and tone will vary and need to fit in with the rest of the site but there are a list of features you need and features that would give added value:

Essential are:

- List of jobs with detail about each of them and how they fit into the organization – sophisticated sites will have search facilities and the capacity to set up a job profile so new roles which match individuals' interests can be identified and sent to them.
- Details on how to apply for a job.
- Information on the company, the working environment, equal opportunities and data protection policies, and career opportunities.
- Awards and standards you have achieved: Top 100 company to work for, campaign wins, positive about disabled people, industry awards, etc.
- A strong 'must-have' as it builds a talent pipeline is the capacity for people to register with you for updates. Although this may require extra functionality, having the kinds of candidates you may wish to employ approaching you instead of having to go and find them is worth a development investment and is likely to be paid back so long as the data is then used in a proactive way.

The following provide added value:

- values and high-level organizational structure of the business;
- rewards and benefits;
- career development, training and learning opportunities;
- advice and tips on how to have a successful career in the sector which your business operates in;

- profiles of successful people in the business showing how they have progressed and developed – from all areas of the business so all applicants can find someone to relate to;
- video showing a day in the life of part of the organization – ideally of a team at work;
- separate graduate section showing the development programme and what graduates can expect;
- statement from the CEO;
- news on apprenticeships, work experience schemes, training programmes;
- links to other sites you are likely to have career opportunities posted on.

You can see from this list that the 'essentials' are simply information based while the 'added values' build a rich picture of what it might be like to actually work in your organization. Your candidates will be able to picture working in the business and having a great career with good rewards, and you'll get motivated, qualified applicants who match your profile.

Entering and winning awards

Every industry will have its 'Best of' awards which you may want to enter and hopefully win. The award will then attract people experienced in your industry and enable you to draw staff from the competition. There will also potentially be some local awards which may be regional variations of the industry awards or stand-alone. If you are a regional employer these can be very helpful.

Alongside this in the UK there is the *Sunday Times* Top 100 Best Companies to Work For awards, which are arguably the most widely recognized competition for organizations. There are two categories – small and medium. There is a range of other awards in the same vein: companies women want to work for, fastest-growing companies, regional recruitment awards – which offer a more targeted opportunity to be recognized – and a host of others.

Winning awards will have a good impact on both internal and prospective employees and can be a good investment, as while they may take up time and energy, they will offer sound payback in terms of attraction. They also drive genuine improvement as you need to be prepared to make progress on areas in the business which your people are feeding back on so you can either maintain or develop your position for next year, which, of course, regardless of award positioning, genuinely creates a strong environment for people to work in.

One CEO I know says every award saves him a minimum £40,000 in unnecessary recruitment fees as it increases the talent contacting the business directly to explore opportunities – and that's before he begins to count the improvements in retention.

Gaining national standards

For some people and organizations it will be motivating and reassuring to know that they work to a range of nationally recognized standards. These are almost certainly more important in larger, particularly public sector, organizations rather than smaller entrepreneurial ones but can offer real value again both to internal employees as well as prospective ones.

In the UK these standards will include the Matrix Standard, Investors in People, ISO and BSI, to name but a few. Most public sector organizations will have national standards of operation across a wide range of sectors, from education to management. Organizations that invest in working to those standards will have a strong story to tell staff.

Recruiting and developing young people

Apprenticeships Apprenticeships used to be the traditional way of learning a trade or craft. Leonardo da Vinci worked as an apprentice for six years. Companies offering modern apprenticeships still exist and this can be a great way of attracting future talent into your business, especially those candidates who may not be academic but interested in getting out to work. 'Not going to university' (www.notgoingtouniversity.co.uk) is a website set up by a young school leaver who found few opportunities available other than university after A levels. It carries news of gap years, courses and jobs as well as success stories of young people who decided university was not for them. As a result of declining university funding, more young people will consider getting out into the workplace after school and more companies will offer them meaningful training opportunities.

Most organizations that offer modern apprenticeships usually combine this with further study at a local education provider to complement the learning in the workplace and leading to a nationally recognized qualification. The National Apprenticeship Service supports, funds and coordinates the delivery of apprenticeships throughout England. The average wage is about £170 per week, but an employer only has to fund the employment costs; education and training are funded by the government. There are a range of apprentice roles available through the schemes and it would be great to see more companies offering these opportunities.

Graduate recruitment It is a misnomer that all graduate recruitment has to be for a formal graduate training programme with defined aims and objectives and career paths. Any role in your business could be suitable for a graduate-level hire, so long as the hiring criteria are valid. Most often this is because you are looking for a proven level of academic ability and the capacity to learn quickly and to a certain level.

However, it is true to say that the best academically qualified graduates – those from Russell Group universities as well as Oxbridge and Durham – are looking for a more structured career with development and career opportunities. Clearly there are exceptions to this but it is generally true. However, this still leaves a lot of highly employable graduates; those from other universities and those without 2:1s may be ideal for many roles where a more practical approach to work is required or where there is a specific role rather than a training programme.

You may therefore decide to invest in future talent by developing a formal graduate recruitment programme. Most of the major companies have them and annually compete for the best talent leaving university each year. If you are thinking of developing one for your business, research how you can draw talent to your business.

Succession planning and internal moves

Many companies overlook this and fail to maximize the existing talent in the business, thus increasing the number of external hires needed. A good succession planning process will work on behalf of both the business and the individual, aiming to satisfy both needs. According to the CIPD, planning declined in the 1990s due to flatter structures and less certainty in the workplace, certainly in a historical perspective. People no longer stayed with firms for a lifetime. How to succession plan in this changing environment becomes challenging – and is therefore often not done at all. To make the most of the internal talent pool there must be a number of elements in place.

Culture If it is not in the culture of the organization for people to move around the business, they probably won't. Often this culture change can start with graduates who consistently move around different departments or operating companies, which means moving around becomes more normal. This can also be tackled through career development planning where people move sideways in organizations rather than just upwards. Too often career development is seen as promoting someone rather than developing them more widely, and whether people move from one organization to another or within organizations there is much potential for people to develop more widely and in a more rounded way by moving sideways more regularly before moving up.

Senior management support In a business where a senior manager or the board does not support losing their best staff and does not encourage them to move on and gain new, fresh experience, the movement of people can stagnate. Often managers are fearful that they will not replace that person or they have made that person indispensable in their mind. To change this culture, managers need a sense of abundance and the recruitment or the HR team can be helpful here in introducing potential new hires into the management team for interview so they can experience choice and options rather than feeling 'robbed' of their best people. Making change the cultural norm will also help manage the senior management agenda and the board can set promotional targets internally to support this. In truth, succession planning needs to be owned and promoted by the chief executive. HR and recruitment can then support it.

Internal promotional mechanism Succession planning may focus its efforts on a specific group in the organization. The board and a couple of levels removed may be the focus of proactive efforts in the business and considered to be the succession talent pool. However, the movement and opportunities for other staff around the business facilitate new thinking into parts of the organization and fuels the movement of existing staff into the succession talent pool in the first place.

The business needs a good engaging way of advertising new roles. This needs to suit the business, so a high-tech company will have a job board with great functionality as part of the intranet, a less high-tech one with a branch distribution may still work on noticeboards and posters. Either way it is the role of recruitment and HR to make the attraction process of jobs internally as attractive and enticing as if they were being advertised externally. Too often one sees dusty dull job specs posted on cupboards in kitchens as a substitute for great recruitment advertising.

There also needs to be a 'safe' method of applying for a job internally, so that if an employee is unsuccessful in applying for a new role, their relationship with their senior manager is still intact. This relates back to the mindset and behaviours of senior management in general but also to the process by which someone applies for a role. It may be helpful for someone to be able to explore a role internally informally before making an application. It is also important for the business to balance the need for openness, fairness and non-discrimination, with inevitable disappointment for people who were encouraged to apply for roles they were not qualified to be appointed to. Avoid encouraging people to apply for roles that they will not get.

This leads on to how to attract candidates directly – and one of the methods is indeed using your existing workforce, incentivizing them to refer their friends, family and ex-colleagues to your business as potential candidates.

Direct candidate attraction methods

In this section I look at a range of general methods and finish by paying particular attention to attracting young people into your business through modern apprenticeships and graduate training schemes.

Employee candidate referral scheme (ECRS)

This can be a really valuable way of recruiting and should form an integral part of any recruitment strategy. Assuming your people are good and you value them, recruiting more people like them seems to make sense (there will be some diversity disadvantages around this but these can be addressed in other ways). It is hard to get figures detailing the percentage of hires recruited through an ECRS but it looks like the norm is to recruit maybe 5 to 10 per cent of staff through this route, and most organizations have some form of scheme ranging from 'It pays to have friends', 'A grand in the hand', 'Refer a friend', 'Friends and family referral scheme' through to 'Rewarding friends' and a whole range in between.

The larger a business is, the greater the opportunity to drive through more hires from this route. It should be possible to raise this to 20 per cent of hires with a degree of effort and visibility.

Top tips:

- Make sure the scheme is promoted widely and then given a facelift or promotional shift each quarter to rejuvenate it. Give it a name (which works with your wider employer brand identity), a brand identity, logo and use noticeboards and the company intranet to ensure everyone knows about it.
- Ensure that the value associated with the scheme is not so great that all your staff spend time headhunting for candidates to join you, but equally ensure it is of value and helps people take the trouble to have conversations with friends and past colleagues.
- Your values as a business will direct you towards the kind of reward: either cash value or a choice of gift or vouchers. This alone will say something about the scheme. When setting up the scheme, bear in mind how much it costs to recruit someone from a recruitment agency and consider linking it to the applicant's salary so that you don't pay the same for candidates on the lowest and highest pay scales.
- Make a big fuss when there are successes. Shout about it and consider paying it visibly in cash if you have a large open-plan office or making a presentation at a team meeting. Success breeds success. At the very least give the reward on the very first day a person joins. Consider splitting the reward across Day One and six months in, which gives your recommender a good reason to mentor their recommendee.
- Put some obvious rules in place about claiming a reward for someone sourced for one's own team, and create some distance between recommending and the hiring process so that people in the business are not involved in the hiring process of someone they have recommended.
- Make your ECRS active, not just passive. If you have an in-house hiring team, recommend to participants that they simply suggest to friends and ex-colleagues they start a conversation with the hiring team so that next time they feel they are ready for a move they know who to talk to at your organization. This way the hiring team can build a pipeline of good people.
- In a similar vein, when you identify a role to hire, make a list of possible organizations that this person might come from and then search the existing employee database to see if there is anyone who has recently worked for this organization and would like to make a referral. You can even help people in what they should say when they call an ex-colleague. Care needs to be taken with this approach, of course, and this active scheme needs to stop short at coercion! If the person is reluctant, simply ask for a name referral and have someone in your existing recruitment team contact them. You may want to

make a separate award for name identification and referrals from a 'full CV' from someone interested in a role.

Make sure you both communicate with referrals themselves really well (you'll want to be communicating with all potential employees really well, of course, but nothing will stop an ECRS in its tracks more than the word getting out that 'no one calls the referrals anyway') and also give feedback to the referrer during the recruitment process.

Advertising

This subject is so vast it could take up a whole book on its own. In the previous chapter there are some guidelines on how to recruit for Beech.co.uk's digital marketing manager role in Scotland. In this section the broad guidelines are discussed and the different options identified.

Advertising is useful to attract specific candidates to a specific vacancy or opportunity. It is also sometimes used to direct large numbers of applicants to open days or information sessions when a new office or branch of a business is opening that requires a large number of brand-new staff. So advertising can be either finely targeted or generalist for a large number of staff. In order to be effective, you'll need to have identified that the staff required do exist and you know what media they read. If staff for a particular role are tough to find and a scarce skill, you would be better served by conducting a specific search.

Advertising choices are:

Internal:
- intranet;
- posters;
- noticeboards;
- word of mouth;
- ERCS.

External
- press: local, national and trade offline (print) advertising:
- online advertising;
- billboards;
- radio;
- Job Centre or shop-window advertising (often still a branch recruitment agency's and retailer's method of choice).

Print advertising used to be one of the main ways of developing a brand presence as a key recruiter, especially for professional and senior roles. This has shifted largely online and the proliferation of high-profile sites like The Ladders and Executives Online has placed online advertising at the heart of any recruitment strategy. This has driven cost down and value for money up, particularly at the senior end of recruitment where a senior role could easily cost £15,000 in a prominent *Sunday Times* advertisement. The last recession meant that many companies were able to take advantage of all online methods of attraction and deliver their attraction strategy with much less money. In the graduate recruitment market the traditional print-based advertising media are struggling as Generation Y eschews the paper-based word, preferring to gather all its information online. Estimates suggest that over 300,000 jobs are advertised online every week. Not all of these will be new jobs but a large proportion will be.

Whichever advertising method you choose, however, it really pays to make an effort with the wording and style of the advertisement to attract the best candidates. It's still easy to get it wrong and the challenge now is not so much the waste of money on a poor ad that fails to attract but more the waste of time which ensues from wading through inappropriate responses.

Fail-safe advertising method

The following mnemonic – AIDA – works well as a framework to write a good compelling advertisement. Considerations are different for print-based and online copywriting. The way ads are found and searched online and in the press is completely different, so you'll need different copy for press-based advertising from online. You'll also have a lot more space when writing press advertising and the capacity to develop a clear brand and image, much of which is lost online. However, the mnemonic and process of crafting an advertisement are the same.

A = attention. The most important aspect here is to grab the reader's attention. One of the benefits of advertising is that you might hope to capture the attention of someone who might not generally be looking for a job but your eye-catching compelling advertisement caught their eye. This is about crafting a good headline which is pertinent to the reader. Imagine wandering past a newsstand and you decide which paper to buy on the basis of its headline. Writing a job advertisement is the same principle. The headline in press advertising can afford to be more brand building, creative or quirky but it must carry the job title too to be clear what it is.

Online the job title as headline and sometimes key skills are all important as full consideration must be given to how people search for jobs online. Typically jobseekers will pop into a search engine 'marketing jobs' or 'jobs for graduates' or 'nursing jobs in Norwich' or 'SAS developers' jobs in London' or 'JAVA developer job in Edinburgh'. So when writing an online advertisement, always include skills for IT in the title along with the job title and the location, as that is another key factor for people to choose whether to apply for roles or not.

Table 8.2 shows how to build an advertisement using AIDA for five specific roles. The headline carries the essential qualification factors in the role for an applicant. Qualification means that an applicant can quickly qualify themselves in or out of the role:

- Is the job title relevant to me? Do I do that job? Could I do that job? Do I like the sound of that job?
- Is that location one that works for me or would I relocate?
- Is that the sort of company or environment I might want to work in?
- Does that salary represent what I think I am worth or a step forward for me, or if not, is there some other commensurate benefit?

I = interest. Assuming the potential applicant has qualified themselves into at least reading more of the advertisement, the next part is to build interest further in the opportunity. This section serves to develop more interest in the role and to deepen the candidate's feeling that this is something they should pursue. Although the examples in the table are for online advertising, this section can be much deeper and larger and would be likely so in a press advertisement.

D = desire. In this section you'll try to create desire. This needs to be strong enough to withstand the need for applicants to have certain qualifications and experience in order to apply. Advertisements which put the needs of the role first and the qualifications required for the role without building interest and desire look as though they have nothing to offer in return and are unlikely to attract interest. At this stage we are simply interested in attracting a good range of candidates who more or less match the skills you need. If you are working in a candidate-short market you'll want to be more flexible around the skills and experience needed, but if there is a large number of potential candidates out there who will think they match your requirements you'll want to make these much more stringent to reduce your administration time of handling all the applicant responses.

Not all advertisements take advantage of building the picture and strength of desire; typically ones appealing to people out of work in candidate-rich areas will not bother.

A = action. This last section is the point at which you want candidates to take action. Here you can build a good sense of urgency but this last line must match the content of the ad stylistically. You can include your requirements either at the end of the desire section or just before the call to action – and sometimes it's worth adding a key selling point before the call to action as some of the examples in Table 8.2 have done.

It is easy to miss an opportunity with a call to action, particularly online as in many advertisements the 'apply now' button is relied upon. When good candidates are scarce it is important to maximize every possible application: 'If you meet the criteria for this role, call me, Sarah Smith, and I will arrange an immediate interview.'

This is in stark contrast to some agencies who are posting in advertisements: 'We endeavour to respond to all successful candidates within 72 hours. Therefore, should you not hear from us within this period, please assume that your application has been unsuccessful on this occasion. Thank you for your interest.'

There is little excuse not to respond to candidates directly after you have assessed their CV with the sophisticated systems available.

TABLE 8.2 AIDA advertisement build

	Chief executive role	Global tax marketing Manager	Practice nurse	Service engineer	Oracle database developer
A	Chief executive Not-for-profit research and training, southern counties, £100k plus comprehensive benefits and relocation	Global tax marketing manager, Top Four accounting firm, London	Practice nurse. Three locations in London and Essex. Walk-in centre. £30–36,000	Service engineer, London and South-East England, £25–28,000	Oracle database developer, major dotcom, London, £55,000
I	This organization is recognized as holding an absolute standard of excellence in both research and learning and development	X's global tax marketing team has an opening for an experienced marketing manager. The candidate will work directly with assigned global transformation initiative leaders, drive the development and growth of the global tax marketing identity and related matters, leverage others in marketing as required to serve global service line leaders and interface with other senior leaders within the countries and regions.	This leading growing group of drop-in centres requires a practice nurse for its brand-new centre.	A large company specializing in security systems, alarms and CCTV is currently looking for service engineers due to expansion.	This is a fantastic opportunity to join an industry leader who provides excellent career training and development.

D	This is a high-profile post which will entail not only taking responsibility for overall strategy but also playing the pivotal role of interface to both the customers and stakeholders	X provides audit, tax, consulting and financial advisory services to public and private clients spanning multiple industries. With a globally connected network of member firms in 140 countries, we bring world-class capabilities and deep local expertise to help clients succeed wherever they operate. X's more than 168,000 professionals are committed to becoming the standard of excellence. X's professionals are unified by a collaborative culture that fosters integrity, outstanding value to markets and clients, commitment to each other, and strength from diversity. They enjoy an environment strengthening corporate responsibility, building public trust, and making a positive impact in their communities.	The centres are part of a growing network of services this company provides, with developing opportunities for furthering your career.	This company has clients all over the south-east and is very busy installing new systems every day.	The role is really important to the overall team and will make a major contribution to the projects delivered.
A	You will need 5 to 10 years' experience as an executive at director/general manager/ managing director level, preferably within a not-for-profit organization and be qualified to business degree,	This role combines marketing expertise with strong project management skills. The ideal candidate will possess the skills to successfully drive projects forward, including extremely strong verbal and written communication skills, marketing expertise, critical thinking skills, proactive problem-solving abilities, a strong collaborative mindset and solid project management skills. X's professionals are unified by a collaborative culture that fosters integrity, outstanding value to markets and clients, commitment to each other, and strength from diversity. They enjoy an environment strengthening corporate responsibility, building public trust, and making a positive impact in their communities. Apply online.	You must be able to assess patients, carry out relevant tests and arrange follow-up while offering advice and information. You must be able to demonstrate	Must have knowledge of fire alarms, access control, CCTV and intruder alarms. If you wish to apply for this job select the 'apply now' button below.	You will have solid experience of Oracle 9i/11G, PL/SQL development and have experience of using source control systems (Perforce/. Subversion).

MBA, Certificate in Company Direction or Chartered Director level. To discuss how this position may make a positive contribution to your career development, call X today for an informal initial discussion.

critical-thinking skills in clinical decision making. You will have the ability to work effectively as part of a multi-professional team within a fast-paced environment, in line with protocols and policies. To be eligible for this post you will need a nursing diploma, be registered with the NMC and have three years' experience. Apply now.

Having experience of working with Oracle Fusion in an SOA environment and having Agile development experience are preferred. Apply now for immediate consideration. Apply for this job online or by e-mail.

Direct proactive approaches to candidates

If you have an internal recruitment team or you are a line manager with a good HR business partner, you may be in a position to try a more focused individual approach. To do this you'll need a good candidate database with all candidates for similar past roles captured, access to LinkedIn and other social networking tools, and some time and capability to contact or re-contact potential candidates directly. Recruitment consultants earn their fees by talking to good candidates consistently even if they have nothing immediately for them, as they may be able to help in the future.

CASE STUDY

Elizabeth Frankland from Frankland Associates, who offer recruitment and search services in all sectors across the UK, gives her advice: 'Speak to people in the industry even if you think you don't or probably won't have any opportunities for them. Even a five-minute conversation can establish a working relationship with that person which may pay dividends in the future. We received the CV of an MD/operations manager, a role that we don't have a lot of experience in recruiting for, or much demand from clients to find. I had planned to ring the applicant to have a quick chat anyway (it's what we do – time spent with people now will more than likely be beneficial in the long term). Then out of the blue, an hour or so later a regular client phoned to say he needed an MD/operations manager. As it happens, this particular applicant was exactly the right level, and also had experience of working in the client's sector.'

This is a similar long-term approach to that of the LinkedIn one led by internal recruiters on behalf of senior managers, and the focus is on building long-term relationships which at some point will recoup their initial investment.

Approaching previous applicants

Start with candidates who have applied to you before, as you know they have an interest in the business and applied for a similar role in the past. It should be a simple process to reconnect with them by e-mail or letter to let them know you have a similar role available now should they wish to apply for it. It is surprising how few companies one hears of doing this. You'll need to be sure that any candidate sourced through an agency is out of their ownership period, of course, but candidates who applied to you directly as a result of advertising or internal referral would be a first port of call. You could then ask the agencies to keep in touch with good candidates they have presented that you would like to stay in touch with. It will be helpful to screen those you send out to, so you are not in the position of regularly inviting people to apply for roles which they are unsuitable for – not a good brand-building exercise. When building your database, segment those who made the long list as they are the ones you would at least be happy to interview. Siphon off those you would not consider for any role.

Figure 8.1 suggests a letter or e-mail you could use or adapt for this.

New potential candidates

In the section on indirect methods of attraction I said that LinkedIn and other social networking sites are predominantly useful for brand building, creating a presence and driving traffic through to your website. If, however, you have the capacity internally, they can also be used for making direct approaches to candidates, through the paid-for 'inmail' system on LinkedIn, the introductions system or the friend system on Facebook (useful in the creative industries or for creative recruitment). You can also simply use them as a large database from which to gather names and identify potential people.

There are many guides on how best to use the social networking sites, so I don't propose to detail this at length here. For more information, check out the guides themselves on LinkedIn. Most agency headhunters and consultants will use LinkedIn as a primary method of candidate attraction and network building, so there is no reason why an organization with the skills and time should not do the same (as explained by one of the case studies in an earlier chapter). If you don't have either, subcontract this to a recruitment agency.

How to approach candidates directly

There is some detailed good information on this in my previous book for recruiters, *The Professional Recruiter's Handbook*, co-authored with Ann Swain, the chief executive of one of the largest recruitment industry trade associations. In there you'll find suggested scripts or things to say when approaching candidates. I use the AIDA mnemonic to explain how to create a good approach call.

There are some golden rules, however, which are worth exploring here.

Golden rules of direct approaches

You might find it helpful to have a clear structure to your approach call:

- Be clear about what you want from the call. Are you calling to approach this person directly about a role? Are you calling because they might have a network of people whom you'd like them to tell about your role? Plan the content of your call and your objectives accordingly.

FIGURE 8.1 Letter to identified talent

Dear

I'd like to let you know about a new role that we are recruiting in XYZ Co. It's similar to the one you applied for some while ago and therefore I thought you might be interested in hearing about it.

It's a new role working in the channel marketing team as a manager. We have taken a wider range of channels to market through an exciting development in our strategy. This has worked really well. We now need someone to manage these channels, develop the relationships and maximize the opportunity we have put in place.

You'll need experience of channel relationship management through channels and be able to show how well you can influence and develop relationships to drive revenue – this may have been with a direct competitor or within another industry.

The role is based at head office and carries a total package of around £75k.

If you'd care to apply, we'd be delighted to hear from you. Please get in touch with me directly rather than going through the careers site, so we can discuss the opportunity in more detail. If this is not the right time for you or the role is not right, please feel free to pass on this information to anyone else with a similar background to yourself and suggest they get in touch.

In any event we hope your career is going well at the moment and if at any point you'd like to revisit your interest in XYZ, feel free to get in touch directly or apply for a role on the website. We'll also try and keep you in touch with potential roles we think might suit you directly.

Yours

Recruitment Director

- Before you call, have your opening sentence prepared. Think what might be 'in it for them' to take the call and ensure that your opening sentence reflects that. It's easy when working in-house or for a business to assume that everyone will find your business as fascinating as you do. Recognize they may not have heard of your company, and even if they have, they will not know who you are and what you are calling about. Therefore make your introduction meaningful to them.

- Say: 'It's Sam Smith here from XYZ Company – we're a leading provider of management consultancy to the education sector, as you'll know. I'd like to chat to you about a project we're working on at the moment.'
- Assuming you have grabbed their attention (in a good way!) check this is a good time for them to speak. Chances are you've reached them at work. Arrange to speak in an evening or some other time to suit them.
- Say: 'Is this a good time for a brief chat?'
- Provide a link statement and maintain their interest.
- Say: 'I have a possible opportunity which I thought worth talking through with you – it may or may not be right for you at this time.' (You might add: 'If not, maybe you could point me in a different direction,' which sets you up for asking for a referral and takes any perceived pressure off the candidate immediately.) 'We need someone to head up a high-profile project we've just won. Is this something you'd be interested in having a conversation about?'
- Never make assumptions about the person you are contacting. Your role is to explore more about them, not to railroad them or assume interest.
- Instead use open questions (questions which enable them to talk and open up) to establish initial rapport and start to understand what's important to them.
- Say: 'So I can understand whether the content of this role might work for you, if you were considering a move either now or in the future, what would be important to you?'
- Use this type of question as well if they say they are happy where they are currently. Make the most of any call by keeping the door open for future conversations and maybe gaining referrals.
- Say: 'Most of the people we recruit at very happy in their current roles and sometimes it's a couple of years before the timing is right for them. We'd very much like to keep in contact with you as we see your skills as very valuable in our space. Tell me, what sorts of roles would you like me to let you know about in our business for the future? (Reassure them you are not planning to contact them every week, just from time to time!)
- Always leave the door open somehow for future contact. Most good people recognize it's of value to build relationships with recruiters and especially with companies they may be interested in later.
- If your contact is not interested themselves, ask them for a referral.
- Say: 'Who else should I be speaking to about this role? Who could you refer me to that you think would be qualified for this role?'
- If you are given a referral, always check if you can use their name as recommender. This will add weight to your referral call – and always

use the name if you can. Too many recruiters say they have been recommended to speak to someone when they have not and people rarely believe this now unless it is supported by evidence.

- Always tell the truth in approaching people. This should go without saying but it can be tempting at an early stage in the process to gain attention to embellish somewhat. This will always unravel later and my advice would be to follow the code of conduct for the Association of Executive Search Consultants (AESC), which can be found on their website. It says that their members commit never to misrepresent themselves. Remember you are representing your business in the open market and integrity is a key value for most people and their businesses.

Attracting apprentices and graduates for schemes

This is a great way of building talent, as we have already discussed. Attracting these candidates, to make sure you get the best candidate pool you possibly can, is of paramount importance. The attraction process with these schemes is likely to be quite specialized and different from general talent hiring so it needs specific attention paid to it.

Attracting young apprentices

The government website www.apprenticeships.org.uk has all the information you might want on apprenticeships available and how to set them up within your business. It aims to begin significant growth in the number of employers offering apprenticeships. The site offers a search facility for roles available to young people and would seem an ideal space to promote your apprenticeships on. Your local Job Centre would also be a good starting point but for real success aim to develop relationships with local schools and colleges. As apprenticeships are aimed at 16–18-year-olds predominantly (although opportunities are open to a wider range of people), these potential candidates are likely to be living locally to your business and/or just finishing education to a certain level. Offer to go into school and run an event or speak in a teaching session, offer work experience to students and maybe sponsor a competition so you can be building interest in your business and what you can offer an apprentice. You may want to set a target to recruit five apprentices (or any number suitable to your business) from each local feeder educational provider in your area. Candidates recruited locally are likely to have a high degree of loyalty and really build the skills in your workforce for the next generation.

Liaising with local colleges and universities

You may develop a range of activities with the college or university to drive and generate interest in your organization or you may simply post job advertisements on their website or noticeboard. Major employers seeking to attract graduates will target the top 50 universities and develop relationships with their careers services to identify the courses they might target or generally to help create awareness of them as an employer.

The Association of Graduate Recruiters (AGR) holds a three-day conference each year which among other things aims to bring university careers people together with top employers to create a dialogue about graduate recruitment. Employers may well run workshops and visit universities to attract potential graduates. Most universities hold job fairs twice a year and offer stands to employers who in turn encourage potential students to talk to them about a career with them and what opportunities these might hold. Traditionally this was known as the 'milk round'. Employers still do the 'milk round' but tend to limit it to courses or universities which they have identified. Direct graduate recruitment has otherwise moved on to web-based sites like graduate-jobs.com.

Local employers may well take the same approach with local colleges, from offering speakers and work experience opportunities to influencing the choice of curriculum to enable potential staff to be well prepared at the end of their course or education there. Many local employers work with their local college to generate interest from students in them as an employer. Sponsoring an activities day or an interview skills day may well help identify the best talent for your business. Offering good work experience which shows what working with your business may be like, as opposed to them learning the photocopier inside out, can drive a good stream of candidates towards you at the end of their course.

Advertising to graduates

There has been a distinct shift from print-based advertising to online. Many graduates (some of whom are perhaps not as organized as they might be!) simply type 'jobs for graduates' into their search engine and have a look at the first site or two they come across. Others are more organized and at the beginning of their final year, if not before, will be identifying the companies they are interested in working for.

Online advertising may in due course obviate the need for paper-based advertising and information-based tools (in other areas of recruitment advertising) as the current generation becomes more used to a paperless environment, but many employers see value in using both at this time.

As in any recruitment advertising campaign, it's important to measure results and track directly where applicants and hires are coming from. Some media may generate a lot of candidates but no hires. The media which generate a smaller number of qualified candidates and then the most hires will of course be most cost effective. Most recruiters will want to cover all bases and want to cover a range of methods. A whole campaign may include:

- print-based advertising with, for example, Prospects/Hobson's directories;
- own careers site;
- liaison and relationships with universities;
- online advertising with, for example, graduate-jobs.com, graduate-women.com, future-talent.com, second-jobber.com;
- posters and flyers in universities;
- events in universities.

An interesting example of how events can attract a high level of candidates is a recent project developed by one of the major consulting firms.

CASE STUDY

The consultancy wanted to find a way of reducing costs of their graduate recruitment. Like most businesses in a recession, they were seeking to cut costs. And like many organizations who set out to achieve one thing, they also achieved another objective: a brilliant and effective attraction tool. They decided to run 'boot camp', a two-day retreat in an old manor house for potential applicants to their business. There was no obligation to apply to the business as a result of the session but they did recruit a high number of candidates. The boot camp involved group work, self-awareness development, presentation skills, problem solving and, most importantly, was not an assessment centre. Delegates were simply allowed to experience the learning they were able to access. As a result of the new initiative the consultancy both drove up the quality of its applicants and reduced its cost.

So far I have focused on how to recruit staff using your own resources, both setting up the right environment for strong hiring and making direct approaches to a candidate community. However, you are unlikely to manage all of your hiring alone, so you'll want to use an agency.

Using recruitment agencies

Sometimes the best way to find a particular skill is to use an expert in their field. Internal recruiters cannot always deliver every role directly even if you have one and managers will not have the time. An internal recruiter, however, will evaluate the need to go externally for you.

CASE STUDY

Joe Perez, recruitment manager at Dainippon Sumitomo Pharma, suggests that the best way to work with outside placement recruiters is to engage them after the corporate recruiter has done a due diligence search. 'My standard line to hiring managers when a position becomes available is as follows: "Give me a couple of days but no more than a week to search the job boards, my contacts in LinkedIn, employee referrals and posting responses. If we do not identify viable candidates through those sources, we can engage a search firm."

'If we do not identify a candidate via the aforementioned sources, then it makes sense to pay an agency if they find us the right candidate. We have also lessened the possibility that candidates we could have sourced on our own are being presented by the agency. Why pay a 25 per cent fee for a candidate I could identify on my own as a corporate recruiter?

'On the other hand, if it is a hard-to-fill position and the outside agency adds value to the recruitment process by identifying candidates from competitors and we select one of those candidates, then the agency has earned the placement fee.'

Working with an agency can be the fastest and most efficient way of attracting candidates. It gives you fast access to a wide range of candidates who are actively looking for roles and in some cases those who are not. In effect a recruitment agency will do all of the work described so far, including building its own brand so that both candidates and clients flow into them. Michael Page, Joslin Rowe and Major Players are three examples of strong brands, some in the broader market, some in their own sectors, which have built their name to the degree that they no longer have to look for clients or candidates, as they simply come to them. For clients this means that they will have a ready flow of great candidates and for candidates this means they will have the best jobs.

Agencies tend to offer services in temporary, freelance, permanent, interim and contract staff. Some will specialize in certain sorts of hires and others in market sectors, some a combination of both, but they will all have some degree of specialization now even if that specialization is purely a geographical one.

Typically an agency will work on most roles on a contingency basis, but often an agency is retained to work for a client financially either through a monthly retainer or against a specific role. This tends to be either a search or selection firm or an RPO/outsourced recruitment model or in a skills-short market for specific skill sets.

One of the advantages of working with an agency is their capacity to represent you and market your role really well. Their ability to do that, however, will be entirely down to the relationship you build with them and the time you spend briefing them. You do need to be clear who to invest your time in.

Preferred supplier list (PSL)

Typically most companies who use agencies frequently will develop a list of people they like to work with regularly, set up terms with them and develop a relationship so that when a role becomes live they don't have to find someone from scratch. The advantages of this approach are that companies have better buying power and suppliers get to know the business and how to position it well in the market. They also build valuable relationships with the hiring manager and can save HR and the line managers a significant amount of time in briefing and seeing unsuitable candidates. If the list is too compact, however, it may mean you miss some good candidates; no agency will ever have every single candidate (especially those on a range of PSLs) on the market, and only a few will go out to find you the best candidate. You need a balance between a tight and manageable PSL and accepting speculative CVs from agencies you don't know so that you ensure a supply of great candidates. Companies which do not accept speculative CVs may think they are being structured and organized but the cost will be the missed talent acquisition opportunity to go with this. The best solution is a hybrid solution where you have a PSL which you brief with new roles coming but you and your line managers will accept great candidates from other agencies – though only when terms are negotiated before any engagement with them. This way you have the best of both worlds.

Negotiating terms

You may have your own terms you want agencies to work to. This is increasingly common in large organizations that are hiring significant quantities of staff. If not, do ensure you agree terms with the agencies you are dealing with. There is little worse than negotiating 'after the event' either when you have interviewed or offered someone. It puts both you and the agency in an extremely difficult position. You are both dealing with the lives and career of a person and negotiation of terms after an introduction reduces this person to a commodity, not a value which most organizations would be proud to call their own today.

Negotiation will revolve around fee rates (normally a percentage of first year's remuneration including guaranteed bonuses, car allowances or other cash benefits) and rebate periods. A rebate period is the amount of time a person stays with you and within which the agency can provide a new candidate or has to refund your fee. This is a tricky area and one which is ripe for development. I would prefer to see agencies share some of the retention risk with their clients. This could mean 75 per cent of the fee on candidate start date and the final 25 per cent after six months or even a year. This would place some emphasis on the agency to support you retaining your staff member. It would mean the agency would need to be careful whom it negotiated these terms with – businesses with a poor reputation for staff treatment would not be a first choice – although that is likely to be the case anyway. However, as companies want ever lower and lower fees, they render this service impossible for an agency to provide.

Although the agency has no influence over the behaviour of the business and therefore over retention, I do think it would encourage more of a partnership approach to sourcing and retaining people within organizations. It might be interesting to open the conversation with your agency.

The agency relationship

As the recruitment industry develops, relationships between suppliers and organizations have improved. Like any relationships, they need investment of time and energy to make them successful and you are likely to get far more value out of your suppliers if you treat them well, share information with them and keep to the terms of your negotiated agreement.

The hardest thing for an agency to work with is lack of communication. Too often they are briefed on a role, brief their candidates, gain permission for them to be submitted to a role and then hear nothing back from their client. This makes them look foolish to their candidate – or, if they pass on your lack of activity, it makes your own brand look disorganized at best and wastes their time, so another time when you want them to do something urgently for you, they are less inclined to do so.

You might consider agreeing a service level agreement so that you both know what's expected of you and you can then keep to this. This might include agreements on:

- times of briefs submitted and exclusive working opportunities;
- CV/candidate submission turnaround time;
- feedback expectations;
- interviews – timings and speed;
- quality and format of CVs;
- number of CVs per brief;

- responsiveness in general;
- how the business is to be represented;
- recruitment process of the business and the agency role within that – offer management, for example.

Include anything else you think would be useful for each of you to understand and agree on. The key message is that working together in partnership will generate stronger results and improve your capacity to attract great candidates.

This chapter has covered a great deal of ground in how to go about attracting candidates. Great candidates for your business are the lifeblood of any recruitment, HR or even line management team. Without great candidates and a strong pipeline of them, you can have the best assessment and on-boarding processes out there but it will make little difference. However, assuming you are now an expert in generating a brilliant shortlist, the next chapter looks at how to separate the great from the good and the not good at all. Of course, as you'll already know, it's harder than it sounds.

Assessment

09

Assessment is an inexact science. Recruitment success cannot be predicted more than about 70 per cent of the time and this makes recruitment very expensive. Yet without at least an effort at an assessment process the risk inherent in recruitment increases costs significantly. The costs of poor hiring decisions far outweigh the costs of good assessment, even though that may mean some initial investment in evaluating and developing the best approaches for you.

Assessment is a broad church with numerous options on the market, including the traditional interview. This chapter covers the whole assessment process, starting after the attraction phase and continuing through to pre-offer. The legislative and compliance framework is explored, as are the different assessment options for a range of roles. Like most things you'll want different assessments for different roles as they will need different capabilities, although there will almost certainly be some common needs running across the business and therefore some common assessments. The more you are able to assess by application screening online or 'en masse', the more you are able to reduce the cost of assessment – yet this needs to be firmly balanced with the necessary rigour of the process.

It may be that currently your form of assessment is purely based around the traditional interview conducted by your line or hiring managers. You may be a hiring manager keen to improve your hiring capability; maybe too many people have been leaving your team or your new hires don't perform the way you thought they would from your interview. It's not easy getting assessment right, which is why a chapter is devoted to it. Everyone will recognize the mistakes we all make even just interviewing. Here are some of them:

- **You like or dislike the look of the candidate when you meet them**, so you decide to spend the rest of the interview proving or disproving your view to yourself. This means you ask lots of leading questions or phrase things negatively to gain a negative response. 'I am sure you've always got all of the management accounts in on time, haven't you?' or 'I am sure like the rest of us you often don't manage to get the management accounts in on time, do you?'

- **You ask someone why they want the role they have applied for** and take this as evidence of what would motivate them in the job if they were to be offered it and that they would be well suited to the role.
- **You assume if you ask someone what they would do if...** that they will tell you what they would actually do and you can rely on this as good evidence.
- **You ask each applicant different questions** depending upon their background and what they have done before because you need to tailor each interview.
- **You unconsciously let your own personal prejudices and stereotypes** (and we all have them) impact your assessment of their capability. 'You'd have thought at his age he might have got over the long-hair phase' or 'They went to a good university, so they must be clever and work hard' or 'They went to my university, so they must be like me, which is good'.
- **You spend the interview worrying about your next meeting** with a tricky customer and forget to listen to the answers. So you give either a favourable or unfavourable assessment depending upon your mood or the way they shook your hand when you met them.
- **You assume because they are good at one thing** they will be good at everything else and ignore the one crucial competency that they must have.
- **You don't check how well they might fit into your organization** – you assume their values and ways of working will be the same, especially if you feel they are like you.
- **You think telling them all about the business, your role, your background and what you want from someone in the role** followed by asking them 'about themselves' is an interview.
- **You don't take notes** because the one you remember will be the best one to hire.
- **You really like this candidate** because you really need someone in this job today.
- **Despite following the carefully defined interview press set out by HR,** you discuss with your colleague afterwards in subjective terms – 'I didn't think they'd fit in with the team – they didn't seem that motivated,' 'I didn't think they were that bright' – rather than using the evidence you have gathered.

And of course there are many more ... and these are mainly just to do with the interview and don't even begin to cover pre-interview unconscious bias about people who 'belong to the caravan club' or 'live in Sidcup', meaning a whole tranche of candidates may never even make it to the interview phase.

Typically in many organizations, different roles are recruited in exactly the same way: a couple of interviews, the first with the hiring manager and the second with them again and often their boss. Both interviews are broadly the same and cover the candidate's background and what they have done before along with why they want the job. More often than should be the case, candidates are offered the role after or at their first interview. Sometimes one 'visit' might be appropriate but rarely would one short interview for a permanent hire be a good investment.

So you'll need to work hard to make sure your processes are both fit for purpose for each job category (type of job) and free of bias or subjective view as far as you possibly can, while retaining the equally important intuitive judgement you or your hiring managers will have as part of the process. It's not easy. It is equally important not to 'over-cook' the process. You may well have a high turnover of staff but this may be a transient student population who provide a high proportion of your labour and need no more complex assessment than you are already doing because they will always move on anyway. The focus of assessment needs to be on full-time long-term employees who need training and investment to be able to do their jobs really well and are expensive and costly to replace if it is found after hiring that they are unsuccessful.

Table 9.1 shows some examples of roles and suggested assessment processes. You may want to use an occupational or chartered psychologist to help you, you may want to simply design something yourself if it doesn't

TABLE 9.1 Assessment processes

	Trainee hires	Experienced hires	Senior/ hard-to-fill/ headhunted
Application form	☐		
Right to work	☐	☐	☐
CV screening	☐	☐	☐
Qualifications screening	☐	☐	☐
Telephone interview	☐		
Telephone assessment		☐	☐
Ability testing	☐	☐	
Psychometric testing		☐	☐
Behavioural interview		☐	☐
Assessment centre	☐	☐	☐
Motivational and aspirational fit	☐	☐	☐
Knowledge tests		☐	☐
References	☐	☐	☐

involve skilled occupational testing. The decision about which of these routes to take will depend upon the volume of hiring you are doing and how well this is working. If you have a very high turnover of staff through poor performance, it would be worthwhile investing in some external expertise to help you improve your recruitment process and methods. If, however, you are simply looking to drive up quality in your own hiring to make modest improvements rather than fixing something which is very broken, then following some of the advice in this chapter may well suffice. Just take care not to invalidate your efforts by employing complex psychological methods without being qualified to do so, as you may end up worse off than you were before.

CASE STUDY

The research mentioned before by DDI looked at what 600 organizations do to assess. They found that the most used methods were application forms and interviewing, with the interviewing method split between situational (hypothetical – what *would* you do *if*... featuring as number three in my 12 deadly sins list) and behavioural. Quite a number also used assessment exercises and questioned around motivational fit to the organization.

They also asked organizations what they planned to change over the next couple of years and the result was a significant increase in the use of behavioural-based interviewing (upon which I base the detailed section on interviewing at the end of this chapter) and computerized résumé selection. Their survey also shows that in the next three years, many organizations will increase their use of knowledge tests (22 per cent), performance/work sample tests (17 per cent), ability tests (14 per cent), and motivational fit inventories (13 per cent).

So organizations recognize the need to get smarter in selecting their staff.

CASE STUDY

One recruitment agency which has married both the sourcing and attraction of applicants with assessment to create a seamless service and then based their fee on its success is standing out from the norm. Roger Philby of Chemistry and its sister Chemistry Consulting explains they are an agency which puts service and predictive success at the heart of their business model. They cite a range of large businesses – Energis, Yell and Harrods – which use their services. They assert that by including occupational assessment in their recruitment service they can increase the average hire success rate of 25 per cent to 75 per cent, and although they expect you to pay something up front for their service, they'll also share the risk of hire by holding back 25 per cent until the candidate has been with the business for six months.

Any assessment process, as an integral part of your recruitment process, needs to be done within a legislative and compliance framework. It is incumbent on you as an employer to make legal compliance a part of your assessment process.

Legislative framework

If you are developing your own assessments, they will not have not been validated on a wider population, which means you could run the risk of them being discriminatory. This can particularly be the case with IT testing, which could sometimes rely on the applicant's use of English. This may not be crucial for good performance in the particular role and may therefore be held to be discriminatory. There will be plenty of tests on the open market which will be validated and that you can buy for in-house use.

Discrimination

In the UK at no point in the recruitment or employment process may you discriminate, directly or indirectly, in favour or against anyone because of their gender, race, religion, nationality, sexual orientation or disability. The recent Equality Act strengthens and combines all previous laws in this respect and adds a range of new conditions which anyone recruiting needs to familiarize themselves with.

Make sure you assess skills, knowledge and behaviours rather than anything else. Do check, though, that everyone you are assessing is able to meet the demands of the role. Some employers may worry that they cannot ask candidates if they can travel for the role or work a night shift. The key is to ask if the candidate can meet the demands of the role rather than to enquire about personal circumstances and to ensure you ask the same question of all candidates.

You'll also need to ensure that tests, assessments or questions at interview do not directly or indirectly discriminate – and if you are in doubt, get them checked out by an expert in recruitment or assessment.

Right to work

Since 2007 it has been unlawful to hire someone who does not have the right to work in the UK. This means that all potential employees have to have a passport check or a letter of right to reside in the UK from the Home Office before you can offer them employment. A good habit to get into is to have everyone bring their passport to the first interview. You are responsible for personally checking the passport is in date and valid, and for scanning it in. A photocopy will not do. If your candidate does not have a passport there is a range of other documents which the Home Office would consider valid but you need to check all this out on the Home Office website, which is clear and helpful.

It is equally possible to recruit staff on a visa so long as they meet a range of criteria and you accept they may not be able to stay after their visa expires. There is a range of tiers of visa available and it's important to familiarize yourself with them so you know what each of their implications are. They are also subject to relatively frequent change. It is possible to sponsor someone from overseas but you will need to prove that it has not been possible to recruit someone locally with those skills.

Once you know that you have the right sorts of processes in place and you understand the legal requirements, you are in a good shape to begin to determine your assessment process.

Developing your assessment process

The process you develop can then be adapted for each role you recruit. You may have a business with a very wide range of roles, all of which could need assessing in different ways. The way one might assess a doctor, for example, will differ greatly from a teenager's first Saturday job in a shop and similarly a senior executive in industry or the civil service versus a building site manager. So you'll need a range of assessment methods for differing categories of job, though there are some common guidelines of good practice which will flow across all methods.

You may be in one of a range of situations:

- no assessment in place other than CV shortlists and biographical interviews;
- assessment processes in place but you think they are not working as too many new hires are unsuccessful;
- assessment processes in place but you are losing good people within a year of starting;
- a range of assessments for a range of job categories across the business but interested in reducing the costs of assessment and/or improving its effectiveness.

As with any improvement process you'll need to:

- assess where you are now and the effectiveness of your approach;
- research and identify the potential of where you could/should or would want to be in the future;
- work out what the gap is and develop a project plan – including a budget – to get there.

Determining who to hire and what to assess

Your assessment will focus on evaluating the skills, competences, behaviours, attitudes and sometimes potential needed for the role you are hiring for. Sometimes this will mean looking at what makes people in those roles successful currently, so you may need to extrapolate and work backwards. To assess your upcoming graduate intake, for example, you may need to look forward to your most able senior managers and determine which characteristics and behaviours they have which you may be able to uncover in your graduate applicant base at assessment.

CASE STUDY

When I personally recruited graduates for the recruitment industry we looked at the top recruiter performers and explored the competences and behaviours they exhibited. We also interviewed the top performers and found out what motivated them in their roles and enabled them to use the skills and competences in their job to make them successful in the particular environment they were working in. It was important for us to pay attention to the environment as those same top performers might well not have been successful in a different environment. I chose an assessment centre rather than an interview as it allowed us to look for a range of skills. Recruits have been evaluated over their early years to see how successful they are being so we can refine the recruitment process.

To assess other roles you'll need to look at them in the same way. Identify your best performers and explore what makes them that way. I outline below what they are and how to go about them so you can decide which is right for you. What is important is to assess people against a clear standard, derived from what people who do well in your organization say and know, and how they behave.

What 'good' looks like

What qualities and behaviours do top performers have and use to get their jobs done so well?

Identify your top and bottom performers through appraisal results, succession plans, fast-track schemes, tangible data and by asking line managers. If you don't currently use any of these, then decide in some measurable way who is successful in their role currently.

Some traps to avoid are:

- choosing your favourite and least favourite people rather than effective people;
- assuming the people with less strong social skills are not effective at their role;
- assuming the people who are 'talking the best talk' are also 'walking the best walk';
- assuming that someone with lots of good ideas is a top performer. Do they implement them or get them implemented? What return on those ideas is generated?

In other words, look underneath the surface behaviours for evidence of actual achievements and results. Aspects to look for:

- evidence that the role holder is delivering the right, measurable results;
- behaviours which contribute positively to their team and the business;
- a results-oriented attitude; this may not always conform to our ideal (which is to have that managed with charm) and may involve questioning everything, but it is one which gets things done and done well;
- people who deliver projects on time and to budget, managing them well along the way.

In other words, look beyond first appearances and impressions for those people who are delivering actual achievements and results.

What you want to end up with is a list of behaviours (or competences). How do they deliver what they do? What do they say and do and know?

How to get started

Take either your entire team or a random sample of the team, including top, middle and poor performers. The most robust method of profiling will be a combination of psychometric testing, ability testing and individual interview to validate and explore the testing and uncover motivations. However, you can make progress by good interviewing.

Your sample will need to be large enough to validate your results. The larger the sample size, the more likely you are to be accurate. Most psychometric houses suggest a minimum sample of 100; however, something is better than nothing and some helpful results can also be obtained from a much smaller sample.

A word of caution. As I suggested earlier, often the suggested top performers can be the ones the hiring manager particularly likes rather than the ones who are actually successful. A hiring manager may give you a profile of 'Tony' to assess and say they want all of their people to be like him. Tony is the most successful person and the manager imagines that with a team of Tonys the bright lights of success are just round the corner. There is real danger in this approach. Without extrapolating out what it is that Tony does well, says well or knows, it will not necessarily be the case that another Tony will be equally successful – if by 'another Tony' we mean a white male from the Home Counties who has a degree, is very sociable and is married with two children – in fact the opposite may well be true. The proven key to successful teams in business is diversity. A diverse team will get better results every time. What if one of your clients doesn't warm to Tony and we only have a team full of Tonys? That client will go to the competition where Nisha, say, will be far more to their liking. The key to success is a balanced diverse team with different backgrounds, ideas and modus operandi. Yet there will be underlying behaviours that both Nisha and Tony will display: they get back to people really quickly, they are naturally curious and therefore ask lots of questions, they are very organized and plan each day out in advance. The choice of candidates to assess as top and bottom performers needs to be based on solid data and performance evidence.

Use quantitative data

With a sales team this is relatively straightforward – you will base their assessment on a combination of sales achievements and key performance indicators such as the number of times they are meeting clients, making client contacts, following through, following a process, cross-selling if appropriate. You'll look at ratios such as first cold call to sale, number of calls required to make a sale, client visits to sale, and look at the quality, not just the quantity, of what they are doing.

With many other teams, such as customer service, finance, shop, factory workers and teams of operatives it can also be straightforward. How many calls are answered in what time? How many queries are outstanding at any one time? How quickly are claims handled? How many customers buy? How quickly do queues go down? How under, on or above target are they processing according to the plans? How quickly do they finish their allotted tasks and what is the quality measure? How quickly do they process the sales ledger and how many queries are outstanding on payroll? How many errors are made?

For managers equally so: how many of their people are performing at above satisfactory from appraisal, how much staff turnover do they have in their team, to what degree are they meeting their objectives, sales, processing or otherwise? How many new ideas have they implemented this year?

It is important to evaluate someone by what is required of them rather than what the evaluator thinks they should be doing!

There are a few roles which might be harder to gather data on. You'll need to find out how they are doing so well. What makes them more successful than their colleagues? Is it because they know more or their skills are stronger? Use observation and interviewing to find out.

Gather some qualitative data

Use observation in the office to analyse exactly what the person is doing every day which makes them successful, or use an in-depth interview to find out exactly what they do, how and why. Observation and a combination of telephone call recording, correspondence analysis and visit accompaniment backed up by an interview should give a really clear picture of what your top performers do really well. It's also important in the interview to explore their motivation: what gets them out of bed in the morning?

Try and group the behaviours you identify into clusters to form a competence. For example, are they very organized? Do they record every call they make and the next steps and then faithfully follow through? Do they have a plan of campaign? Do they organize what they'll do the next day before they go home at night? How do they handle calls to prospective clients? Do they take no for an answer or are they prepared to argue their case and use persuasive skills? How much will they continue to try and develop that potential client or gain new business, or do they give up easily? In other words, how tenacious are they?

Identifying the underlying belief systems and behaviours of each of your successful team members will help you to identify future high flyers in your assessment process; there will be common threads of behaviours and motivators which can bind a group of very different people together to be successful in a certain environment.

Use the job description

In the previous chapter I covered job descriptions and how to develop them. This is a good place to start with your evaluation. Really look at what is expected of someone and then go beneath that to look at what someone does to make their job description work well. What behaviours do they exhibit?

Table 9.2 shows a job description and next to it a generic competence which would be the underlying skill, behaviour or attitude the role holder would need to have to do this aspect of the role well. These have been clustered into standard competences.

As a result of this exercise it may be that you choose to develop a competency framework for your business – you may already have one, in which case you can use this to support your quest for a 'top performer' profile.

TABLE 9.2 Role specification and competences

Job description – account manager	Competence
Overall Aim The purpose of this role is to take responsibility for a number of client accounts. Ensure maximum business is gained through building solid long-term relationships and ensuring the client is serviced to an excellent standard. This role provides a career path towards management through the development of excellence in account management and direction.	
Expectations of role holder	
Client mapping and strategy: Understand the organizational structure of each account and develop relationships with all stakeholders. Develop relationships with each of the stakeholders. Develop a strategic plan to develop the value of the business with the client over an 18-month timescale.	**Planning and organizing** The role holder needs to be able to systematically work their way across an organization to find out the name of every decision maker.They also need to be able to write a plan and think about the client's needs so they can develop the business won. **Active listening** To build any relationship the candidate needs to be able to listen really well. **Initiating action** The role holder needs to be able to start a relationship through initiating action to do so.
Communication: Contact on weekly or bi-weekly basis to ensure that client is receiving sufficient quality answers to enquiries. Hold quarterly internal meetings with all those working with the client to discuss any issues, successes, news, info, etc. Arrange quarterly client meetings to discuss last quarter KPIs and strategy for next period.	**Monitoring** To check the performance of the teams working on the account and ensure they get feedback on their performance. To take alternative action if the standard is not met (see initiating action above). **Verbal communication** Uses chosen communication methods and strategies to influence people.

Pursue and initiate a formal client appraisal of our service every SIX months.	**Relationship building** To deliberately develop a good relationship through face-to-face communication with both internal and external clients. **Sensitivity** The ability to recognize and understand situations and empathize. **Problem solving** Knows how to solve a problem using a defined process.
Service management: Take responsibility for negotiating and managing the overall terms of business and agree service level agreements across accounts.Ensure the business is offering the highest level of service across all divisions. Maximize the number of enquiries coming through to the business. Improve ratio of enquiry received to sale made. Ensure enquiries are being handled to minimum standards.Advise and communicate on industry issues, marketplace, trends, best practices. Develop added-value programmes where possible, eg seminars to client about relevant industry practices.	**Goal oriented** The capacity to work towards a defined goal until it is achieved, evaluating the options of how to achieve the goal. **Developing others** Uses a range of ways to encourage and support others to learn and develop, eg feedback, coaching; offers suggestions and directs where this would be developmental. **Creativity** Able to come up with a range of ideas to support the sales effort and add value to the client.
Internal management: Ensure all account information is logged and passed on to relevant teams. Ensure invoices are settled and handle any issues. Ensure everyone working on the account is fully informed of any changes at all times.	**Verbal and written communication** As above. **Team worker** Works as part of a team to ensure tasks are achieved and goals are met. Is able to involve others to good effect.

Competency frameworks

A competency is defined as a cluster of job-related behaviours – in other words, a range of things you expect someone to do, say or know, along with the attitude they have towards it, which will make them competent or able in a role. Some organizations may already have a competency framework for the business which various roles will need to a greater or lesser degree or level. It is easy to become caught up in developing a complex competency framework, thinking that without one it won't be possible to assess candidates for roles or people in roles once they have joined, but it is by no means essential to have a competency framework in your business to get good assessment and performance results.

Table 9.3 shows an example of a competence definition. As it shows, the competency may be demonstrated at different levels. Everyone in a business might be expected to be client service oriented, for example, but the junior receptionist might be expected to demonstrate this in a different way and at a different level from a senior account manager.

One of the best and most well-known competency frameworks is the Hay Group's Generic Competencies: Summary, from McBer's Scaled Competency Dictionary 1996. The Hay Group are arguably the leading thinkers in developing job analysis and competency frameworks as well as on how to assess these competences. Many competences have now made their way into organizations' frameworks and most occupational psychologists use them in one way or another. The Chartered Management Institute has a comprehensive framework for managers and leaders.

Table 9.4 shows an extract from a skills matrix which shows how this might apply differently across different roles.

TABLE 9.3 Example of competence definition

Planning and organizing
Definition The ability to visualize a sequence of actions needed to achieve a goal and to estimate the resources required. A preference for acting in a structured, thorough manner.
Behavioural indicators Level 1: Junior manager Manages own time and personal activities. Breaks complex activities into manageable tasks. Identifies possible obstacles to planned achievement. Level 2: Middle manager Produces contingency plans for possible future occurrences. Estimates in advance the resources and timescales needed to meet objectives. Coordinates team activities to make best use of individual skills and specialists. Level 3: Senior manager Identifies longer-term operational implications of business plans. Effectively plans utilization of all resources.

TABLE 9.4 Job skills and competency matrix

		Implementation			Development	
	Associate director	Implementation managers (Senior IMs and IMs)	Business analyst	Associate director	Development managers (Senior DMs and DMs)	Systems analyst, Analyst programmer, Programmer
The role (Key points from the role spec), eg	Profitability of client projects Staffing levels and assignment of resources	SIM Implementation of client projects IM Project management of client projects	Detailed analysis of user needs, creating specifications on client projects	Responsibility of the management of software modifications and development Management of all resources	SDM Overall responsibility for the management of software modifications across clients Manages a JDA development team DM Manages modifications for one or more client projects	SA Produces development estimates and technical specs AP Produces software modules Test plans P Programming

Success criteria, eg	Project meets or exceeds profit targets Staffing needs are anticipated and managed	SIM Assigned projects are delivered and implemented against agreed project plan IM Meets all day-to-day agreed delivery targets	Accurate analysis of user needs Accurate functional specifications that are agreed with clients	Agreed software development cycles must meet agreed timelines Staffing needs are anticipated and managed	SDM Software modifications meet agreed criteria DM Meets all day-to-day agreed delivery targets	SA Design changes must meet functional and technical requirements AP Programme code is well organized and documented
Competences, eg						
Planning and organizing	Level 1	Level 1/2	Level 3	Level 1	Level 1/2	Level 3

Psychometric testing

You may end up with a range of competences which can also be tested psychometrically using a range of personality tests. This sort of test can help build a model which you can use for additional information in the hiring process.

Ask all of your top performers to do one of the leading psychometric instruments such as the 16PF or OPQ. Then you can evaluate the results and look for correlations in your competences, particularly in relation to supporting evidence gained from your observations and interviews. If you are considering using any web-based pre-screening tools, you'll need to model these on your performers as well.

Whichever method you choose, ensure you have a qualified test assessor to evaluate your results and then to put together an overall picture of the core competences of the most successful and the least successful team members. There will be some correlations between behaviours at both ends of the scale. This forms the basis of the competences you will be looking for in your new recruits. Avoid adding requirements that are unnecessary just because perhaps of personal opinion or prejudice:

- 'Surely everyone needs to be able to write good English.'
- 'I couldn't hire someone who hadn't got a 2:1.'
- 'But they weren't born and brought up in the county.'

This approach not only limits your candidate pool but can also be discriminatory. Unless there is a good reason for excluding candidates from a role because of a qualification, background or skill, then it is best not to. Question yourself closely on why a candidate needs a 2:1 instead of a 2:2, why a candidate needs A levels and not just GCSEs and why their written English needs to be good when they don't have to write day to day. If you can justify your answer, and in many cases you will be able to, this is good and helpful; but if you cannot, take care you are not limiting your applicant base and losing the opportunity to develop a more diverse team.

Putting all the information together

You now have:

- data from analysing results of KPIs/appraisal/sales/achievements against objectives;
- observational information about how people are behaving;
- interview information on motivations and behaviours;
- data on which level top performers in their role are operating at;
- results of psychometric profiling.

You may also have your organizational competency framework, which you'll need to include in your evaluation as it may need further development as a result of this exercise.

You should end up with a list of competences which you can use while assessing new potential hires. The competences will include behaviours, knowledge and attitudes which can be individually assessed. The next stage is to decide how to assess each of these elements in your assessment process.

Setting the assessment criteria

The first step is to decide what the application criteria are:

- the right to work in the UK;
- qualifications (must be verifiable);
- essential skills, knowledge and experience (take care not to express this in number of years, as this could be held to be age discriminatory, but rather talk in terms of the size of projects you would like them to have handled, the type of work and the level of responsibility rather than the number of years they have been doing it);
- desirable or preferred skills, knowledge and experience.

Then blend them into your attraction. You may find that some online advertising allows you some questions as part of a screening process and this will help you automatically select or have candidates self-select themselves out of the process. You will still need to double-check criteria manually or have your system do it for you once the applications have found their way through your filter.

Different assessment methods

I'll look at each of the assessment methods in turn and discuss the advantages and disadvantages as well as which job categories they might usefully be applied to and when you might include them in the process. There are no hard and fast rules. You'll then want to choose from a menu of methods for each job category, making more of an investment on hires which you hope will have longevity or those which confer the likely highest return to the business. Once the assessment has been designed – and it will likely take a year to see its effectiveness – it should be reviewed annually.

The general objective is to reduce the number of candidates for the role at each stage of the process. Figure 9.1 shows how this can be accomplished by funnelling candidates down through whatever assessment process you choose until you ideally have two or three candidates to choose from who can do the job and meet all of your assessment criteria. At this point you'll enter into the on-boarding stage, the subject of the final chapter in this book. Figure 9.1 can also be seen as a sample assessment method for a range of roles, although the order of events may change depending upon the candidate population.

FIGURE 9.1 Assessment process

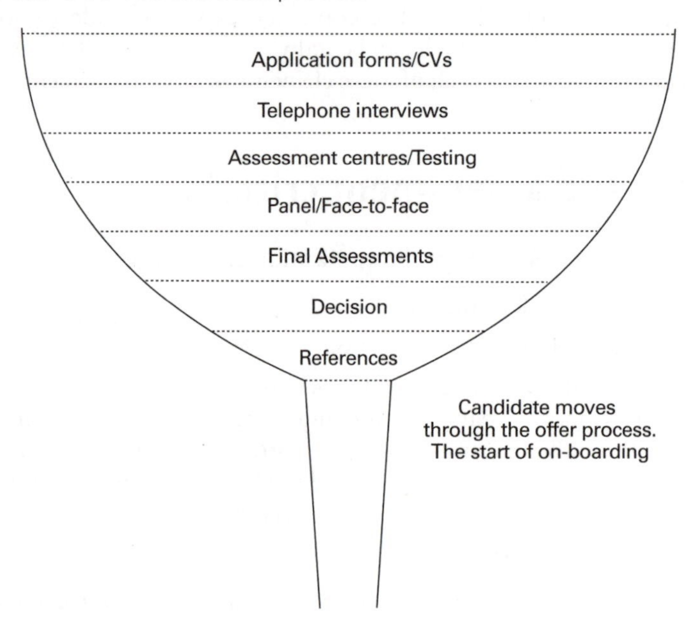

Choosing an assessment structure

Although you will tailor processes to clusters of roles, Table 9.5 provides a general helpful 'rule of thumb', though, as ever, exceptions will exist.

Assessment methods explained

Initial application mechanisms – pre-shortlisting

You can take applications online, on paper or a combination. Your choice will depend on what your potential applicants have access to.

Unless the role is highly skill short, you'll normally find that for volume applications you'll be able to initially shortlist 10–20 per cent of candidates, half of which may then go through to interview. This group could be called your long list and we'll revisit this concept later. It is helpful to sort your candidates into the following categories:

A: meets all the criteria, essential and desirable. Definite progression to next stage.

B: meets all of the essential criteria/meets most of the essential criteria and some of the desirable. May progress to next stage.

C: meets few of the criteria. Unlikely to progress but may suit something else.

D: meets none of the criteria. Reject.

TABLE 9.5 Choosing an assessment structure

Number of applicants		General assessment process
Large volume of applicants for each role/new jobseekers/full-time job seekers/inexperienced workers	=	Initial application form and/or psychometric developed specifically to assess the competences and behaviours in your organization. All of this can be conducted online and without paper but in the recognition that this may reduce your candidate base and impact your diversity.
Low volume of applicants for each role/specific skill set sought/experienced jobseekers/likely to need strong attraction and even headhunting	=	Initial CV or recommendation from employment agency leading to initial face-to-face interview (45-minute 'meet and greet' initially perhaps), followed by line manager first in-depth interview. Can be followed by psychometric tests or assessment centre and then a final face-to-face interview.

Or you may choose a simple 'Yes/No', which is fine until you hit problems with not enough Yes applicants, which may mean revisiting the No group all over again. So some form of 'Yes, Maybe and No' is the best solution.

Writing capability

During your 'What good looks like' piece of work you'll have decided whether it's important someone is able to write well and express themselves both grammatically and fluently. This can be assessed to a degree from a written application. It can never be assumed, of course, that the form or CV has been written by the person applying but it is a good guide. A form, whether online, paper based or offering candidates the choice, can be developed to assess whatever level of proficiency in English you require. You may ask applicants to expand on why they want the role or you may test their writing skills by asking them to write an opinion piece on something. The more opinion oriented you make this, however, the more labour intensive your screening process will be.

The first question to address is whether you want to use a CV or an application form.

Application form

Typically for volume recruitment where you are likely to get a high response it helps to have a standard application form so you can evaluate them all on the same basis. Forms can also be made available for people to collect in person, sent out in the post or downloaded from the internet.

CASE STUDY

Sainsbury's have recently decided to take online applications only and install PCs in their stores to enable people without online access to apply in store with help if needed. They will have evaluated the potential negative impact on diversity of their applicant base but will also be making significant cost savings and arguably at the same time enabling some people who may not use the internet to feel more confident in doing so. Equally, every form will then be looked at on the basis of its content rather than handwriting. An unconscious response to poor handwriting from an assessor may be that they may not be very suitable for the role, even if handwriting is an unimportant aspect, so in this way Sainsbury's is levelling the playing field.

An application form reduces potentially discriminatory behaviours but you'll also need to consider cultural norms. Applicants to the public sector are used to completing application forms and will not consider it strange to do so, yet senior executives in the private sector certainly would do.

Advantages of an application form:

- Reduces the amount of time needed for initial screening over and above telephone interviews, for example.
- Enables an assessor to see the same information about each individual applicant in the same way, so reducing screening time.
- Is easily transferred to a computerized system.
- Tests a level of commitment as more work is required than simply pressing 'apply' and attaching a CV.
- Assessors less likely to make snap judgements on the 'look' of the form, especially if completed online.

Disadvantages of an application form:

- Cannot see how an applicant presents themselves on paper without guidelines.
- Much harder to get a sense of personality through a form as applicant does not have to make so many choices.
- Can be off-putting for candidates to complete, particularly if they have to complete a large number for a range of roles.
- Runs the risk of putting good applicants off applying for the role.
- Has the connotations of a lower-level role when used in the private sector.

CV assessment

Candidates are typically asked to provide a CV as an application to a role and sometimes an accompanying cover letter or letter of application is asked for too.

Advantages and disadvantages are broadly the opposite of those listed under Application form.

Advantages of a CV in the application process:

- Do not have to design an application form.
- Can see how the applicant presents themselves on paper and how they choose to market themselves.
- Easy to see at a glance whether they have the background and the qualifications to be shortlisted.
- Most candidates expect to be asked for a CV above a certain level and will have one ready, making it easier to attract high-calibre candidates to the role.
- Easy to set the criteria to whatever you need them to be.

Disadvantages of a CV in the application process:

- Particularly easy for applicants to respond to job ads with technology today.
- CVs no longer have to be typed or prepared individually and can be presented easily and quickly at the touch of a button, which means there is likely to be a high volume of applicants who may not all be qualified for the role – thereby increasing the workload of the assessor.
- Harder to assess on a level playing field.

Letter of application

Often applicants today will have a standard covering letter which is designed to cover all roles. Asking for a tailored application letter to accompany a CV or a form can be worthwhile as it immediately gives you shortlisting criteria. If the candidate has not written a letter at all, or one not tailored to the application, then you could reject them at this point.

Advantages:

- Enables early shortlisting mechanism if no letter is written.
- Gives a good feel for the candidate, how they express themselves and what their thoughts are on the questions you have asked them.
- Assessment can be made about the salutation they use and how much care they have taken over their spelling and grammar.

Disadvantages:

- Takes longer to assess.
- Disadvantages candidates who may not be so strong at English and writing, so can be invalid if the role does not require these skills.

Open days/job fairs

If a new store or factory is opening or an organization wants to recruit a large number of new staff, they may well combine a positive branding exercise (particularly if they are new to the area) with a recruitment exercise. Equally, organizations interested in recruiting in a particular area or from a particular group will often attend a job fair to generate candidates for their roles. Examples would be graduates being recruited from a particular university at a job fair or a particular candidate group. Forum3 is a specialist recruitment event for the not-for-profit sector. They teamed up with the Pink Paper to try and encourage applications and visitors to their job fair from the lesbian, gay, bi-sexual and transgender community in London. This is really an attraction mechanism but can also be used as a screening tool.

Advantages:

- Immediate candidate capture.
- Good for attracting a large volume of candidates, especially from particular segments. Good value per candidate capture.
- Good branding opportunity as candidates have the chance to interact directly with you and people from the organization.
- Need not accept applications from candidates who do not meet the initial screening criteria, so is a good initial screening process too.
- If the fair or open day is well staffed, then it may be possible to screen people through to interview stage, which will make it effective.

Disadvantages:

- Unless carefully set up to do so, can be very hard to assess as you go over and above 'paper' initial screening, eg qualifications.
- You'll never be really sure how many people will attend and therefore how much resources you will need – and can be an expensive screening mechanism.

However, at the end of the fair or open day you'll at least have a good first-line screened group of applicants and at best a set of shortlisted ones with a date for first interviews set up.

Web-based initial applications

This is a tailored or off-the-shelf package to assess a range of competences; it can take the form of a psychometric test or behavioural assessment which maps exactly to the competences required for the role. It is not recommended you 'do this yourself at home' but there are specialist suppliers who focus on this area. One of the growing areas for web-based applications is in graduate recruitment, where graduates complete a series of tasks to predict future behaviours. Equally, some sales and retail roles are using a similar process.

CASE STUDY

In the USA a major international bank wanted to improve the capability of their customer service staff in the branches. Staff were responsible both for great service as well as setting up loan requests, which was a big part of the branch business. They engaged with a firm, PeopleAnswers, to develop a tool for pre-employment screening to improve the choice of candidates coming through for interview. Candidates completed a simple online behavioural assessment and out of that PeopleAnswers provided a predictive analysis of each applicant plus a report suggesting next-step questions at interview. The result after seven months was a 27 per cent uplift in capability of the staff hired.

You'll need to check that the costs of developing such a process justify the potential which can be gained. With a large business recruiting a high number of staff it would be likely to do so.

Your shortlist

At this point you will have gathered your first shortlist, and these candidates may well be the ones you interview. You could, however, hit a number of problems at this stage, not least of which is that you either have far too many candidates who meet the criteria or you don't have enough.

Too few candidates

Options:

- Revisit the assessment criteria by going back over the applicant base again, applying a wider set of criteria (having sorted your candidates into Yes, No and Maybe shows its advantages at this point).
- Consider re-advertising or re-attracting new candidates or decide to try another set of attraction mechanisms, maybe using a recruitment agency if you were handling the recruiting, or going externally if you have only looked internally up to now.
- Brief and pay a specialist headhunter to find the candidates for you.

Hopefully you will have assessed all this before getting to this point, but it does happen frequently enough for even the most able of recruiters, especially in skill-short markets.

Too many candidates

This is less of a problem. Your choices here depend upon a number of factors:

- What you have done to assess to this point.
- What criteria you have been using to assess the candidates.

Options:

- Consider asking all candidates to complete a psychometric test online if you have one which you use for the business in general.
- Raise the criteria to make the 'desirable' elements' the new 'essential' elements and reread the applications.
- Conduct an initial telephone interview. For some roles, being on the telephone and communicating in this way is a key part of the job. Equally, on the phone you may be able to find other salient information which may not be clear from the application and which would rule someone in or out of the shortlist. You may need to know their location, for example, or how much they are earning.

Table 9.6 is an example of a telephone interviewing form, which you can adapt, of course, for your own use.

Telephone interview

This can be used as part of either the long-list screening process or the shortlist. It's a tool to enable some verbal communication with the candidate but also to confirm some further information about them. It can work well at all sorts of levels. It is a good way of de-shortlisting people from a face-to-face interview and thus saving both you and the applicant time.

Advantages of telephone interviewing:

- Saves time as takes less time than all applicants coming to face-to-face interview.
- Gives you a sense of the applicant over the phone and how they sound.
- Can be used to test someone's capacity to speak English, or any other language necessary for the role – so long as this is valid.
- Can often reduce your shortlist by half.

To make this as fair as possible for the candidate, in the same way as you would set up an interview, set up a telephone interview with an organized time. If you do ring someone to telephone interview them on the spot, take this into account.

Disadvantages of a telephone interview:

- The danger in over-assessing on the phone and reading too much into someone's answers.
- Using it when use of English or telephone skill is irrelevant to the role and thereby creating unconscious bias against candidates who do not have these skills.

TABLE 9.6 Telephone assessment form

Telephone assessment form
Telephone sales trainee

Scoring guidelines:
3: Fully meets/exceeds criteria and offered a place on assessment
2: More than partly meets the criteria and is on hold for assessment
1: Does not meet criteria

Criteria	Score
Sounds positive on the phone with clear diction and good tone	
Establishes rapport on the call	
Listens carefully before responding to questions	
Has some questions to ask about the role or company if you have pre-booked the call	
Shows an interest in sales; can evidence this	
Questions:	
Why have you chosen to apply for a role in tele-sales?	
What have you learned about our company since you first saw the role advertised?	
What experience have you had to lead you to believe a sales career is right for you? Tell me about your existing role (if relevant) and why you've decided to move.	
What sorts of attributes do you think a good tele-sales person will find invaluable?	
What have you enjoyed about a holiday job/ role/internship you have done?	
What have you liked least about a holiday job/role/internship you have done?	
Housekeeping questions about other roles they are looking at (preference to candidates already looking at tele-sales), where they are living, current salary, availability for assessment if called, etc	

Assessing your shortlist

The main assessment methods are:

- face-to-face interviews;
- assessment centres;
- panel interviews;
- testing – psychometric, ability, skills or other, including presentations;
- psychologist interviews.

Assessment order

You'll need to decide what order to do your assessments in.

Testing

There are three broad forms of testing: psychometric, ability and skills. Psychometric testing is a form of personality assessment which assesses the individual's potential competences and motivations. Ability testing is testing for verbal, numeric, data skills or other abilities. Results of the tests are compared against a particular 'norm' group, which is a group of similar people. Norm groups have to be substantial in order to validate the tests and make them statistically valid. Skills testing will assess the capacity of someone to do a particular role. This could be an IT test but it could also be working as a receptionist for half a day to see how well they do. Many organizations will devise their own skills test and so long as this is a valid test this can be helpful in making hiring decisions.

Psychometric testing The main advantage of psychometric testing is that it is likely to give you much more information more quickly about a person that can be gained by interview and possibly more than can be gained by working with someone for three months. This in turn confers strong cost benefits if one assumes it is an aid to decision making.

The main disadvantage of psychometric testing comes from untested instruments being used which have no validity and untrained assessors making judgements on test results.

A further disadvantage can come from any test being used as an entire decision-making tool in its own right.

Most tests are conducted online now, which can mean you can do a proportion of your assessment process without having to have candidates come to your offices or elsewhere on too many occasions. When designing the assessment itself you can place the testing when you want it in the process as opposed to having to fit it in around other interviews.

There is a range of psychometric tests on the market. The major ones, which will help determine future recruitment profiles, are, for example, SHL's OPQ or Cattell's 16PF or 15PF+. These are offered by a range of testing houses. They can be used both to help determine your 'ideal candidate profile' in your 'What good likes like' process and then to assess future potential hires against this profile.

There will be plenty of others on the market too and everyone will have their favourites. When you are choosing a test, do make sure it is valid and that the test itself and the norm groups are rigorously tested and validated consistently. To this end it makes sense to go with one of the leading consultancies. There are too many test houses and tests on the market to list each one but the British Psychological Society's website has a useful list of tests available and reviews each one. The website address for the reviews is http://www.psychtesting.org.uk/test-registration-and-test-reviews/test-reviews.cfm but you can find it simply too by Googling the BPS.

The test houses will also offer consultancy around putting together the best process or do the whole exercise for you and design a recruitment process to follow, often with excellent results. Some clients of SHL, for example, have reduced their recruitment turnover from as high as 70 per cent to nearer 30 per cent.

CASE STUDY

In March 2010, Aberdeen Group studied over 250 organizations currently using assessments, including 74 organizations using SHL solutions. The study showed that in SHL's customer base, marked improvements were being seen over and above other test providers, specifically an improvement in first-year retention by 15 per cent and an 18 per cent improvement in new hire performance.

Most organizations use psychometric testing towards the end of the assessment process, although there is a proportion who use it right at the beginning for every applicant. Using it at the beginning, you can assess people against a set of self-declared behaviours which you know you need from all of your people. This means you are not calling anyone for interview who does not agree with those behaviours, thus saving your time to hire and increasing the quality of your interview candidate base. For some roles with a large volume of similar applicants, this will prove to be helpful. The candidate population will be such that they may be full-time jobseekers or new to the employment market and therefore be happy to partake in the selection process and not be put off by an early online assessment.

For more experienced candidates, however, with some workplace experience, and in a more skill-short arena this will be likely to dissuade candidates from completing the application process and you may find you do not have enough qualified applicants. In this circumstance, the tests will be best placed towards the end of the process, perhaps after a second interview or in between a first and second interview. The same arguments and thought process apply to ability testing.

Alternatively the tests can take place during an assessment centre, which I come to shortly.

Ability testing Distinct from personality-based tests, these tests are designed to assess someone's aptitude for or ability in certain areas.

Advantages of ability tests:

- Give useful information under controlled conditions of the candidate's capability in the area of the test.
- You'll find out whether they can produce profitable quotations/ business in the numerical reasoning and whether they can write well and argue their case in the verbal.
- Specialist technical and mechanical tests will be able to show someone's capability or aptitude in specific areas.

Disadvantages:

- Similar to the personality tests in that if the role does not require this aptitude you could be over-testing.
- If you choose an invalid test either in general or for the role, this may reject some otherwise able candidates.

There is again a wide range of these tests on the market and you need to be careful to choose the right one for your roles, so you may use a range for different roles within the business. Typically numerical and verbal reasoning tests are helpful for many roles.

Types of tests are:

- numerical aptitude;
- verbal aptitude;
- abstract reasoning ability;
- spatial ability;
- technical ability;
- clerical ability (including concentration rate).

You may feel that a certain level of verbal and numerical reasoning is useful for salespeople, for example, or managers, and that spatial ability will help if you are recruiting someone into your production or design team and you want to see if they have the likely spatial aptitude for the role. Technical ability is often used to test candidates joining the emergency services or military, and also in this genre are mechanical ability tests which assess a candidate's ability to find and diagnose faults in electrical systems, etc.

Finally, there are clerical ability tests which will assess someone's capability to move through tasks quickly and accurately.

CASE STUDY

I recall interviewing (with some reservations, which I found hard to put my finger on exactly) and then verbally assessing a senior PR executive and finding that instead of her being in the top 20 per cent in her norm group on verbal reasoning as we might have expected, she was in the bottom 40 per cent. The business decided to go ahead and hire her anyway. Within four months she had left the role as she was unable to keep up with the demands for verbal and written information and communication. In her last role she had generated the ideas and others had implemented them.

Therefore there can be some merit, for some roles, in ability testing as well as psychometric testing. The case also shows that where you have evidence for doubt, you can validate the doubt by using ability tests – although this in hindsight might also have been uncovered at interview.

Ability tests can be used in a range of groups. It will not simply be white-collar staff recruitment which can benefit.

CASE STUDY

Patrick Merlevede from jobEQ tells about a recent project.

'A few years ago, we worked with a growing European shipping company, DDtrans. DDtrans had 120 trucks on the road, and with the business doing so well, they needed 20–30 drivers on short notice. The biggest challenges for their HR department were a high turnover rate and poor performance by drivers (too many accidents and late deliveries). The company had tried other profiling products, but the results were not an improvement. They chose jobEQ because of our unique Model of Excellence tool.

'First, several high-quality truck drivers were interviewed using the iWAM/LAB Profile technology. From these profiles, we build a Model of Excellence, and a jobEQ consultant trained the HR staff to recognize the desired attitude and motivation patterns during an interview. Using these methods, DDtrans has had tremendous success. The number of accidents has been reduced by 50 per cent. Having better employees has also led to reduced turnover. These benefits have even led to lower insurance costs.

Now DDtrans has more than 200 trucks on the road every day, and they continue to use our products. HR coordinator Anje Lagast said this successful recruitment "is envied by our competitors. With these employees we could convince Ford Motor Company to make DDtrans the company of choice for traffic between the UK, Belgium and Germany." '

Investment in testing

Assessments as part of the recruitment process can then be carried through into the on-boarding and development journey for the candidate. Understanding more about an individual can be invaluable in getting them up to speed quickly, and there is more on this in the final chapter.

Assessment centres

This is an event which candidates attend, usually in a group, where they are assessed on a range of competences and behaviours. The assessment takes the form of a range of different exercises looking at how they interact with each other or behave in certain situations as well as individually, and also usually includes the capacity to 'sell' the opportunity to prospective candidates.

Advantages:

- Excellent choice for the capacity to see more than one aspect of the candidate. Research has been done to show the effectiveness of a range of activities so you can be sure that a particular activity is valid.
- Good for either large groups of similar hires, eg graduates or customer service, or senior hires where the investment will pay off.

Disadvantages:

- Untrained assessors can jump to conclusions about candidates and not necessarily look at them in the right way.
- The cost can be expensive but not if compared with the cost of getting the hiring decisions wrong.
- It can be challenging getting all the candidates together on one day.

Organizing your assessment centre

Most centres will take between half a day and a day (BP use a two-day centre for their graduates), so it is reasonable and best practice to offer candidates open feedback after their time investment in your business as well as giving them some indication of what will be expected of them on the day.

The number of candidates you can invite along will depend upon the number of trained assessors you have at any one time. Most professional assessors will suggest one or two assessors per applicant is best, although I have run them to good effect with a range of different assessors at different times of the centre, depending upon the activity, but would never go below one for every four applicants at any point. Numbers also depend upon the type of role, but for junior roles you could consider 10 to 20 applicants per centre and I have heard of 30 to 50. For more senior roles, up to six would be appropriate at one time.

You will almost certainly need more than one centre for volume applicants, though this will not be the case for senior roles. Often candidates are simply expected to attend on the date set or not be considered. For volume assessments you can sometimes expect up to a 50 per cent drop-out rate and nothing can be more frustrating than having 10 assessors lined up to see 20 candidates and only 12 show up. You can improve dramatically on this with good communication and encouragement, including reminding candidates just before the event, ideally by phone. Figure 9.2 gives you a sample assessment centre invitation letter which you can adapt for your own use.

For the venue you'll need either one very large room or a large room with a series of break-out rooms. I have used both and either works well. It's good to have an area where candidates can congregate before they are invited to join you in the centre and once everyone has arrived. This means you meet them all at once.

It's also important to remember that as with any interview, this is an opportunity for you to show who you are as a business and create an atmosphere which might resemble working in your business, so candidates can get a sense of whether they would want to work for you. Assessment centres vary in flavour enormously. Make sure yours is a true reflection of your business and how you work so you are not giving a false impression. This will also help you assess how well your candidates do in that environment. If in your business you always give broad-brush instructions or project briefings and expect people to fill in their own gaps, don't give clear precise instruction on assessment. Brief the assessments and exercises carefully, mindful of how you normally operate.

CASE STUDY

One company I run assessment centres for is Major Players, a recruitment company working within the creative industries. Every candidate says the centres are so different from any of the others they attend as they are really friendly and informal and they feel like they can be themselves and say what they want and that making mistakes is okay. Making mistakes at Major Players is fine and learning from them is also really important. The whole format and ethos of the centres are designed to reflect the unique culture of Major Players, ensuring that the candidates that are selected to join the graduate development programme fit in and feel at home straight away.

FIGURE 9.2 Invitation to assessment

Dear

I am delighted to let you know you have been successful in your telephone interview and as a result we'd like to invite you to an assessment centre which is the next stage of our recruitment process. If you are successful at this you'll then progress to psychometric profiling (a personality questionnaire to give us further information on your preferred working style) and a final set of interviews.

The assessment centre is designed to assess your skills in a range of situations and you'll be working on tasks which have problems you'll need to solve, others where you'll have an opportunity to demonstrate your commercial thinking and some where you'll be working alone and making an individual presentation.

As part of the centre we'll also be introducing you to previous graduates so they can tell you over a coffee all about our scheme and we'll be making presentations to let you know what you can gain from it and how it will work. We aim to make our centres an informal and enjoyable experience, so we hope you will look forward to it!

You have a choice of dates and times below:

9.00–12.30 Tuesday 29 November

2.00–5.30 Tuesday 29 November

9.00–12.30 Wednesday 7 December

2.00–5.30 Wednesday 7 December

The centre will be held at our head office and the dress code will be formal interview style. Please get in touch with me as soon as possible to confirm your time and we look forward to seeing you and meeting you in person.

Yours etc

Graduate Recruitment Manager

Finally, take care with the centre to ensure that candidates can leave having enjoyed themselves, been given an opportunity to shine, maintained their self-esteem, perhaps having learned something about themselves and ideally either very keen to join your organization or having learned that it's not for them but still feeling positive about the whole experience.

Designing the centre

There is a range of types of assessment you can use. I have listed the most typical below. Many of these can be bought 'off the shelf' from a wide range of suppliers or you can design your own. Most of the test providers will also have assessment processes you can buy or they will design and run your centre for you.

Your design needs to start with the competences or behaviours you want to assess. One of the main purposes is to assess how candidates behave in a group situation, as most roles involve working in a team. Exercises which look at a candidate's communication skills, their capacity to relate to and get on with others whom they have only just met, their performance under pressure, and their capacity to take initiatives, influence and persuade others, handle data and assimilate information will give you good information on how successful they might be in your roles.

Once you know what you want to assess, you can then design the exercises to assess it. Figures 9.3 and 9.4 show two typical assessment centres to use as a starting point for designing your own, but do also bear in mind the level of person you are recruiting. You recruit a graduate and a chief technology officer in very different ways.

Group exercises

Introductory exercise This can either be in pairs, fours or with the whole group. The exercise is designed in part as an ice-breaker to create some energy and to enable the candidates to relax, so this exercise should not be too demanding. It can be a good idea to make this quite a social event and ask a range of people in the business to come along to meet the applicants.

- Assesses spoken communication and social skills.

Case study The group is given a case study with some degree of detail and you ask them to make recommendations based on the case given.

- Assesses data handling, exercising judgement and decision making as well as teamwork, as they will have to argue their case to others and be persuasive if there is disagreement.

Group discussion The group is given a topic to discuss or sometimes a scenario and a role each to take. This can be a controversial topic, a business case, a 'balloon' type exercise ('There are eight different people with different qualities or skills in a balloon; who would you throw out?') where you ask them all to argue their case or anything similar.

- Assesses spoken communication skills, persuasion, influence, sensitivity.

FIGURE 9.3 Sample junior assessment centre format

Sample Assessment Centre Agenda

Graduate/Sales/Junior Staff

8.30	Coffee and informal welcome
9.00	Introduction to the day – senior manager/recruitment manager What we'll be doing Setting the tone
9.15	Introductions Candidates all 'interview' each other and then present their interviewee to the rest of the group. Assesses listening skills, rapport building and capacity to speak in front of a group.
10.00	Group discussion Whole group is set a topic to discuss and make some recommendations on – they are asked to report back with recommendations in 20 minutes.
10.30	Speed meeting Bring other graduates into the room and give them two minutes each to ask a question of a graduate or manager about the programme. Existing graduates to give feedback.
11.00	Coffee with existing graduates
11.15	Commercial group task In small groups they are asked to think about how to manage a customer problem – they are told the customer is available to speak to (this is role played by a company member or actor) and they have to come to the most commercially advantageous solution.
11.50	Individual presentations Candidates are given 10 minutes to prepare a one-minute elevator speech about why they would be good for the business.
12.30	Company presentation and questions and answers
13.00	Close

Group activity This may be a task given to the group to make something, design something, develop a business case for something, use physical skills, compete in something or create something. You may then introduce elements of change as you progress through the task. This will test both their teamwork skills and other competences.

FIGURE 9.4 Sample senior assessment centre format

Sample Assessment Centre Agenda

Senior team member

8.30	Coffee and informal welcome
9.00	Introduction to the day – senior manager/recruitment manager What we'll be doing Setting the tone
9.15	Individual presentation Candidates are asked to introduce themselves and spend two minutes telling the group about the skills they have which are relevant to this role.
9.45	Group discussion Whole group is set a topic to discuss and make some recommendations on – they are asked to report back with recommendations in 20 minutes.
10.15	Individual role plays Candidates are asked to role play a challenging situation which they may face within the business. When they are not role playing they are asked to read a case study in preparation for the task following coffee.
11.00	Coffee with other senior managers
11.30	Case study Candidates are asked to discuss and prepare recommendations for the board on a case study problem which they read earlier. The case will be complex and involve both numerical data and findings. They are asked to present an action plan.
12.00	Case study presentations
12.30	Company presentation and questions and answers
13.00	Lunch
1.30	Individual interviews with hiring managers
16.00	Close

Assesses adaptability, creativity, decisiveness, possibly data facility or detail handling depending upon the task, initiating action, judgement, persuasion, planning and organizing, capacity to handle stress, client handling and commerciality. A comprehensive task which will assess a wide range of competences if designed well.

Individual exercises

Tests As so many psychometric or ability tests are online now, you may not choose to ask candidates to complete them in an assessment centre. However, should you choose to use a paper-and-pen exercise you do have the advantage of getting them all completed at the same time and being able to 'wash up' the centre at the end of the session as the assessor will be able to compile the results of at least the ability tests by then.

In-tray/e-tray exercises Again not always paper based but can be in-box based as well. Candidates are given information about the business and their team and a range of issues to deal with. They are expected to prioritize them, delegate, write replies to letters and e-mails, escalate issues and decide how to handle them. They may be asked to present their recommendations on one topic as well.

- Assesses very similar competences to the group activity but on a purely individual basis. Strong assessor of judgement, data and detail handling, planning and organizing.

Presentation This can either be linked to another exercise or stand alone. Candidates can either be asked to bring something with them to present which they have prepared or to prepare something on the day in the time provided. Which of these is appropriate will depend to a great degree on their previous experience and the seniority of the role.

- Assesses spoken communication skills, thinking style, impact and knowledge (particularly if Q and A is run after the presentation).

Interview You may choose to include an interview at this point. This can take the form of an informal initial interview or a more in-depth one. Arguably with one face-to-face individual opportunity to shine, you may miss attributes and analytical capacity which may be important to the role. It depends upon what competences you are looking for as to the type of interview or whether you do one at all.

- Assesses individual competences and gains evidence of past behaviours, showing whether they are likely to have the competence you are seeking. See more about this in the section on interviewing.

Presenting your business

It is important to present both your business and the roles available within it. It is good for prospective candidates to meet other people in the company who may have joined in the way they are hoping to, either informally over lunch or as presenters or part of a Q and A session. Focus on the benefits of the business, the career paths available and what the role might involve. Your presenter needs to remember who your audience is and that they will tell other prospective candidates (their friends) all about the experience, so it is important to make it positive.

As we have said, an assessment centre can take a range of forms and no two are the same. Neither are they placed in the same order in the recruitment process, some taking place as a filtering process and others as a final decision-making tool. The next case study is an example of the latter.

CASE STUDY

Tracey Richardson, former managing consultant at specialist public sector recruiter Tribal Resourcing, is called in by local authorities to recruit senior staff. She recently recruited the CE of one of the most exciting authorities in the UK. Following first interviews, six candidates were progressed to a two-day rigorous assessment process led by Tracey, a colleague and her assessor team.

The process included psychometric profiling, testing, business analysis cases, group discussion, a presentation and competency-based interview with the member panel, meetings with key external stakeholders and a drinks party with many representatives from local groups. Exhausting for all, but a fantastically rigorous process from which to make decisions.

At the end of the two days Tracey led a thorough discussion on each candidate and a decision was made on who to appoint. The leader of the council made the call to the successful candidate and Tracey then rang the others that same day.

Interviews

This is by a long way the most common and popular form of assessment and can take place as part of an assessment centre or as a stand-alone assessment. It is also the one which has the capacity to be done least well. For some reason interviewing is not always seen as something one needs training for, in the way you would need training in how to drive or use a lathe. Interviewing, rather often like management, is seen as talking and therefore a skill which we already possess.

This section aims to equip everyone with the basics of interviewing well. Ideally before you start any recruitment process, equip everyone involved with the core skills of assessment and most specifically interviewing.

The bad interview

Alongside the 12 deadly sins earlier in this chapter you also should not:

- regale the candidate with everything about the business, the team and you, and then realize the allotted time is up;
- phrase each question with 'We find here that X works really well – don't you agree?'
- make assumptions;
- accept every answer;
- go where the mood takes you with questions;
- interview on your own, forget to take notes and find the only thing you can remember is what they vaguely looked like and base your assessment on that;
- interview with someone who is 'the nice interviewer', while you take the role of 'nasty interviewer' – good cop, bad cop;
- be sexist, racist or discriminatory in any way;
- ask questions to throw someone and see how they cope;
- leave the candidate feeling as if they have failed;
- deliberately give someone a very hard time to 'see how they cope under pressure'. If you run this kind of business you can make more money by changing the culture rather than recruiting more of the same.

The list can be endless as there are more mistakes made at interview than almost anything else and it is no wonder so few recruits are successful in their roles. So, what makes an interview successful?

The good interview

There is a range of different techniques and methods and the one you choose will depend as ever upon the role you are interviewing for. However, there are a few rules of thumb:

- Plan and prepare before an interview. Read the candidate's CV and review your pre-prepared interview process for the role.
- Make sure you have allocated enough time in the diary and be prompt to meet the candidate. Being late suggests you are more important than they are, which does not augur well for a prospective employment relationship.
- Relax your candidate so they feel at ease. This enables them to perform their best and you can see what their best looks like.
- Tell them what you plan to do at the interview and check they are okay for time.

- Ask every candidate the same questions. This will enable you to compare them more easily, is less unlikely to be discriminatory and is fairer.
- Focus on asking questions which are not hypothetical, eg not 'What *would* you do...' but 'What *did* you do when...?'
- Tell them all about the company and the role on offer at the end of the interview.
- Allow plenty of time for candidate questions at the end.
- Tell them what happens next and make sure you stick to that.

In this section I'll outline two types of interview: the biographical interview and the competency- or behavioural-based interview. Both have commonalities but differ in the main purpose of the interview. First we'll look at the commonalities and then go on to look at each type of interview.

Preparing for and conducting an interview

There are numerous interview plans and structures. It does not really matter which one you choose, so long as you choose one and cover all bases. An interview might take anything from 40 minutes to over an hour. On average 50 minutes would probably seem ideal for a first-stage interview.

A simple one is detailed here:

W: welcome and rapport;

I: introduction;

G: gathering information;

G: giving information;

S: selling and closing.

The types of question you use in each section will help determine the flow of the interview and also whether you get the information you want. Table 9.7 outlines the range of questions to use and some examples of them.

W: welcome and rapport

Introduce yourself. Put the candidate at their ease, offer drinks, etc. Make some small talk to start the interview off. You will get more from your candidate if you are friendly and warm but professional. Say how long the interview will last and what you plan to cover. If you are planning to use any evidence-based (competency or behavioural) questions it will be useful to let them know that now. Reassure them they will have a chance at the end of the session to ask lots of questions about either the role or the way in which you suggest you both work together. Check the timing works for them. Say that notes will be taken. Check they are happy with that and ready to start.

Use *closed* questions to check the candidate is comfortable with what you have explained will happen. 'Are you happy with that?' 'Does that work for you?'

TABLE 9.7 Question types

Question type	Purpose and when to use	
Open questions: where the other person talks more than you	To get someone talking	How, Why, What, Who, When? How did you come to take your current role?
Open/demand questions: as open questions	To take control or assert authority	Tell me, Take me through, Explain to me, Show me, Talk to me about… Take me through your current role.
Probing questions: allow you to find more information on a topic	To develop the conversation further	Can you say more about that? Can you give me an example of that?' Go on…
Reflective questions: alternative to probes – reflect back someone's answers and keep the person talking	In client meetings When you want to find out more about someone or something When you want to help someone talk	You're not happy with the current service then? You're looking for a longer-term option, you say?
Direct questions: ask for information	To elicit specific information	What's your base salary/hourly/daily rate? What's your current journey time to work? How many people report into you?
Closed questions: person answers yes or no only	To gain confirmation To take control of the conversation To change the subject	You'd be happy with Birmingham, then? Do you feel you could work with the team?

Evidence-based questions (competency, behaviour or capability questions): to uncover evidence of particular capability; also use probing and direct questions	When conducting competency-based or behavioural interviews If running a selection or search	Can you think of a time when you were able to persuade someone to change their mind? What was the situation? (S) What did you want to achieve? (T) What did you do? (A) What was the outcome? (R)
Hypothetical questions: asking what someone would do, if…	Rarely; this will not tell you what someone would do, only what they like to think they would do	If you took this role, what would you do first?
Leading questions: tell the listener what you want to hear	If a candidate needs relaxing or reassuring, but not if you want to find something out. Dangerous if used with clients as it is easy to make false assumptions	I'm sure you'll agree our website is great. I think drawing up a balance sheet is the easy part, isn't it?
Multiple questions: asking more than one question at once	Never	Did you enjoy your interview, how long did the journey take and did they ask you back for a second?

I: introduction

Tell them a brief couple of sentences about the company you are working for. This is just to further relax the candidate but also a mini sales pitch to remind them of why you are both meeting and what the benefit might be to them. Resist the temptation here to tell them 'all about' the job or your company as you don't want to tell them everything so they can then tell you what you have told them you want to hear! Let them answer the questions you are about to ask and give them more information about the business later.

G: gathering information

This is the largest section of the interview. Here you need to collect the following three chunks of information: details on their current situation, a brief look at their career and what they are looking for next.

Current or last employment and personal details Location, salary/pay rate and benefits/expenses, their minimum and what they want, willingness to relocate (if relevant) and criteria for doing so, working hours, any personal circumstances which affect their work. At this point you can be matching what they say they currently have with what you are offering.

Use *direct* questions in this section but in a relaxed manner.

Career highlights and reasons for moving on This covers a broad biographical account of their career history: why they have taken the roles that they have and then moved on. This section may form the bulk of a biographical interview, but if you intend doing a behavioural-based interview this section should take 10–15 minutes. You might ask your candidate something like 'Take me through your CV for 10 minutes or so, focusing on the career direction and choices you have made. Tell me why you chose each role and what made you leave and then we'll look more at the detail of each job.'

Cover any gaps in the CV and find out what they were doing and why.

Use *open/demand* questions here to get the candidate talking but avoid 'Tell me about yourself' as it leaves the candidate unsure what sort of thing you want from them. Be a little more directive if you want to use this approach: 'Tell me why you have applied for this role' or 'Tell me why you are thinking of leaving your current company.'

Motivations and aspirations What is important to them and, crucially, why they want a new role now and their career aspirations for the future. This will help you think about whether the role you are interviewing them for will not only suit them now but also in the future or what their career path with you might look like.

Use *open* questions in this section: 'What did you enjoy most in your last role?' 'What was the least enjoyable aspect?' 'What thoughts do you have about your longer-term career goals, if any?' 'What other roles are you looking at currently and with whom?'

G: giving information

You may wish to bypass this section or use it fully. You may have decided that you will not progress your candidate to shortlist and therefore will not be giving detailed information on your company. If you might progress the candidate, this is when to go into more of a sales mode and ensure they are interested before you finish the interview.

S: selling and closing

In this last section you'll want to give your candidate a chance to ask questions but you'll also want to tell them much more about the business and the role. Tell them what the next steps are and when they will take place – and make sure you show the candidate out yourself. You want your candidate leaving your interview feeling good about themselves and very positive about your company. Then show them out, keeping the atmosphere relaxed as you do so by chatting further.

Every interview should then follow whichever standard format you have chosen regardless of type, and the same questions and even to a large degree probes should also be used. The difference may come in the type of interview.

Use *closed* questions here to check their interest in the role and in coming back for the next stage.

Biographical interview

This interview focuses on the background of the candidate and presupposes their experience and skills can be assessed through discussing their previous roles. If this interview is conducted in the same way with each candidate it can be effective for some recruitment processes where the technical knowledge and detail are specific – for example, using a particular type of machine.

It's important that an interview structure and process are adhered to and each candidate has the same interview in order to compare at the end of the process. Bear in mind that knowledge and competence in a certain area are only part of the equation, and environment as well as clarity of purpose must also be taken into account.

During this interview the interviewer will generally expect the candidate to talk through their CV in detail and the interviewer will ask questions about each of the roles they did, to see how they relate to the role they are interviewing for.

Take care not to assume that because they seem to have done a similar job elsewhere they will be successful in your business.

Competency-based or behavioural interview

There are some good resources available on this type of interviewing, so this book aims to give you an overview of what this type of interview looks like and how to go about designing one. The idea is that what someone has done in the past, all other things being equal, is what they will be likely to do or behave like in the future. In other words: past behaviour predicts future performance.

The job of the competency-based interview is to gather evidence of past behaviour in detail, drilling down to find out what a candidate actually did and said in certain situations. Many candidates will be able to give a broad answer but using probing questions as in Table 9.7 will enable you to really understand a candidate's behaviour.

Interview plan

Use the WIGGS structure or something similar as a base.

Decide which competences you want to assess.

Use the competences table to come up with some questions around those competences.

Use *probes* to dig down into the competences

The competency-based section takes place in G: gathering information. You may start by asking your candidate to go through their CV briefly, as suggested earlier, but you'll then spend the next part of the interview exploring evidence of their ability in the competences you are looking for.

To introduce this you might say 'I'd like to move on to the competency-based section of the interview now and I shall be asking you questions focused on the competencies we have identified as important for this role. So I may ask if you can think of a time when you have had to persuade someone to change their mind. Please take your time to think about the answers as it's not always easy to have an answer at the front of your mind.'

If you are using competency-based interviewing, Figure 9.5 may be useful. When you are asking your candidate questions it's easier to gather evidence by framing them in this way. Each question has four distinct parts and the idea is to get an answer to each part.

Contra-evidence

If you are getting a significant quantity of evidence in favour of a particular competency, you also need to seek some contra-evidence. Ask for times when the candidate has not been able to persuade, when they have failed to meet a deadline, when they made the wrong judgement. No one gets it right all of the time, and someone who cannot identify where things have gone wrong or cannot give an example of a mistake would be unlikely and throws doubt over the other answers to their questions.

FIGURE 9.5 STAR interviewing

Evidence-based interviewing

For each competency, capability or behaviour you are assessing, this is a useful framework for gathering answers.

S	Situation	What was the situation?
T	Task	What did you want to achieve?
A	Action	What did you do?
R	Result	What happened as a result?

If you do not have a full STAR and cannot achieve one through more probing, then it is unlikely the candidate can meet that competency, capability or behaviour.

Interviewing as part of the overall process

It is more than likely that you will be conducting more than one interview for promising candidates. You may progress two or three to final-stage interview and this stage may be with a more senior manager or again with the hiring manager.

For both your own judgement and the candidate experience it is good to evaluate a different set of competences at the second stage: ideally those which are desirable rather than mandatory. It is also a good chance to cover a competency you were concerned about earlier or one which is very important and that you'd like more examples of. It can be helpful to complete a feedback sheet at the end of the first interview which you then pass on to the second interviewer. You can see an example of a simple one in Table 9.8. You may want to hold this back as well, however, so that the second interviewer can give an unbiased opinion and you can share notes at the end – this does not preclude you from asking the second interviewer to focus on a particular competency you felt you would have liked more evidence of or contra-evidence.

Some senior roles rightly need a comprehensive set of interviews and often companies will involve their clients if it's a really important appointment to work with that client. You'll need to ensure the process you design around interviews is fit for purpose, that the candidate sees as many people as they need to and that you are making a robust hiring decision. The longer the process, the greater the level of commitment you are expecting from the candidate – and generally the more influential the role, the longer the process. Some organizations will go to 16 interviews or more for a senior hire.

The most important thing is to make the assessment process fit for purpose. You are assessing aspects of a candidate that you have identified as being important to the role and that you have proven to work over a period of time. You want the candidate to have a good experience at any event you run as part of your assessment, and you want the process to be cost effective, bearing in mind the costs of getting it wrong. And you want your ensuing retention rate to be where you want it to be.

TABLE 9.8 Interview evaluation form

Interview evaluation sheet	First interview	
Competence, knowledge or skill	Key words candidate says plus grade 1–5 (5 is excellent, 4 is very good, 3 is satisfactory, 2 is development is needed, 1 is has no skills or competence)	Grade 1–5
CV assessment – 15 minutes: Take me through your CV in 15 minutes, focusing on the highlights and lowlights and why you joined and left companies.		
Business development: Tell me about a piece of new business development you have been successful at. Have you ever been faced with a brick wall when trying to develop a relationship with a client? Tell me about a relationship you have built from scratch.		
Successful/least successful campaign: Tell me about the most and the least successful campaign you have been involved in.		
People management: What do you do on a day-to-day basis in your management role? (Look for how they manage and what they say.)		
Job motivation: What do you most enjoy about your role currently – and least enjoy?		

Adding value: Tell me about a time when you added value to a client's business – and to the business you were working for. Can you think of an example of creative thinking which enabled you to have success for the client?	
Interview evaluation (including feedback for candidate)	
Progress to final interview?	Yes/No (delete as appropriate)

Once you have decided the candidate is right, you'll need to get them on board. Much effort and cost go into the process up to this point, so you'll not want to fail in making them the right offer or making the most of their skills as soon as they join, as well as ensuring they stay. The next and final chapter deals with on-boarding, from making the offer to signing off on their probation.

On-boarding

10

This final chapter looks at the importance of bringing someone over the threshold into your organization well. I look at maximizing the value you can gain from, and bring to, a new person when they join your business. Although the focus here is on a permanent employee, the same process can be applied, albeit in less detail, to a contractor or freelance person if they are likely to be with you three or more months rather than days.

The on-boarding process starts with making and negotiating the offer and goes through to the end of the person's probationary period, which tends to last between three and six months. Clearly the effort involved is likely to be greater at the beginning, but much can be gained from close attention and evaluation at each stage. As soon as the person passes their probationary period they then move through to the stage of performance management with their line manager and it becomes more 'business as usual'.

Often one of the difficulties with on-boarding is that when recruitment and on-boarding (often recruitment and HR) are not working closely together the on-boarding team do not know what has been said to the candidate during the recruitment phase and vice versa. During the recruitment process the realities of the role may differ somewhat from what is 'sold' and even in the most 'joined-up' organizations new joiners may have made assumptions about the culture of the business or their level of authority. So if the two teams organizing recruitment and on-boarding do not work together then, they need to make great efforts to smooth the transition from the pre-nuptial to the nuptial stage of the relationship. Part of this will be completing the recruitment process.

Completing the recruitment process

For any role you will end up with a few candidates on your shortlist, assuming all has gone according to plan. One or more of those you may be happy to offer, others you will need to turn down.

Rejecting a candidate

This may seem an odd place to deal with this but making an offer to one candidate automatically generates the likelihood of having to turn others down. A general rule of thumb is while you want to pay good attention to every rejection and ensure it is delivered fairly, responsibly on time and helpfully, the more time a candidate has given up in interviewing with your business, the more personal a rejection you should make.

Assuming the candidate has become close to getting the role you are hiring for, the chances are that they may be right for something else in the business. You want to retain this candidate as a potential pipeline candidate for future roles.

Every business will set its own rejection policies but a good rule of thumb is:

Application form/letter/CV: Letter or e-mail rejecting the candidate with a non-personalized reason after the details have been evaluated. The practice of sending an acknowledgement which also serves as a rejection is not ideal for candidates, although organizations facing large volumes of responses struggle with this. New systems are coming along which will allow candidates to track their own applications and see where they are in the recruitment process, giving applicants greater control, and this would seem a potential solution to the challenge for both applicant and hirer.

After first interview: Non-personalized letter of rejection but being clear this is post-interview. If the candidate is working through an agency it is helpful to both the candidate and the agency to give feedback on why the candidate was not suitable, so the agency can hone their own evaluation of future candidates on your behalf.

After second/final interview: Personal letter or phone call from the agency, HR or hiring manager. You'll make your own judgement as to what feedback to give. Avoid assuming the candidate will welcome and value detailed feedback, especially if elements of it are of a personal nature, but they may value understanding where their skills and competences were not as strong as other candidates'.

Figure 10.1 shows an example of a possible rejection letter for a candidate you were very close to hiring, Figure 10.2 after a first interview and Figure 10.3 for one you have not progressed at all. Figure 10.4 is sadly all too common and the one to avoid if you want strong engagement. You'll want to rewrite any of these templates according to the style of your business, of course.

If you have used psychometric tests it is good practice to give detailed feedback on the results, ideally face to face during part of the interview process, but of course you'll make it clear that these have been a decision-making tool rather than criteria for success.

FIGURE 10.1 A rejection letter template for a close-to-hire candidate

Dear

We've very much enjoyed the chance to meet with you for interview for the role of [JobTitle] over the last couple of weeks.

As you know, we have been interviewing a wide range of candidates for this role, and indeed had over [number] applications. Each step of the process has been very challenging for us to reduce the number of potential candidates. This last section of final interviews has been the most difficult of all.

We ended with three candidates who were all well qualified to do the role and therefore had to choose the one that we felt has in the past, to the greatest degree of all of you, demonstrated the sorts of skills and knowledge that we are looking for in the role holder.

Unfortunately this time we have decided to offer the role to another candidate and they have accepted it. We felt, however, that you have some exceptional skills as well and would have been a valuable addition to the team and are sorry that we do not have more than one opportunity at this time.

We would urge you to keep in touch with us, keep an eye on the website to see if anything else suitable arises and to apply for it if so, as we really would be keen to welcome you on board for the right next role.

Thank you so much for all the time you have put into interviewing with us. We hope that it has been worthwhile and hope our paths cross again in the future.

Yours sincerely

FIGURE 10.2 A rejection letter template post interview

Dear

Thank you very much for coming along to interview with us recently for the role of [JobTitle].

We have had a very high standard of applications and interviewees for this role, so the decision about whom to progress to the next stage has been very challenging.

However, we have decided to progress those applicants whose skills, background experience and knowledge most closely match those of the role we are recruiting for at this time and are sorry to let you know that on this occasion we will not be progressing with you.

We would urge you to keep an eye on the website to see if anything else suitable arises and to apply for it if you would like to as we did feel you have some valuable skills.

We hope you found the interview experience with us of use and that you learned more about our business for another time.

Yours sincerely

FIGURE 10.3 A rejection letter post CV/application form

Dear

Thank you very much for applying to us recently for the role of [Job Title].

We have looked carefully at your application in relation to the role we are recruiting for and have decided we will not be inviting you to interview for this particular role because other candidates match our brief and specification more closely at this time.

We are very pleased that you are interested in our organization and would encourage you to keep an eye on the website to see if anything else suitable arises and to apply for it if it is of interest.

We wish you every success in your next career move.

Yours sincerely

FIGURE 10.4 A poor example of a rejection letter

Dear

Thank you for your application to join our company. Unfortunately due to the volume of response we get, unless you hear from us to the contrary please treat this acknowledgement as notice that we will not be progressing your application further.

Yours sincerely

Some processes will require more interviews but the process and guidelines still hold good. If a candidate has been through a significant recruitment process (four or more interviews) with you and is unsuccessful it is always good practice to offer them the opportunity for a face-to-face debrief and an opportunity to chat through possible future options with your business or elsewhere.

Offering your preferred candidate a role

If you have more than one preferred candidate it may be wise to offer the one you prefer, give them a deadline on responding to your offer and hold off on rejecting your second choice until your first choice has accepted. This way you stay in control of the process and are less likely to lose your second-choice candidate.

Your offer will be made up of a range of factors and any candidate will be considering all of them. Their focus will probably be on pay and benefits at the final stages as many of the other aspects will have been dealt with at interviews.

Factors to an offer:

- reward: salary and benefits;
- role and opportunity for learning and development;
- career path in the future;
- opportunity to achieve and be recognized;
- working environment and prospective colleagues; culture of the business;
- work–life balance.

Trying to acquire a candidate for lower than their required salary can lead to resentment and disappointment. Managing, or mismanaging, the expectations of the candidate starts right at the beginning of the interview process and if not handled well will lead to problems when you come to making an offer.

To ensure that this stage does not adversely impact your employer brand, ensure that when you make an offer you follow a few rules or remember a few points:

- Remuneration is a good indicator of capability and seniority. If not explored at an early stage because 'money is not a primary consideration', this will lead to disappointment. It is dangerous to make assumptions about the package at any stage in the process. Offers will fall down when everyone leaves it until the final interview to explore money. Money and package should be dealt with at an early stage. Once the principles have been agreed and it is clear there is common ground, then this can be safely ignored (in general) until offer stage – at which point it all becomes about the data.
- You establish the likelihood of the candidate accepting the offer before you make it to them formally. This way they are able to give some feedback before the formal offer stage which will help you frame the offer in the right way for them.
- There is equally no need to overpay people. Establishing their ideas at the beginning will make this process seamless.
- The likely shape of the offer is not a shock. As in an appraisal, the offer stage is not the time for the candidate to find out that they are

not as highly rated as you have led them to believe or that the role doesn't pay as much as they had thought.

Finding a win–win for both parties

When you make the offer you want it to work for both parties. To make this happen you need to have a clear picture of what your candidate wants. During the interview and assessment phase you will have explored with them their aspirations: what they want in their career and what they are looking for in their next role. You will also have explored what sort of offer they will accept, including their minimum salary and benefits. Equally you will be aware of what you are able to offer and what constraints you have. Rarely will a candidate accept a role paying less than they are currently earning unless there is some other significant gain for them or they are currently not working. Avoid the temptation for someone who is not working to get them at a much cheaper salary than they had been earning; you may find that instead of being grateful for a job (your hope), they never really forgive you and find another role as soon as they can.

Offer guidelines:

- Pay someone what they are worth for the job within the finances you have available.
- Ensure your offer is above the minimum they will accept.
- Test an offer on a candidate first: 'Any offer we might make is likely to hover around the X mark. At that level would you accept it?
- Give a verbal offer before sending an offer letter so you can negotiate (if necessary) before the letter is written.
- Send an offer over e-mail and then by post as well.
- Decide before someone negotiates what your top and bottom level package will be so you can make decisions clearly and don't end up paying them something you'll regret. This can be tempting with a key hire in a smaller business.
- Be sure you want to make the candidate an offer, as any offer forms the basis of a contract.

Find an offer which sits in the 'magic circle'

In my last co-authored book, *The Professional Recruiter's Handbook*, I referred to the 'magic circle' for trying to find a package which will suit both parties. Figure 10.5 shows the most common pattern of package negotiation. This is where both parties try and find a sum they are both happy with which sits ideally in the centre of both of the minimum and maximum ranges. The greater the size of the 'magic circle' in each case, the easier the task for both to accommodate each other.

FIGURE 10.5 The magic circle

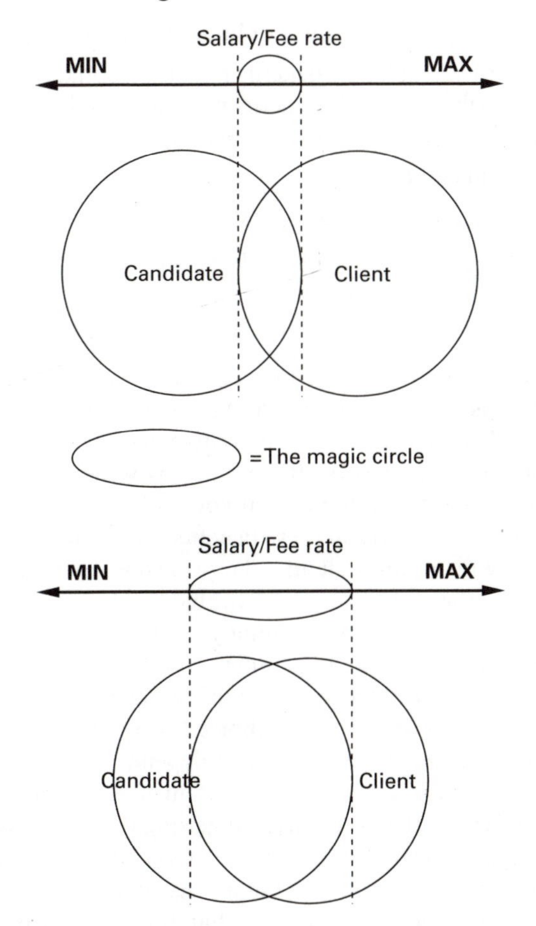

SOURCE: *The Professional Recruiter's Handbook*

If you have a recruitment consultant working on your behalf they will take the pain out of this element for you and will establish both your and the candidate's circle so they can suggest a mid-point for both. If you are lucky enough to have a skilled recruiter this can be a massive value-add. Most of the work in making a placement goes in up to this point, so no recruiter will want to fail from potential offer through to start date. If you are managing the process yourself, you need to pay it a similar amount of attention.

Decide in advance what you are prepared to negotiate and what you are not. You may have few choices around this as your business may already have constraints and how much your candidate is prepared to bend what they want will depend upon how good your business is and how much you have been able to show them that in the recruitment process.

Likely negotiating areas:

- pre-booked holiday in advance of holiday entitlement;
- adjustment of variables on benefits to suit personal requirements – businesses without flexible benefits may find candidates would prefer to spend their benefits money themselves;
- bonus elements and criteria;
- car type or choice of allowance instead;
- pre-arrange pay review against criteria (option if your candidate would prefer a higher salary);
- flexible working/working from home.

If your business is continually getting requests on a particular area of the working conditions or package, then it may be wise to investigate this area further and see whether you are uncompetitive in your area or sector in this regard. If all of your competitors offer a four-day week, a job-share scheme, child-care vouchers and you don't, then you will struggle to compete for a demographic segment for whom these benefits are important.

Of course, it will be difficult in a large business to treat people very differently and neither would it be desirable as the administration costs would outweigh the benefits to the employees. It may be tempting to do so in a small business, but if you are planning to grow your business you may want to start as you mean to go on, with a flexible structure in which everyone can operate with a level of choice for all. The capacity to which you are able to offer flexible working will depend upon your organization and its client's needs. Legally in the UK you need to take a reasonable approach to this within the boundaries of getting the work done.

On-boarding is a question of balance. A good employer will want to try and meet the needs of the employee but at the same time balance the needs of the business and the customers of that business. A little individual flexibility with people who work in your business, however, will go a long way in gaining their loyalty and engagement.

In your offer letter and when you offer verbally, ask the candidate when they are likely to come back to you. Many candidates will accept at the verbal offer subject to receiving the written offer. Some will want a while to think about it and others will want until they have other offers come in that they want to choose from. Many graduates sit on four or so offers until September, causing havoc for graduate recruiters who find, a month before their cohort is about to start, that they are a candidate short and have to start the recruitment process from scratch. Some of the candidates who want to think about it may be the ones you have to negotiate with, as already discussed.

If you follow the advice and guidelines given, especially pre-testing an offer, and you have listened hard to your candidates through the process, you will finish with a successful acceptance from your preferred candidate.

The offer letter

Obviously there are legal considerations. Any offer letter forms the basis of a contract of employment but there is no reason why this cannot be a warm letter or in plain English. You may wish to get any letter you write checked out by a lawyer. Even if you don't provide contractual terms initially, The Employment Rights Act 1996 requires employers to provide most employees with a written statement of the main terms within two calendar months of starting work. Most employees will feel uncomfortable if they do not have clarity about their terms before accepting a job offer if this is a permanent role and they are making a serious career move which involves them leaving their existing business.

The letter should be warm and welcoming and confirm discussions already taken place. Again, here there should be no surprises.

Figure 10.6 shows an example of an offer letter you could write. You may not want to be quite as informal as this, but equally there is nothing in the HR rule book to say you have to be formal either.

You'll want to write this in the style which suits your organization. I have written this example as deliberately informal and friendly. If you work for a more corporate firm you might want to change the language to reflect the operating culture and conditions of the offices and client environment. The point is that the offer letter should be congruent with the organization writing it. Just as with the offer, there should be no surprises or sense of confusion in the candidate.

Employment documentation

If you need access to any type of documentation you can find a range of online suppliers with templates to download. Some offer free resources, including a 'rejection after interview' letter like http://www.redtapedoc.co.uk/, and others offer contractual documents written in plain English such as www.netlawman.co.uk. One with a specific emphasis on contractual law is http://www.employment-contract.org.uk/ and some will enable free access to all documents on a subscription basis, others on a piece-by-piece basis. Check before you buy that the documents have been drafted by a qualified lawyer and if so this can be an easy way to kit yourself out with all of the documentation you require. Bear in mind they have not been written with engagement in mind, so there may be a market opportunity lurking there for a smart solicitor.

Look at all the documents you are planning to use from a candidate's perspective. Ask yourself how they might feel about the letter you are sending. It may be that you can remember receiving your own offer letter and recall what that was like.

Once you have made the verbal offer, ensure your administration is able to get the confirmatory letter out quickly, as candidates may have other interviews and offers and are unlikely to forgo those until they know they have an offer in writing. Your objective is to make the whole offer, the resignation process from their existing role and their start with you as smooth, swift and seamless as possible.

FIGURE 10.6 Informal offer letter

Dear

We're really thrilled to offer you the role of Chief Dishwasher at Friendly Local Restaurant. We think you're going to make a fabulous difference to the way we wash our dishes and that you will add a huge amount of value to the business. We also hope you'll enjoy it!

We plan for you to start as soon as possible and so we can make sure everything is ready for you, please let Susie in HR (Susie@friendly.co.uk) know as soon as you have your start date. We're putting together a welcome pack for you so you can settle in as quickly as possible, get to know everyone and understand your role – and of course we look forward to welcoming you to 'welcome coffee' on your first morning. You already have a buddy arranged; she is called Manesha and her job is to make you feel like you have worked here five years by the end of the first day – but in a good way! Manesha will show you round, introduce you to everyone, collect you for breaks and make sure you know your way round the place really quickly.

You'll have noticed that attached to this is your Contract of Employment. Please do check this over carefully and make sure you are happy with it and all the terms are clear before signing it and popping it back in the post to us. If you have any questions about it at all – however small – please do just give me a call and we can chat things over.

We are really looking forward to you working here with the team at Friendly – we're a great bunch and cannot wait for you to start.

Best wishes

Sarah

HR Manager

Managing the resignation

Once the offer letter has been received and the candidate is happy with it they will need to resign from their current role. A good recruiter will have addressed this before you get to this point but if not it is worth asking when you make the offer how their current employer is likely to react to them leaving. You may ask if people are routinely counter-offered at their firm. This can be a real problem in organizations with staff with scarce skills. Often organizations do fail to look after their own people in favour of hiring new ones and it is not until they have a resignation that they then take any action.

Here are some checklist points.

Your own staff:

- Check all your people get reviewed regularly.
- Ensure they all know what their next career move is, how to work towards it and most importantly that it is something they want to do.
- Keep a very open dialogue with your teams.
- Treat staff as a priority and avoid moving reviews or appraisals, being late with planned increases in salaries, stopping learning and development or anything which disengages people.

If your business is in professional services, technology or science, where skills are scarce and both costly and hard to replace, it makes sense to focus on keeping your existing people and protecting them from the external offers they are bound to be receiving. It is easy to focus on hiring to the exclusion of retention.

People you are hiring:

- Check what happens in their company when key people resign. Ask if counter-offers are made.
- Ask your candidates what will happen when they resign.
- Ask if they are likely to be counter-offered.
- Ask how they will feel about a counter-offer. Point out that if they are thinking of taking any counter-offer they need to ask themselves what their motivation for moving is. If it is simply about money, ask if they have addressed this with their company up to now. If they say no, suggest they may find a counter-offer coming along and to be prepared for this. If they say they have, advise them this won't preclude a counter-offer but to remember clearly the salary they offer will be for their convenience and benefit, not that of the candidate. If they wanted to benefit the candidate and retain them, they would have offered before.
- Let them know that 80 per cent of people who accept a counter-offer leave within six months. The reality is that few of us only move jobs for money. We may be tempted away by a better offer but money is rarely the only driver. Not being paid enough for your role, however, can be a real driver to move.
- Get the hiring manager to invite them in for lunch and to meet the team if they have not already done so, show them where they'll be sitting and let them know about an exciting new project (hopefully there is one!) that they'll be working on and how that will contribute to the overall business and their own development.

Candidates rejecting offers

This is an important metric, as discussed earlier in the book. If you have a significant quantity of candidates rejecting your offers in favour of other organizations, you'll need to look at your hiring process from start to finish and identify where some of the problems might lie. This can stem from any aspect of the process but typically the key areas to explore are:

- How well the business is 'selling' its proposition; often organizations fail to get either the process or the tone of the recruitment right. Sometimes there is too long a gap between interviews or the interview process is too one-sided.
- How realistic the candidate market you are approaching is. Are you always offering less money, benefits, learning and development, career options, etc than your competitors? Do a competitor benchmarking analysis to see how you compare, particularly if you are finding candidates rejecting your offer in favour of one competitor.
- What sorts of questions you are asking candidates through the interview process. How well are you identifying what's important to them and what will be their decision-making criteria for their next role?
- How close are you to what other options candidates have?
- How are you recruiting? If you are using an agency and they have several other options for your candidates, this may be disadvantageous. Ask the agency what the candidate choices are and enlist their support to get the candidate you want. One way of doing this is to make sure you have not negotiated so hard on rates that it makes it harder for the consultant to advise in your favour if there are two similar options.

If you are a successful company in high demand and people want to work for you, eg Google, then you should be aiming for 95–98 per cent acceptance ratio. An average business might expect 75–80 per cent. Most recruitment consultants would be aiming for 85–90 per cent, so a rejection is an exception. Over six months and say 12 placements they may lose one or possibly two offers. Anything less than 70 per cent needs attention. It may be, of course, that you know why your hire rate is low and you are constrained by factors out of your control. In this case it would be useful to consider changing your target audience as rejected offers are very expensive. Although there is no recruitment consultancy fee to pay, a considerable amount of management time will have gone into recruitment and the payback needs to be good.

Taking up references

Once you have agreed terms with your candidate and they have resigned, you'll need to take up references on them. You may also do a range of other checks on them, depending upon the role. You will know what checks you need for your business, from medical to criminal, right to work (everyone needs to do this) to qualifications, security clearance and the Criminal Records Bureau. Set up a painless process to do this and at least take up previous employment references along with the right to work.

Additional value can be gained by taking up verbal references from a line manager or a previous one. This will give you a chance to find out information not only to confirm your offer to the candidate but also how to help manage them in the future.

Period between resignation and joining

It is not risk free to assume that your candidate who has accepted their role is going to join you on the first day. It is not entirely unusual for people simply not to arrive for work, so it pays to keep in close touch with them up to the start date. Make sure you involve them where you can in your business, invite them to any social events and if they would like to be, involve them in reading or offering access to the intranet so they can start to become familiar with the business. This way, once they start on their first day they will feel an immediate sense of familiarity, which will help them and guard against any other opportunities which may have not have quite finished prior to your offer.

Using assessment tools for development and understanding

In the previous chapter we identified a sometimes missed opportunity to make the most of the tools you use during assessment. These could be the results of a psychometric assessment, ability test or observations made at a group assessment activity.

Often these data are kept confined to the recruitment team, but value can be gained from handing over the candidate from the assessment and recruitment process into the management and on-boarding process.

At the very least, share information gathered with the new line manager and ideally have them then share it with the new joiner so they can use it as the basis of an on-boarding development conversation. Some of the reports provided by assessment houses can also be broadened out to include more information than is strictly necessary for recruitment purposes.

CASE STUDY

Malcolm Menard, commercial director at Team Focus, explains how the 15FQ+ (the evolved 16PF) can be used to explore conversations with candidates and new joiners. The report explores the candidate's preference for working styles. Assuming they have completed it honestly and have an average degree of self-awareness, the report can provide valuable insights into what people thrive on and enjoy as well as areas they may find more challenging or not so much to their liking. It covers their interaction style, their interpersonal and influencing styles, how they manage pressure and their thinking and decision-making style along with their overall work style. Often it can be several months before managers and new starters have this level of open discussion about potential performance and development. Using a profile such as this with the resulting report can short-circuit the first three months' discovery phase and lead to an immediately greater shared understanding and a positioning of the new person to succeed by allowing them to play to their strengths.

On-boarding from Day One and beyond

Just as it is critically important to be clear about your vision, purpose and goals before you start recruiting, it is as important to know what you need someone to do before they join you. This is not just about writing a job description, this is about priority and letting someone know what is expected of them.

Marcus Buckingham and the Gallup organization see the question 'Do you know what is expected of you?' as one of the top six questions to ask to see how happy and satisfied, and therefore engaged, someone is at work. I had an early experience in my career where I was hired to deliver 'marketing programmes'. Bizarrely (now) I wasn't entirely sure what they were. Indeed, I never did find out as I was promoted some few months later to manage the team, which I found a whole lot easier to get to grips with. It seems extraordinary in today's workplace that I almost sat there for several months wondering exactly what I needed to do (asking left me none the wiser) and was on the point of leaving when the situation changed.

The overall objective of induction or on-boarding should be that your new recruit can get up and running and effective as soon as possible. That creates a win–win for both them and you as an organization and creates a culture of high performance right from the start.

A further couple of questions that Marcus Buckingham asks are 'Do you feel that someone cares about you as a person at work?' and 'Do you have a best friend at work?' At one organization I was asked to consult to, they had had someone leave after their first day as on that day they had been given a manual to read all day and nothing else. Human contact at work and the capacity to belong is both one of the reasons we work and one of the values we can gain. The importance of making someone feel welcome and creating a sense of belonging, right from when they accept their job offer, is crucial to longer-term success, as the following case studies show.

CASE STUDY

Major Players, the recruitment consultancy to the creative industries, really works hard to make new people feel welcome. It doesn't run inductions; it runs 'welcomes', which comprise a welcome note at reception for new people, a goodie box on their desk with champagne and chocs as well as their 'help' book with lots of key information in it, a buddy who shows them round and introduces them to everyone and then looks after them for the rest of the week, a schedule of events helping them to get to know the business and what everyone does as well as specific training on the system , meetings with the MD and the various teams, lunch with their own team and at 5 pm on their first day a high tea with everyone else in the business. The welcome continues over the first few weeks in a systematic way so people feel thoroughly at home by the end of their welcome programme.

None of the things that Major Players do costs very much money but it does require quite a high degree of time and attention. If 'Welcome' doesn't suit your business, why not call it 'Great Start'? It gives a completely different feel and tone. This attention to detail will bring commercial advantage through engagement, retention and well-being, however, as the next case study shows.

CASE STUDY

Enterprise Rent-A-Car cites their holistic on-boarding approach as one of the key reasons for their success at retaining the best talent they work hard to attract and recruit: 'With a current retention rate of 75 per cent, we are certain that our holistic approach to induction and on-boarding – ensuring the smooth transition of new employees into our organization – is one of the key reasons we are able to successfully retain such a high percentage of our new recruits.

'At Enterprise Rent-A-Car, induction is critical to our company's success. We have fundamental beliefs that we should reward hard work and high performance. Therefore, promotion from within is a core principle in how we run our business – developing and educating employees about how to become great leaders.

'In the UK we have over 3,000 employees, of whom 99 per cent have been promoted from our graduate training programme. Giving employees an exceptional on-boarding and induction experience helps them clearly understand our culture, values and customer service philosophy. We understand there is a connection between a high-quality induction process and building a high-performance culture.

'On-boarding, the socialization of an employee into the organization, takes centre stage in our induction programme. We take a systematic and comprehensive approach to making the employee feel welcome, which results in an increase in performance, productivity and engagement of the employee at an earlier stage in their career. We do this through employee interaction, mentoring and role modelling rather than e-on-boarding or website approaches that some companies use.

'Our on-boarding programme is focused on socializing the new employee and aims to build connections between people that help new recruits to build, understand and navigate newly formed organizational relationships. Focusing on relationship building as well as process throughout the induction process helps bring our new employees up to speed faster and more effectively.

'For us the on-boarding process starts as soon as the candidate accepts the job. Once a candidate has accepted, they receive constant communication from the recruiter who took them through the interview process as well as their new manager, right up until the date they start. We send birthday cards and good luck cards prior to exams. We also invite new employees to attend social, business and specifically designed networking events prior to their start date. New recruits receive a letter from the managing director welcoming them to the organization. A welcome letter is also sent to the family of the new employee.

'At Enterprise, all members of management and human resources have a role to play within this process. Senior managers are heavily involved in our on-boarding process. All orientations include presentations from department managers and our managing directors personally meet and talk to every new hire at some point throughout the induction process. Senior managers are also often chosen as mentors to new employees during induction. Incorporating senior management into the induction process helps managers understand how to support the new hires to be at their best.'

As the case study above indicates, there is significant evidence to show that networking is a key to successful on-boarding, career development and retention in general. In *Driving Results through Social Networks*, Rob Cross and Robert J Thomas outline findings from an investment bank. The bank discovered that its senior executives had very different networks from their junior executives. Seniors had much more diverse networks than juniors, reaching across divisions and roles, so the bank arranged a series of events aimed at supporting junior executives to develop similar networks to their seniors.

I am not surprised that the senior executives all had good networks. In my experience those executives will have become senior though their willingness to embrace other people and their understanding of the value others can bring to an everyday problem or a career. Senior people are much more available to headhunters not because they are mostly looking for a new job but because they recognize the value of the contact. So supporting new people who join a business through the process of networking across the wider business will not only develop their skills and capacity to do the job, it also means you are likely to retain their talent in the wider organization.

CASE STUDY

Simon Mitchell of DDI explains the work that his organization is doing with new leaders into organizations through their on-boarding programme and cites networking as a key example of a crucial skill and element of the first 90 days. Their research and work show clearly that there is a strong link between developing relationships within the business and high performance and that many key relationships are formed within the first ninety days.

Of course, it is not only in the on-boarding phase that those relationships can be developed; this can happen later in their time with the business.

CASE STUDY

Hala Collins, HR director of Randstad, cites the value of networking gained from her recent innovative 'Leaders in Action' programme which brings together the leaders of a range of businesses, who might not otherwise meet, to share a leadership development programme. The side benefit has been the relationships they have developed along the way and the value being generated from those relationships will be immense in terms of both engagement and joint client opportunities which may not otherwise have been identified.

To gain maximum benefit from people and to create for them a sense of belonging and 'at home', the earlier in their career with your company you can do this the better.

Developing your on-boarding programme

The core tasks of on-boarding can be seen like this:

- Keep the new joiner's engagement high after they have accepted the role; help them step over the threshold into their new role and familiarize themselves with the business before their start date.
- Help someone make friends.
- Help someone develop their network to get things done.
- Let them know where to find everything they need.
- Let them know what's expected of them.
- Help them with the culture: 'how we do things round here'.
- Develop and deliver a first-class induction or welcome programme which gives them a systematic programme of events and activities to bring them over the threshold of the new organization.

Five things *not* to do:

1. Forget they are starting!
2. Have your new starter fill in forms or read manuals on the first day all day.
3. Simply tell them the jobs people do, rather than who they are.
4. Arrange two weeks of wall-to-wall one-to-ones where people tell them what they do.
5. Leave them to it at their desk, expecting them to find out who's who and what's what.

You only have one chance to make a first impression. When I developed the employee joining cycle (Figure 3.1 in Chapter Three), I indicated that the highest point of engagement to date is when the new employee accepts your offer. From this point on you'll be on-boarding them. To keep engagement high you'll need to make on-boarding simple, easy to access, interesting, ideally good fun, and consistent.

Transitioning into your team

You'll need to ensure you create a good team environment for this new person to operate within. Any new person in a team provides a level of disruption and change, and change is always a challenge. Your team may still be sad to see the other team member leave and not be looking forward to a replacement, so they may not be as welcoming as possible. It is the manager's job to make sure that any challenges like this are overcome by finding a way to help the team bond together. Simple things like a team lunch or drinks, getting-to-know-you sessions and talking openly about how hard it is sometimes to change and to accept new people but also to be accepted will help this period move through more smoothly and some of this can be done before the person joins.

There are three clear stages of on-boarding:

1. Pre-start date.
2. First week or two.
3. First three months: post weeks one and two.

The best programmes have designed activities and programmes in each of these stages but many organizations focus simply on Stage 2. For many businesses Stage 2 involves a health and safety briefing and being introduced round the office (once) and shown where the coffee machine is.

I am going to look at each of the stages in turn and suggest good ways to help new colleagues step over the threshold into your business, to be a success and feel happy that they made the right choice. Table 10.1 shows a very brief outline template for an on-boarding programme.

Pre start date

There is a balance here, particularly between those people who are working and those who are not. Expecting someone to make meetings and events and read weighty documentation sends the wrong message about the new role and is unreasonable, so take care not to overburden your new recruit.

Equally and with this is mind, it is also possible to completely ignore them until they start. Enterprise Rent-A-Car gave some good examples in their case study above and you may also want to try the following:

- Invite them to social events both with their team and with the company.
- Have your MD drop them a note welcoming them to the business.
- Have the manager send them a note telling them that they are looking forward to them joining and that they are planning their welcome/induction programme to help them get up and running as easily as possible.
- Invite them over to meet the team one lunchtime or early evening, particularly if their present office is nearby.
- If you have a large cohort of people joining at the same time, throw a welcome drinks party and ensure everyone gets to know one another so everyone has a friend and recognizes others from the first day.
- Allocate them a buddy (someone who is their first friend on Day One) and have the buddy call them up to welcome them and have a chat.
- Send them some background reading but take care this material is interesting and not the health and safety manual – also take care it is not too commercially sensitive as they have not started yet and you just need to take a little care around that.

TABLE 10.1 An on-boarding template

On-boarding activity	With (name)	When	Where	Why	Completed
Your first week					
Breakfast meeting	Sarah and Mo		In the cafe next door	To discuss your marketing plans	
Health and safety briefing	Your PC! e-learning	Day 1	Your desk	So we can keep you safe	Yes
Your second week					
Meeting with No 3 client	Mary		On the client site. Research for client can be found at www. **** and internal database	So you can begin to take over the account	
Your second fortnight					

- Deal with all of the 'housekeeping' issues of joining: sending in P45s, bank account details, benefits decisions, car choice, etc.
- Give them information on 'how things are done round here' so on Day One they don't get up to go to lunch when it's an unwritten rule (rightly or wrongly) that lunch is a working sandwich and it is not culturally acceptable for them to go out for an hour lunch break.

First week or two: the first day

This sets the tone for the rest of the week and on-boarding process, so it's important to get this exactly right. Your objective is to have your new joiner leave the workplace at the end of the first day feeling excited and useful!

- Perhaps ask them to start a little later on their first day so they can be sure people are ready for them. This is less important if they are going straight into an organized group induction. Otherwise for their manager there should be no more important task than collecting their new starter from reception on time.
- On the day someone starts, make sure their physical tools of the job are ready for them – that they have a desk, a phone, computer or whatever equipment they need.
- Let other people know they are starting. Have their manager send out a welcome e-mail to the team or the wider business telling the team a bit about their background plus something on a personal level: they like bowling, recently returned from Cambodia, have three cats and hate tomato soup.
- Ensure that very quickly they have support to learn whatever they need to do their job; so if there is a computer system, get them trained on this quickly; similarly if there are some products they need to understand. In other words, make sure they have the tools to do their job well.
- Do everything you can to see that they get to know some people; you can carry on the buddy system from before the first day, arrange lunches, coffees and other meetings with key people and avoid them sitting behind their desk on e-learning much of the day – although some quiet time to get familiar with the role and the business is also important.
- Take care not to overwhelm them with information so they end their first day having been 'talked to' for eight hours; not only will they not have taken this in, they will feel exhausted and not stimulated. Find a good balance between them discovering things for themselves and others talking to them.
- Try and give them a chance to contribute to something. In some roles they will be up and running really quickly and others will take longer to learn, but if possible have them actually doing some work in the

first day rather than just listening to or watching others, even if it is a simple task or a series of meetings where they can ask questions and learn for themselves.

First week or two: the first week

By the end of the first week it's good to ensure your new starter:

- understands the overall vision and purpose of the business and how their role fits into that;
- understands their own role, its purpose and what's expected within that role on both a day-to-day and bigger-picture basis;
- has all the tools they need to do their job to the degree you expect them to be able to do it at this point; they may continue to develop their skills and knowledge, of course, and for some this may be a longer-term process, but they need to be able to meet your immediate expectations;
- has completed all of the 'housekeeping' aspects of starting a new job if this has not been done prior to the first week, and has covered all the health and safety elements of the business, ideally in Day One – in other words, all the 'boring but necessary' bits;
- understands who the rest of the immediate team are, what they do and how they contribute to the whole;
- has developed an understanding of the cultural norms of the business;
- has met some of the senior management team;
- knows how to present the business if this is part of their role; understands why it is successful and why it does well;
- knows who the clients or customers are and understands the ethos of dealing with those customers;
- has begun to develop a wider network.

How you achieve this will depend on the size of your business, the resources available and what has worked well and what not so well before. If you are a large distributed business, guard against using the intranet and e-learning to the exclusion of all else. These solutions can be cost effective and good, especially in a 'better than nothing' scenario, but where it is at all possible to make much of the on-boarding activities human centred, then new joiners will benefit much more. It is good, however, to have intranet- and web-based tools there for a 'just-in-time' service for information at the point when it is needed. It is equally unhelpful to have the MD deliver a great presentation on the structure of the business once and to have nowhere where this can subsequently be checked out again.

If you do use an intranet, try and make it as accessible and interesting as possible; notice how much time you spend on websites you like as opposed to those which are very dry and just have words – but this again will depend upon the budget available. Better to have big colourful posters in the office with people's pictures, names and jobs on them than a dry list of names in a Word document.

It is a great idea to have an 'FAQ for new starters' page on the intranet or in a welcome pack. This can be sent out in the pre-start phase as well.

First three months (post weeks one and two): the first month

By the end of the first month it's good to ensure your new starter:

- feels part of the business;
- has made some work friends to go to lunch with, make coffee with and just hang out with in a down moment;
- is feeling confident about what their role is and that they can complete it well;
- understands the priorities of the role and what to start with and where;
- has developed a business network or strong peer groups across the organization to call on to get things done and ask advice;
- has developed a good relationship with their manager and other team members;
- has developed a good relationship with their team if they are a manager themselves; has had an in-depth conversation with every team member and has listened to their thoughts and opinions;
- still feels important and valued;
- is still excited about the business and the role;
- has a picture of the business as a whole and what departments and companies do what and how that fits together.

And at the end of this month it makes sense to arrange a formal catch-up or meeting between the new joiner and their manager to check in, see how things have gone and to look forward to the next two months. Table 10.2 suggests a format for doing this.

Once this first crucial month has passed, the rest of the on-boarding phase will vary dramatically. Senior people will be expecting to deliver recommendations for improvements, requests for resources and potential reorganizations during this period. In some roles, after the first month the new starter will be up and running, doing their job well and needing regular normal reviews to check all is well. As a general rule of thumb, however, it makes sense to touch base with all new people every week in the first month – and every month as a minimum thereafter to ensure all is well. This touching base needs to be over and above the general day-to-day work topics and conversations and focus solely on how they are getting on in the business.

TABLE 10.2 On-boarding meeting format: post month-one meeting

Manager	How? (Probe)
We're meeting to see how your first month has gone with us, what has gone well, what not so well and to look forward to the next couple of months as well.	
So, how do you feel that the first month here has gone?	
Looking through your first month's checklist, can we just identify any areas which you've not managed to complete or that have been missed? What plan can we make to ensure they are covered?	
What have you enjoyed the most about this month?	And why is that?
What have you found most frustrating?	And what ideas might you have to change that?
What have you identified that you need more help or training with?	
What have you noticed that you think we could do better?	
Where do you think your focus for the next two months will lie?	
What feedback do you have for me on the business, the team and how you and I have been working together?	
How could we improve this process for others?	
What else?	
Manager offers feedback	I've noticed that when you do 'X' the impact on the team is energizing. That's been great to see and I'd like to see you doing more of it. I've noticed that when you are not sure it can take a while before you seek help. I'd like to see you taking a more pro-active approach to asking for help or advice when you need it. I really value people who ask others and see it as a real strength as we are such a strong team-oriented organization.
Let's then put together an action plan for the next month and catch up at the end of that.	Action planning session

Three-month evaluation

Although this is an ongoing process, a three-month checkpoint is important to make sure you have both chosen well: the right company and role and the right person. If good attention is paid during this period, problems can be addressed and solved. Lack of attention means issues may not come to light until nearer the six-month point. Probation periods range from three to six months and close attention needs to be paid to on-boarding throughout this process.

At the end of three months your new starter:

- will have a clear sense of what needs to be achieved in the new role and have developed plans to make it happen;
- will have a good understanding of the wider business, how it is structured and how each of these areas contributes;
- will have developed a good network within each of these areas and spent time building relationships with the key stakeholders;
- will have settled into the cultural norms of the business and be someone who perpetuates them rather than follows them;
- will have developed knowledge and competence in their role;
- will have a clear picture of what's needed next.

On-boarding into performance management

Once the new starter is successfully on-boarded, they transition through into the normal methods of performance management. They become a fully fledged member of your team who, if you have recruited and assessed them well, on-boarded them with care and look after them on an ongoing basis, will be with you and your business for years to come.

'Joined-up' recruitment

You'll have learned about collecting metrics on the success of the hiring process and also on retention, but the effectiveness of your recruitment process and everything that surrounds it, from your employer branding to your manager's interviewing skills and how you sell your business, needs continual evaluation. Employment markets and businesses and their objectives change. Recruitment needs to change with them to add the value I hope your business is now able to derive from a more 'joined-up' recruitment approach.

Recruiting people who stay with your organization for years to come is where this book really started. To gain competitive advantage and provide great careers, fulfilment and opportunity to people who work with you, it pays to become really good at recruiting them. As I've hopefully convinced you, recruitment is best placed in an environment with all elements working harmoniously together: attracting great people to your business through a great employer brand, assessing them really well to ensure they are in a job where they can thrive, develop, contribute widely and progress, and engaging them so they feel emotionally attached to the business and want to stay. If you do all these things well your business will hold on to its top talent, ensuring advantage over your competition. But for me by far the most important, you will have the satisfaction of doing a great job of creating the best place to work for you and all the people around you.

INDEX

NB: page numbers in *italic* indicate figures or tables

ability testing 192–93
- advantages 192
- disadvantages 192
- types 192–93

Accenture 134
Adecco 104
advertising 148–58
- AIDA 149-50, *151–53*
- external 148
- graduates 159–60
- internal 148
- proactive approaches 154
- websites 148
- *see also* attraction, job advertisement

Age Discrimination Act 2006 131
Ambler, Tim 134
Apple 134
application form 8, 184
- advantages 184
- disadvantages 184

appraisal 173
apprentices 144
- attracting 158

assessment 31–33, 67–68, 165–212
- ability testing 192–93
- application form 183–84
- case studies 168, 168–69, 171, 184, 187, 193, 193–94
- centres 8, 171, 194–200
- choice of structure *183*
- competency framework 174–79
- criteria 181, 187
- CV 185
- group exercises 197–98
- interviews 31–33
- invitations 31
- letter of application 185–86
- methods 181–200, 182--85
- mistakes 165–66
- open days/job fairs 186
- pre-shortlisting 182–83
- processes 6, 7–8, *167*, 170–71, *182*
- psychometric testing 180, 190–94
- putting the information together 180–81
- qualitative data 174
- quantitative data 173–74
- references 226–27
- shortlisting 187 quantitative 88, 190
- telephone interview 188, *189*
- types 8
- web-based initial applications 186 quantitative 87
- what 'good' looks like 172
- writing capability 183

assessment centres 8, 171, 194–200
- advantages 194
- case studies 195, 201
- designing 197
- disadvantages 194
- group exercises 197–98
- individual exercises 200
- invitation to *196*
- organising 194–95
- presenting your business 200–01
- sample formats *198*, *199*

Association of Executive Search Consultants (AESC) 158
Association of Graduate Recruiters (AGR) 159
attraction 27–28, 66–67, 125–26, 134–64
- advertising 148–58
- careers page 142-43
- developing recruitment brand 134–37
- employee candidate referral scheme (ECRS) 146–48
- employee value proposition 135–36
- graduates 144–45
- identifying needs 137
- methods 28, 32, 129, 138, 138–39
- previous applicants 154–55

social networking 139–42
target candidate communities 135
young people 144

Balfour Beatty Workplace 106
Barrow, Simon 134
Beech.co.uk case study 115–33
BP 194
brand *see* employer brand
British Market Research Bureau 129
British Psychological Society 67, 191
Buckingham, Marcus 228
BSI 144
business growth 5, 116
recruitment and 17–20
see also recruitment strategy

candidates 187–88
assessing 7-8, 165–212
attracting 27–28
direct approaches 155–58
managing resignation 224–25
negotiating job offer 33
offering a job 219–20
rejecting 28–29, 214–18
self-esteem 32
career development/progression 42–43, 52–53
checklist *44*
learning opportunities 53
Caterek 141
Cattell 190
Chartered Institute of Personnel and Development (CIPD) 14
Resourcing and Talent Planning Survey 2010 *36*
Chartered Management Institute 177
Chemistry 168
Coca-Cola 24
colleges/universities 159
Collins, Hala 34–35, 231
Collins, Jim 21, 52
communication 52
competency
definition 176
competency frameworks 176–79
example *177*
job skills and *178-79*

Corporate Leadership Council 34
Engagement survey 34, 45
costs 13–20
hidden 13, 14, 15
labour turnover *15*
overt 13, 14
recruitment 16
replacing staff 14, *15*
Cross, Rob 230
culture 54–55, 145
definition 54
customer relationship management (CRM) system 27
CV (curriculum vitae) 185, 206, 208
advantages 185
disadvantages 185

Dainippon Sumitomo Pharma 161
Data Protection Act 1998 115
Davis, Penny 106–07
DDI 139
case studies 168, 231
DDtrans case study 193–94
DS Connections 51
diversity of workforce 91–92, 173

employee candidate referral scheme (ECRS) 146–48
employee engagement *see* engagement
employee value proposition 135–36
employer brand 10, 21, 134–37
awards 143
communication 137
employee experience 135–36
employee needs 25
guarding 26
measuring 136
meeting national standards 143–44
employer branding 23–25
employer of choice 23
employment documentation 223
employment legislation 169–70
discrimination 168
right to work 170
employment life cycle 6, 7,9, *22*, 22–23
engagement 8–9, 21–34
rational/emotional commitment 34
survey of 34, 45

Enterprise Rent-A-Car case studies 91–92, 229–30, 233
Equal Opportunity for Women in the Workplace Agency (Australia) 23
Equality Act 2010 131, 169
Evans, Sue 51
exit interview *38*, 83
  case study 39

Facebook 32, 155
Ford 42
Fortune 54, 74
Frankland Associates 154
Frankland, Elizabeth 154

Gallup 228
GE 35
Generation Y 25
Gilbert, Stephen 104
Google 16, 25
graduates 25, 144–45
  advertising to 159–60
  case study 160
Gratton, John 39
'great place to work', creating 50–55
Great Place to Work Institute 9, 49, 50

Hammond, Carol 105-06
Handy, Charles 91
Hay Group, the 177
  Generic Competencies 177
Hays 104
Herzberg, Frederick 45
Hesburgh, Theodore M 51
hiring requisition form *118*
holidays 123
HP group 139
HR team 6, 11, 64–65

induction 8
Infosys 139
insourcing 92–93, 106–07
interview questions *204–05*
  closed *204*
  direct *204*
  evidence-based *205*
  hypothetical *205*
  leading *205*
  multiple *205*
  open *204*
  open/demand *204*
  probing *204*
  reflective *204*
interviews 8, 31–33, 201–12
  bad 202
  behavioural-based 168, 208
  biographical 207
  competency-based 208
  contra-evidence 208
  evaluation form *210–11*
  evidence-based *209*
  gathering information 206–07
  giving information 207
  good 202–03
  introduction 206
  mistakes 165–66
  plan 208
  preparing for/conducting 203–12
  question types *204–05*
  selling/closing 207
  STAR *209*
  telephone 132, 188, *189*
  welcome/rapport 203
Investors in People 44, 144
ISO 144

job advertisement 129–30
  example *130*
job applications, acknowledging 28, *29*, *30*
Job Centre 158
job description *119*, *121–22*, 174
job offer 33, 219–24
  letter 223, *224*
  'magic circle' 220–22, *221*
  negotiating areas 222
  references 226–27
  rejection of 228
  win-win 220
jobEQ 193
John Lewis 25
'joined-up' approach 5–12

Kellaher, Emma 141
key performance indicators (KPIs) 9
  internal promotion 44

labour turnover 35–36, *79*
leaver's metrics *39*, *83*
recruitment metrics *78–79*
use of data 36–37
King, Spencer 91–92
Kit Kat 24

labour, types *88–90*
agency workers *88*
apprenticeships *89*
casual *88*
diversity *90*
external consultants *88*
fixed term contracts *89*
freelances *88*
full-time *90*
geographical spread *90*
graduate trainee *89*
interims *89*
internships *89*
locations 90
part-time *90*
project workers *88*
temporary *88*
leadership 46–47, 51
checklist *47*
leaver's metrics *39*, *83*
Lego 24
letter of application 185–86
advantages 185
disadvantages 185
LinkedIn 139, 140, 154, 155
case study 140–41
Lloyd, Peter 108
London Business School 134
L'Oréal case study 40

'magic circle,' the 220–22, *221*
see also job offer
Major Players 161
case studies 39, 165, 229
Marks & Spencer 25
Maslow, Abraham 54
hierarchy of needs *54*
Matrix Standard 144
Menard, Malcolm 227–28
Merlevede, Patrick 193
metrics *see* key performance indicators
Microsoft 123
Mitchell, Simon 231

National Apprenticeship Service 144
National Health Service (NHS) 25
National Online Recruitment Audience Survey (NORAS) 129
networking 230

Ochre House 104
offer *see* job offer
on-boarding 8, 33–34, 41, 213–40
case studies 227–28, 229–30
checklist *43*
completing recruitment process 213–28
core tasks 232
developing programme 232
first day 235–36
first week 236–37
first month 237
making people welcome 228–31
meeting format *238*
pre-start date 233
stages 233
template *234*
three month evaluation 239
transitioning into team 232–39
see also job offer
open days/job fairs 186
advantages 186
disadvantages 186
Forum3 186
organizations 17–20
as a community 53–54
commitment to people *48*
culture 54–55, 145
reputation 24, 31–32
strategy 52, 55, 85–87
values 48
vision and purpose 50–51
see also employer brand
outsourcing 92–93, 94–96, 102–06

P & G 140
Palfrey-Smith, Graham 31, 114
pay/benefits 45–46, 70, 124
bonus 123

case study 124–25
checklist *46*
commission 123
holidays 123
pension 12
performance-related pay 123
salary 122–23
share option schemes 123
Peabody 103
PeopleAnswers 187
Perez, Joe 161
person specification *120*, *121–22*
PESTLEC analysis 75, *76*
Phelps, Richard 14
Philby, Roger 168
Pink Paper 186
PPS 103
PricewaterhouseCoopers (PwC) 14
case study 14
Pruden, Shirley 16
psychometric testing 180, 190–94
case study 191
feedback 214
15FQ+ 227–28
16PF 180, 190
OPQ 180, 190

Randstad 34–35, 104
case study 231
recruiting lifecycle of organization 17–20, *110*
recruitment 41, 59–70, 108–33
assessment 67–68
'at the heart' of an organization 10–12, *10*
attraction 66–67
budgeting 68
business plan and 111
case study 114, 115–33
checklist *42*
employer brand and 26–27
costs of poor 13–20, 165
'fit for purpose' 112
focus on 63–64
HR business partners 94–95
hybrid model 96
insourcing 92–93, 106–07
internal team 64–65, 93, 128–30
IT systems 114–15
'joined-up' 5–12, 239-40
metrics *78–79*
mistakes 111
objectives 111–12
on-boarding 213–28
organizational structure and 62-63
outsourcing 92–93, 94–96, 102–06
passion for 63
people evaluation 61
process 65–66, *109*, 113, 115–33
reward 70
role evaluation 60–61
shared service model 96
shortlisting 130–33
speed/cost/quality balance *67*, 67–68
strategic methods/choices 92–96, *97–101*
successful *60*
supplier relationships 65
temporary labour 94–95
recruitment agencies 160–62
case study 161
checklist 127
choosing/engaging 126–28
negotiating terms 162–63
preferred supplier list (PSL) 162
relationship with 163–64
recruitment consultants 6–7, 102–06, 221
recruitment strategy 11, 62, 71–107
benefits of 71–73
case studies 80, 87
design/development 85–87
diversity of workforce 91–92
fledging business 85
gap analysis 82–83
insourcing 106–07
labour market external research 77
larger city company 86
metrics *78–79*
objectives/goals 80–82
offshoring 105
outsourcing 102–06
PESTLEC analysis 75, *76*
rural factory 86
situational analysis 73–80

small business 85–86
SMARTER goals 81
strategic labour choices 87, *88–90*
SWOT analysis *74*, 74–75, 77
vision 80
references 226–27
rejecting a candidate 214–18
template letters *215–18*
remuneration 219
see also pay/benefits
retention 9–12, 34–49
advantages 35
benchmarking 36
career development 42–43
commitment to people *48*
definition 34
drivers 35, *36*, 41–49
exit interview *38*
external factors 40
gap 84–85
internal factors 37
leadership 46–47
metrics *79*, *83*
on-boarding 41
pay/benefits 45–46
profit and 49
recruitment 41
reward package 122–23
see also pay/benefits
Richardson, Tracey 201
right to work 170, 181
role specification *175–76*
Roosevelt, Theodore 52
Ruddy, Ian 104

Sainsbury's case study 184
search engine optimization (SEO) 116, 139, 141
SHL 190, 191
shortlisting 130–33, 182–83, 187–88, 190
criteria 130–31
Sky 134
'smashability' 24
Snelling, Alex 40
social networking 139
Stanford Research Institute 74
strategy 52
development 73-87
see also recruitment strategy
succession planning 9, 61, 145–46
Sun Microsystems 35
Sunday Times Best Companies to Work 50, 81, 143
suppliers 11, 65
Swain, Ann 155
SWOT analysis *74*, 74–75, 77

Taylor, Frederick 45
Team Focus 227
Telefónica 104
The Times Graduate Recruitment Awards 23
Thomas, Robert J 230
Traynor, Maria 66
Tribal Resourcing 201
turnover 36, 173
gap analysis *83*
metrics *39*, *79*
see also retention
Twitter 32, 139, 140,
case study 141–42

UNESCO case study 80

values 48, 147
verbal/numerical reasoning tests 8
Virgin 134

web-based initial applications 186–87
Welch, Jack 35
Westaff 23
Williams, Mark 140-41
working mothers 23
working patterns 23
Wyatt, Gerry 108